Women Society : Struggle and Problems

Women Society : Struggle and Problems

Edited by

P. Kumar

GLOBAL PUBLICATIONS
NEW DELHI-110 002 (INDIA)

GLOBAL PUBLICATIONS
4378/4B, G-4 JMD House
Murari Lal Street, Ansari Road
Daryaganj, New Delhi - 110 002
Phone : 23278062 (Off.)
e-mail : omega_publications@yahoo.com

Head Office :
79/23, Laxmi Garden
Near Satya Jyoti School,
Gurgaon (Haryana)
Mob : 9213562438

Women Society : Struggle and Problems

First Published : 2011

ISBN : 978-93-80833-48-4

PRINTED IN INDIA

Published by Ishwari Prasad Garg for Global Publications, New Delhi-110002 and Printed at Suman Printers, Delhi

Preface

Life may go on today; it can fight or run away, that it may be here to fight tomorrow; and by a process of division it can create a new life so that its existence may continue across the generations. With such units it is quite conceivable that life might go on through all eternity, death following birth, were it not that protoplasm contains within itself a principle of change. Life and change are synonymous. And this change moves ever toward a complexity, which we call development, where cells unite in a larger life, and functions and organs are specialized. Thus there comes a time when the part split off carries with it power to eat and digest, to fight or run away, but only half the power of procreation. This half unit, this incomplete individual, is either male or female, and from this time on, the epic of life gathers around the search of these half-lives for their complements. The force that impels to this search, while at first valuable only for the perpetuation of the generations, gathers into itself modifying feeling and desires and, at a later period, ideas and ideals, which finally, when men and women appear, make it the greatest of all the shaping forces in life.

It is, of course, conceivable that these two halves of the biological unit might have been made, or might have developed, alike in everything except the sexual function. At least they might have been as much alike as men are alike. They might have been of the same size, possessed of the same strength, of the same figures and gestures, complexion and hair. Their voices might have been alike. They might have had the same kinds of nervous systems, with the same desires, feelings, ideas and tendencies. In the assertions and arguments born of intellectual, industrial, social and political readjustments, it is often assumed that this is the case. Differences are minimized or denied, and an attempt is made to resolve the world of men and women into a world of human beings capable of living together in mingled competitions and cooperations, regardless of sex, except where the reproductive process is considered. But this view is superficial; born of argument it breaks down when confronted by any body of significant facts.

The major topics dealt in this book are : *Introduction; Women in Education; Economic Independence of Women; The Feminizing of Culture; Political Life and Women; Women in Industry; The Modern Family; Parasitism; Women and Labour Problems; Female Parasitism; Woman and War; Sex Differences; Certain Objections; etc.*

No doubt, these will serve the purpose of trainees and trainers, professional and policy planners in the field. Since the sources of information are all secondary, we express our gratitude to the scholars whose works are cited or substantially made use of. We are thankful to all those who rendered ready help and cooperation while working on this project.

I express my gratitude to various scholars, teachers and friends for their assistance and guidance. Finally, I thank the publishers for bringing out this book in very limited time.

—***Editor***

Contents

Preface (v)

1. Introduction 1-24
2. Women in Education 25
3. Economic Independence of Women 40
4. The Feminizing of Culture 49
5. Political Life and Women 61
6. Women in Industry 93
7. The Modern Family 106
8. Parasitism 134
9. Women and Labour Problems 155
10. Female Parasitism 175
11. Woman and War 198
12. Sex Differences 213
13. Certain Objections 222

Index 274

1
Introduction

If we go back to the earliest forms of life, where the unit is simply a minute mass of protoplasm surrounded by a cell wall, we find each of these divisions to be a complete individual. It can feed itself, that its life may go on to-day; it can fight or run away, that it may be here to fight to-morrow; and by a process of division it can create a new life so that its existence may continue across the generations. With such units it is quite conceivable that life might go on through all eternity, death following birth, were it not that protoplasm contains within itself a principle of change. Life and change are synonymous.

And this change moves ever toward a complexity, which we call development, where cells unite in a larger life, and functions and organs are specialized. Thus there comes a time when the part split off carries with it power to eat and digest, to fight or run away, but only half the power of procreation. This half unit, this incomplete individual, is either male or female, and from this time on, the epic of life gathers around the search of these half-lives for their complements. The force that impels to this search, while at first valuable only for the perpetuation of the generations, gathers into itself modifying feeling and desires and, at a later period, ideas and ideals, which finally, when men and women appear, make it the greatest of all the shaping forces in life.

Of course, in such a sweeping statement as this, one must include under sex hunger all the forces that drive men and women to seek each other's society, rather than that of their own sex. In this sense, it can be truly said that it gives a motive for our care of offspring, and for all our other most self-forgetful devotions, our finest altruisms, our most polished expressions in language, manners and dress. It justifies labor, ambition, and at times even self-effacement It underlies nearly all the lyric expressions in art; furnishes almost the only theme for that delineation of modern life which we call the novel; and is a main support for music, painting, statuary and belles-lettres. It gives us the institution of the family, which is the parent of the state; it is closely allied to religion; and in our individual lives it lifts us to the heights of self-realization and happiness, or plunges us down to the depths of degradation and tragedy.

While this sex hunger belongs equally to men and women, it has come to be associated with women, until we even speak of them as "the sex." Hence, when we are discussing women, we are generally discussing the sex interest common to both men and women, and this disturbs our point of view. The fact is that sex interest is a common possession, that the unit in human life, even more than among lower animals, is always a male and a female bound together by love. Just as a body can function in sleep or under the influence of a narcotic, for a time seemingly independent of the mind, so a man or a woman can live for a time in seeming independence of the opposite sex; but from any biological point of view, such a separate existence of male and female is only a transient effort. The half-life must find its mate or, after a few brief days, it dies, leaving its line extinct. For all the larger purposes of life, man is but a half-creature, and woman is equally a fragment.

It is, of course, conceivable that these two halves of the biological unit might have been made, or might have developed, alike in everything except the sexual function. At least they might have been as much alike as men are alike. They might have been of the same size, possessed of the same strength, of the same figures and gestures, complexion and hair. Their voices might have been alike. They might have had the same kinds of nervous systems, with the same desires, feelings, ideas and tendencies. In the assertions and arguments born of intellectual, industrial, social and political readjustments, it is often assumed that this is the case. Differences are minimized or denied, and an attempt is made to resolve the world of men and women into a world of human beings capable of living together in mingled competitions and cooperations, regardless of sex, except where the reproductive process is considered. But this view is superficial; born of argument it breaks down when confronted by any body of significant facts.

Again, it has happened that in the long struggle of developing civilization, sometimes one and sometimes the other sex has gained what has seemed an advantage over the other, just as in the development of any man's individual life, his brain may gain a seeming advantage over his stomach, so that it has more than its fair share of nourishment and activity. Arguing from such a case, we might declare the brain superior to the stomach in power, health and function; but in the long accounting, all such temporary superiorities are wiped out. So with men and women, seeming advantages for either are gained only at the expense of the common life; and in the last analysis, men and women are now fairly established on the quantitative side. Marshall has shown that if we compare brain weight with the stature in the two sexes there is a slight preponderance of cerebrum in males; but if the other parts of the brain are taken into consideration, the sexes are equal. Havelock Ellis has carefully gathered the results of many investigators and declares that woman's brain is slightly superior to man's in proportion to her size. But these quantitative differences are now felt to have comparatively little significance; and of the relative qualities of the brain substance in the two sexes we know nothing positively. In fact, if we give a scientist a section of brain substance he cannot tell whether it is the brain of a man or a woman. It is very probable that the average woman's mind is capable of much the same activity as the average man's mind, given the same heredity and the same training. They are both alike capable of remarkable feats of imitation, and an ordinarily intelligent man could probably learn to wear woman's clothes, and walk as she generally walks, so as to deceive even a jury of women, if there were a motive to justify the effort Women also can perform, and they do perform, most of the feats of men.

At the same time it is desirable to note present differences in modes of thinking and feeling, for while they may have been produced by environment and ideals, and may hence give way to education, they must be reckoned with in making the next steps. In the chapter on education we shall discuss certain academic peculiarities of women's minds, but here we are interested in seeing what fundamental differences characterize the thinking of the sexes.

Women seem more subject to emotional states than men; and this general observation agrees with the fact that the basal ganglia of the brain are more developed in women than in men, and these parts of the brain seem most intimately concerned with emotional activity. Whether emotion follows acts or leads to acts remains a disputed question, but certainly emotion gives charm and significance to life and distinguishes modes of thinking. Particularly in the dramatic art, this quality of mind gives women special excellence. The fact that she more often appeals to emotion than to reason, as cause for action, in no way marks her as inferior to man, but simply as different As Ellen Key says: "There is nothing more futile than to try to prove the inferiority of woman to man, unless it be to try to prove her equality." Most women think in particulars as compared with men. The individual circumstance seems to them very important; and it is hard for them to get away from the concrete. On the other hand, a man's thinking is more impersonal and general; and he is more easily drawn into abstractions. It is true that woman's domestic life would naturally develop this quality but we are not now concerned with the question of origins. Most women find it easy to live from day to day; the man is more given to systematizing and planning. Thus in offices, men are more efficient as heads of departments, while women handle details admirably. In public life we have recently seen thousands of women eager to depose a United States Senator, accused of polygamy, without regard to the bearing of the concrete act on constitutional guarantees. Women have done little with abstract studies like metaphysics; they have done much with the novel, where ideas are presented in the concrete and particular.

This habit of dealing with particulars, and disinclination for abstraction, leads easily to habitual action. It is easy for women to stock up their lower nerve centers with reflex actions. This, of course, goes along with the general anabolic characteristics of the sex. Hence women are the conservers of traditions; rules of conducting social intercourse appeal to them; and they are the final supporters of theological dogmas. Women naturally uphold caste, and Daughters of the Revolution and Colonial Dames flourish on the scantiest foundations of ancestral excellence. Man, on the other hand, is more radical and creative. He has perfected most of our inventions; he has painted our great pictures; carved our great statues; he has written music, while women have interpreted it.

Along with these fixed qualities of action, women have a tendency to indirection when they advance. We say they have diplomacy, tact and coquetry, while man is more direct and bald in his methods. Of course, one easily understands how these qualities may have arisen, since "fraud is the force of weak natures," and woman has always been driven to supplement her weakness with tact, from the days of Jael and Delilah down to the present day adventuress.

These qualities of mind naturally drive women to literary interests which are concrete, personal and emotional. Men turn more easily than women to the abstract generalizations of science. Of course, there are marked exceptions to these general statements, in both sexes. Madame Curie, who was recently a candidate for the honors of the French Academy, and who, in 1911, was given the Nobel prize for her distinguished services to chemistry, is but one of many women who are famous to-day in the world of science. Still the private life of these women, as in the case of S6nya Kovalevsky, seems to bear out our general conclusion. Men, on the other hand, as milliners and editors of ladies' journals, show marked skill in catering to women's tastes; but on the whole the differences indicated seem important and widely diffused.

Another profound difference between men and women is the woman's greater tendency to periodicity in all her functions and adjustments to life. In all normal societies the life of the man is fairly regular and constant from birth to old age. He moves along lines mainly predetermined by his heredity and his environment, his habits and his work. Even puberty is less disturbing in its effect upon a boy than upon a girl; and often by eighteen we can anticipate the life of a young man with great accuracy. The one element in his life hardest to forecast is the effect of his love-affairs.

With a woman, it is quite different As a girl, the period of puberty produces profound changes; and after that, for more than thirty years she passes through periodical exaltations and depressions that must play a large part in determining her health, happiness and efficiency. In the forties, comes another great change which affects her life to a degree strangely ignored by those who have dealt with her possibilities in the past.

But the great element of uncertainty, always fronting the girl and young woman, is marriage. Marriage for her generally means abandonment of old working interests, and a substitution of new; it brings her geographical change; new acquaintances and friendships; and the steady adjustment of her personal life to the man she has married in its relation to industry, religion, society and the arts. If children come to her, they must inevitably retire her from public life, for a time, with the danger of losing connections which comes to all who temporarily drop out of the race.

A boy, industrious, observant, with some power of administration, studies mining engineering, moves to a mining center and expresses his individual and social powers along the lines of his work until he is sixty. The women who impinge against his life may deflect him from the mines in California to those in Australia, or from the actual work of superintendence to an office; or from an interest in Browning to Tennyson; or from Methodism to Christian Science. The girl with industrious and observant interests studies stenography and type-writing, moves to the vicinity of offices, but is then caught up in the life of a farmer-husband who shifts her center of activity to a farm in Idaho where she must devote herself to entirely different activities, form new associations, think in new terms, respond to new emotions, and adjust herself to her farmer-husband's personality. When, after twenty-five years, she has reared a family of children, and when improved circumstances enable them to move up to the county seat, she confronts many of the conditions for which she originally prepared herself, but with farm habits, diminishing adaptability and diminishing power of appealing to her husband. His powers are still comparatively unimpaired, and as a dealer in farm produce or farm machinery his interests undergo slight change. In general, it may be said that a woman's life falls into three great periods of twenty-five years each. The first twenty-five years of childhood and girlhood is a time of getting ready for the puzzling combination of her personal needs as a human being, her needs as a self-supporting social unit, and her probabilities of matrimony. The second twenty-five years, the domestic period of her life, is a time of adjustments as wife and mother, which may instead prove to be a period of barren waiting, or a time of professional and industrial self-direction and self-support. The third twenty-five years is a time of mature and ripened powers, of lessened romantic interests, and if the preceding period has been devoted to husband and children, it is often a time of social detachment, of weakened individual initiative, of old-fashioned knowledge, of inefficiency, of premature retirement and old age.

On the moral side, as Professor Thomas has so admirably pointed out, women have evolved a morality of the person and of the family, while men have evolved a morality of the group and of property. Since men have had a monopoly of property and of law-making they have shaped laws mainly for the protection of property, and in a secondary degree for the protection of the person. Under these laws a man who beats another nearly to death is less severely punished than one who signs the wrong name to a check for five dollars. Man's katabolic nature and his greater freedom have given him almost a monopoly of crime under these laws which he has made. Offences against the coming generation, against health, social efficiency and good taste have until recently been left to the tribunal of public opinion as expressed in social usage; and here, as we have seen, women are generally the judges and executioners. In this, her own field of moral judgment, woman is idealistic and uncompromising. If one of her sisters falls from virtue she will often pursue her unmercifully. If a man, on the other hand, commits a burglary or forgery her sympathy and mercy may make her a very lenient judge.

In aesthetics, the differences follow the same general law. Women express beauty in themselves; jewels are for their ornament; and rooms are furnished as a setting for themselves. The lives of millions of workers go to the adornment of women. In painting they sometimes excel, but a Madame Le Brun does her best work when she paints herself and her child, and when Angelica Kauffmann would paint a vestal virgin, she drapes a veil over her own head and transfers her features to the canvas. Sculpture and architecture are too impersonal and abstract to attract much attention from women at present. Even a sculptor like Mrs. Bessie Potter Vonnoh finds her truest theme in statuettes of mothers with their children about them.

During the past few years psychologists have paid great attention to secondary sex characteristics of the mind, and doubtless many qualities of the thought and feeling of men and women owe their origin to the same source as brilliant plumage, antlers, combs and wattles. Thus the shy, retiring, reticent, self-effacing, languishing, adoring excesses of maidenhood and the peculiar psychological manifestations of the late forties must probably be understood from this point of view. So, also, must the bold, swaggering, assertive, compelling bearing of youth be interpreted. The shy or modish, dandified, lackadaisical cane-carrying youth is naturally disliked as a sexual perversion.

Women alone, whether individually or in groups, tend to develop certain hard, dry, arid qualities of mind and heart, or they become emotional and unbalanced. Losing a sense of large significances, they become over careful, saving, sometimes penurious, while in matters of feeling they lavish sentiment and sympathy on unimportant pets and movements.

Men, when alone, become selfish, coarse, and reckless; their judgments become extravagant and their pursuits remorseless.

Thus it is certainly true that men and women supplement each other in the subjective as in the objective life. Man creates, woman conserves; man composes, woman interprets; man generalizes, woman particularizes; man seeks beauty, woman embodies beauty; man thinks more than he feels, woman feels more than she thinks. For new spiritual birth, as for physical birth, men and women must supplement each other.

To be a woman then, is to be for twenty-five years a girl and then a young woman, capable of feeding and protecting herself, possessed of preparing and conserving powers superior to her brothers. After that, for twenty-five years, she is a human being primarily devoted to romanticism, finding her largest fulfilment only in wifehood and motherhood, direct or vicarious; in the last twenty-five years, she should be a wise woman, of ripe experience, carrying over her gathered training and powers to the service of the group. All this time she is, like the man, an incomplete creature, realizing her greatest power and her greatest service only when working in loving association with the man of her choice.

WOMAN'S HERITAGE

So thoroughly have modern men fastened their attention upon the problems of the immediate present, that one feels driven to justify oneself in taking up an historical investigation of any subject presented in a popular manner. And yet it takes little argument to show that what we shall be depends in large measure on what we are; and that what we are rests back on what we have been. In anything we try to think or feel or do, we quickly reach a limit; and this limit is determined by the original quality of our nervous system plus the training it has received. For here is the curious fact about this instrument of thought and feeling which at once takes it away from comparison with mechanical instruments. Whatever it does, becomes a part of itself, and then helps to determine what it will do the next time and how it will do it. With the making easy of mental operations through repetition, and with the formation of associations based on our choices, it may be truly said that we become whatever we habitually think and feel and do.

Every choice we make is thus literally built into our character and becomes a part of ourselves. After that, the old choice will help determine the new, and we shall find ourselves being directed by all of our past choices, and even by the choices of our ancestors. Since, then, all our earlier selves are continued in us and make us what we are, we are simply studying ourselves when we study the history of our ancestors. If we would go forward, we must first look backward; for we must rise on stepping-stones of our dead selves.

But history is not merely the story of the past To relate that, would take as long as it took to live it, and the result would be but weariness of spirit. History, to be significant, must select the events with which it will deal; it must arrange these in series that are in accord with the constitution of things; and then it must use the generalizations it reaches to interpret the present, and even to forecast the future. It is obvious that this interpretation will depend on the point of view held by the interpreter.

Hence we must ask in what fundamental beliefs this presentation rests. These are, first, that life tends to move along certain lines that constitute the law of human nature. Just as the infant tends first to wriggle, then creep, then walk, then run and dance, so human nature tends to move upward from savagery through primitive settled life to the complex forms of larger settled units. In this progress, material or economic forces play a large part; but ideas, originally born out of circumstances, but sometimes borrowed from other people, sometimes degenerate remnants of past utilities, also play a large part The progress we finally make is thus directed by this human tendency, by material circumstances, and by ideas. Sometimes it keeps pretty closely to what seems to us to be upward human growth; sometimes it stagnates; sometimes it gives us perverted products; and sometimes it destroys itself.

Thus it becomes necessary to trace the past experiences of woman that we may see with what heritage she faces the future. She is all that she has felt and thought and done. She started with at least half of the destiny of the race in her keeping. Handicapped in size and agility, and periodically weighted down by the burdens of maternity, she still possessed charms and was mistress of pleasures which made her, for savage man, the dearest possession next to food; and for civilized man, the companion, joy and inspiration of his days.

Of woman's position in early savage times we know only what we can learn from fragmentary prehistoric remains, from the structure of early languages, from records of travelers and students among savages of more recent times; or what can be inferred from human nature in general. Most of this data is difficult to interpret, but it is probable that woman's position was not much worse than man's. It is a bad beast that fouls its own food or its own nest; and the female had always the protection of the male's desire. If she could not entirely control her body, she could still control her own expressions of affection and desire; and, without these, mere possession lost much of its charm.

As keeper of the cave, cultivator of the soil, and guardian of the child, woman, rather than her more foot-loose mate, probably became the center of the earliest civilization. The jealousy of men formed tribal rules for her protection; and to these, religion early gave its powerful sanctions. Thus there came a day when the woman took her mate home to her tribe and gave her children her own name. Even if the matriarchal period was not so important as has sometimes been assumed, woman certainly had large influence over tribal affairs in early savage life.

With the increase in population, and the consequent disappearance of game, man was forced to turn his attention to the crude agriculture which woman had begun to develop. The superior qualities which he had acquired in war and the chase, enabled him slowly to improve on these beginnings and to shape a body of custom which made settled society possible. With man's leadership in the family the patriarchal form of government developed, and man's power over woman was sanctioned by custom and law. The woman was stolen, or bought; and while sexual attraction did not play the continuous part which it plays in developed society, it must have done much to protect women from abuse and neglect, at least during the years of girlhood and child-bearing. It is at this point that our historical records begin.

In the pages of Homer, or of the Old Testament, in Tacitus's "Germania," or in the writings of Livy, we find woman's position well defined. True, she stands second to the man, but she is his assistant, not his slave. She must be courted, and while marriage presents are exchanged, she is not bought In times of emergency, she steps to the front and legislates, judges, or fights. It is possible in the pages of the Old Testament to find women doing everything which men can do. Even where the power is not nominally in her own hands, she often, as in the cases of Penelope or Esther, rules by indirection. Her body and her offspring are protected; and the Hebrew woman of the Proverbs shows us a singularly free and secure industrial position. Such was the condition in primitive Judea, in early Greece, in republican Rome, or among the Germans who invaded southern Europe in the third and fourth centuries of our era.

Man's jealousy of his woman as a source of pleasure and honor to himself, and to his family, must have always acted to limit woman's freedom, even while it gave her protection and a secure position in society. With the development of settled government in city states, like Athens or early Rome, the necessity for defining citizenship made the family increasingly a political institution. A man's offspring through slave women, concubines, or "strangers" lived outside the citizen group, and so were negligible; but the citizen woman's children were citizens, and so she became a jealously guarded political institution. The established family became the test of civic, military, and property rights. The regulations limiting the freedom of girls and women were jealously enforced, since mismating might open the treasures of citizenship to any low born or foreign adventurer.

In the ancient Orient, in Greece, Rome, and in later Europe, these stages have been repeated again and again. Woman is first a slave, stolen or bought, protected by sexual interest to which is later added social custom and religious sanction. Early civilization centers around the woman, so that she becomes in some degree the center of the home-staying group. In primitive civilization man takes over woman's most important activities; but she gains a fixed position, protected, though still further enslaved, by political necessities.

But with the increase of wealth, whether in terms of money, slaves, or trade, woman found herself subject to a fourth form of enslavement more subtly dangerous than brute force, lust, or political and religious institutionalism. This was the desire of man to protect her and make her happy because he loved her. He put golden chains about her neck and bracelets on her arms, clothed her in silks and satins, fed her with dainty fare, gave her a retinue of attendants to spare her fatigue, and put her in the safest rear rooms of the habitation. But it is foolish to talk of conscious enslavement in this connection. Rich men and luxurious civilizations have always enslaved women in the same way that rich, fond, and foolish mothers have enslaved their children, by robbing them of opportunity, by taking away that needful work and that vital experience of real life which alone can develop the powers of the soul.

Thus in the Periclean age in Greece, in the Eastern Kingdoms established by Alexander, in Imperial Rome, in the later Italian Renaissance, in France under Louis XIV and Louis XV, in England under the Stuart kings, and in many centers of our own contemporary world, women have given up their legitimate heritage of work and independent thought for trinkets, silks, and servants, and have quickly degenerated, like the children of rich and foolish mothers, into luxury-loving parasites and playthings.

To maintain this luxurious setting for their mistresses, whether wives or irregular concubines, men of the Occident have generally been driven to ever fiercer struggle with their fellows. Thus a Pericles, at the zenith of his powers, facing difficulties which strained and developed all his forces, had for his legitimate wife a woman, bound hand and foot by conventions and immured in her house in Athens. But a man is only half a complete human being, and the other half cannot be furnished by a weak and ignorant kept-woman, no matter how legal the bond Hence the forces always driving men to completeness and unity drove Pericles away from his house and his legitimate children and his mere wife to find the completion of his life.

In these cases, as elsewhere, demand creates supply, and there were to be found everywhere in Athens able and cultivated foreign women, many of whom had come over from the mainland of Asia Minor; and one of these, Aspasia, became the mistress of Pericles and bore him children. She was no adventuress of the street, but an educated and brilliant woman, in whose home you might have met not only Pericles, but also Socrates, Phidias, Anaxagoras, Sophocles and Euripides.

This is the stage that always follows the period of the luxury-loving wife. It was so in Imperial Rome, in later Carthage, in Venice, and in eighteenth-century France But the normal human unit is the man and woman who love each other, not these combinations of illegality, law, lust, love and dishonor. Such a triangle of two women and a man rests its base in shame, and its lines are lies, and its value is destruction. So virile republican Rome swept over decadent Greece and made it into the Roman province of Achaia; later the chaste Germans swarmed over the decadent Roman Empire and then slowly rebuilt modern Europe; the ascetic Puritans destroyed the Stuarts; while the French Revolution was the deluge that swept away Louis XVI and put the virtuous, if commonplace, bourgeoisie in power.

So far we have dealt with the position of women as though it depended alone on human hungers, passions and environment; but while these are the driving forces of life, they are very subject to the repressing and diverting power of ideas, working in an environment of economic conditions. These ideas may themselves date back to earlier passions and economic conditions, but they often survive the time which created them, and then they enter into life and conduct as seemingly independent forces. These ideas played a large part, even in the ancient world.

The Jews organized their religious and political practices about a patriarchal Deity ruling a patriarchal state; and their tradition handicapped all women with the sin of Eve, the sin of seeking knowledge. The Greeks, on the other hand, gave woman a splendid place in the hierarchy of the gods, and idealized not only her beauty in Aphrodite but her chaste aloofness in Artemis, her physical strength in the Amazons, and her wisdom in Athena and Hera. They covered the Acropolis with matchless monuments in honor of Athena, patron goddess of their fair city, and celebrated splendid pageants on her anniversaries. So, too, republican Rome, while it gathered its civic life about patriarchal ideas in which the father was supreme, gave women positions of high honor in its religion, whether as deities or as servitors of the gods. In the Niebelungenlied, the Germans bodied forth their splendid conceptions of female beauty, strength and passion in such figures as Brunhilda. These ideas must have done much to offset the physical weakness and functional handicaps of women in the ancient world.

The Christian ideas, which have dominated us now for nearly two thousand years, are generally considered to have been favorable to women. In their insistence on the value of the human soul, and on democratic equality, they have doubtless helped to raise the status of women along with that of all human beings. But, as between man and woman, Christianity has given every possible advantage to men, and has added needlessly to the natural burdens of women.

From Judaism, Christianity borrowed Eve, with her eternally operative sin, and thus placed all women under a perpetual load of suspicion and guilt The Founder of the new faith never assumed the responsibilities of a family, and he included no woman among his disciples. Example, even negative example, is often more powerful than precept Paul, the most learned of the disciples, in his writings, and as an organizer of the Church, emphasized the older Jewish position. In the new organization, women filled only lesser places, while the men settled all points of dogma, directing and mainly conducting the services of worship. Meantime each woman's soul remained her own, to be saved only by her individual actions; therein lay her hope for the future, both on earth and in heaven. But it was those later developments of belief and practice that gathered around Christian asceticism which placed woman and her special functions under a cloud of suspicion from which she is not even yet entirely freed.

Celibacy became exalted; virginity was a positive virtue; chastity, instead of a healthful antecedent to parenthood, became an end in itself; and monasteries and convents multiplied throughout Christendom. Something of shame and guilt gathered around conception and birth, as representing a lower standard of life, even when sanctified by the ceremonies of the Church. From the second century to the sixth, the ablest of the Church Fathers, Greek and Latin alike, formulated statements in which woman became the chief ally of the devil in dragging men down to perdition. We still hear ancestral reverberations of these teachings in all our discussions of woman's place in civilization.

But ideas can only for a time overcome or divert the primitive human hungers, and slowly Mary, Mother of Jesus, won first place among the saints. Celibate recluses who feared to walk the streets for fear of meeting a woman, and who spent the nights fighting down their noblest passions, starving them, flagellating and rolling their naked bodies in thorny rose hedges or in snow-drifts to silence demands for wife and children, threw themselves in an ecstasy of adoration before an image of the Virgin with the Baby in her arms. So Maryolatry came to bless the world.

But even this blessing was not without alloy, for it gave us an ideal of woman, superhuman, immaculate, bowing in frightened awe before the angel with the lily, standing mute with crossed hands and downcast eyes before her Divine Son. She represented, not the institution of the family, but the institution of the Church. Even when she appeared in representations of the Holy Family, Joseph, her husband, was not the father of her child, but his servant

Chivalry took up this conception, and shaped for us the fantastic lady who stands back of much of modern romantic love. Robbed of her simple, human, pagan passions, she became often an anaemic and unfruitful, if angelic, creature.

For the direct and passionate assurances of a virtuous and noble love she substituted sighs and tears, languishing looks and weary renunciations. This sterile hybrid, bred of human passions and theological negations, must be finally banished from our literature and from our minds before we can have a healthy eugenic conscience among us.

The Protestant Revolution went far to restore the special functions of women to respect Belief in her individual soul, and in its need of salvation through individual choice, was supplemented by the belief that this choice must be guided by her individual judgment. Celibacy ceased to be a sign of righteousness; and the best men and women married. But beliefs cannot be directly destroyed by revolution; they can only be disturbed and modified. The teachings of Paul, Augustine, Tertullian and St. Jerome were still authoritative, and Calvin and Knox reaffirmed many of them. The family was still subordinate to the Church; and marriage still remained a sacrament, with theological significances, rather than the simple union of a man and woman who loved each other. The choice of a mate once made was final, because theological, and it could be broken only with infinite pain and disgrace.

The great political upheaval, which we call the French Revolution, carried in its fundamental teachings freedom and opportunity for men and for women; but like the corresponding revolution in religion, it required time to make adjustments, and so we have been content to live for more than a hundred years in the midst of verbal affirmations which we denied in all our institutional life.

In America, conditions have always been favorable for women to work out their freedom. Among the immigrants who came to our shores before 1840 there were, of course, a few traders, adventurers and servants who hoped to improve their financial conditions; but the leaders, and most of the rank and file, came that they might be free to think their own thoughts and live their own lives. If this selection of colonists, through religious and political persecution, sometimes gave us bigots with one idea, it also gave us people who knew that ideas can change. Along with Cotton Mather it gave us Anne Hutchinson, Roger Williams and William Penn.

Most of these who came in the early days belonged to extreme dissenting sects believing in salvation through individual choice, based on personal judgments. Preaching was exalted at the expense of ritual; and by substituting new thinking for old habits in religion, the American settlers made it less difficult for other adjustments to be made, even in such a conservative matter as woman's position. It is through no accident that Methodists, Friends, Unitarians and the Salvation Army have been much more sympathetic to woman's progress than have the older ritualistic faiths.

And these theological ideas had to be worked out under the material conditions of the New World, which were also favorable to the emancipation of women. Facing primitive conditions in the forest, it became a habit to do new things in new ways. Woman's work and judgment were indispensable; and these picked women showed themselves capable in every direction. They did every kind of work; and when it came to enduring privation or even to starving, they set an example for men.

But while every new movement in ideas always carries with it other radical ideas, the practical difficulties of mental, social and legal adjustment always prevent the full and harmonious development of all that is involved in any new point of view. In the American colonies the need for new adjustments in religion, government and practical living made it inevitable that any very important change in woman's position should linger. In fact, the student of colonial records finds many traces of ultra conservatism in the treatment of women, though the forces had been liberated which must inevitably open the way for her through the New World of America into a new world of the spirit

And before the quickening influence of the new life had time to become commonplace, the struggle with England began. The Revolutionary period was a time of intense political education for every one. War and sacrifice glorified the new ideas; and even the children and women could not escape their influence. Why then did not the American Revolution pass on to full freedom and opportunity for women? For the same reason that it did not forever abolish slavery in America. The vested interests involved were so many, and the changes so momentous and difficult, that only the most imperative needs could receive attention.

But this does not mean that the interest in a larger life for women was not active or that women were making no advance in self-direction. There is evidence that women like Abigail Adams realized the abstract injustice of their position, and the fact that as early as 1794, Mary Wollstonecraft's "Vindication of the Rights of Woman" was republished in Philadelphia shows that her ideas must have had some currency in America.

After the Revolution, the intimate, stimulating influence of Europe, which the earlier colonists had enjoyed, was for a time almost entirely lost. The new States became extremely provincial; and minds untouched by the larger world always tend to conservatism. Noah Webster, in "A Letter to Young Ladies," published in Boston, in 1790, declared that they "must be content to be women; to be mild, social and sentimental." Three years later the "Letters to a Young Lady," by the Reverend John Bennett, were republished in Philadelphia, after going through several London editions. He placed the qualities to be cultivated in this order: "A genteel person, a simple nature, sensibility, cheerfulness, delicacy, softness, affability, good manners, regular habits, skill in fancy work, and a fund of hidden genteel learning." Through the first half of the nineteenth century these ideals struggled along parallel with the new ideas that were everywhere springing up from the colonial forest experiences of the last two generations.

As conservers of morals and as leaders in higher ideals of life, the advanced women of America came early face to face with two outgrown abuses. One of these was human slavery and the other was intemperance. In attacking these abuses, women had to break with all the traditions that defined their position.

The wealthy and intelligent Englishwoman, Frances Wright, who came to this country in 1818 to attack slavery, found herself doubly opposed because she was a woman speaking in public Had not St. Paul declared: "It is a shame for women to speak in the church*'? Lucretia Mott, born in the Society of Friends in Nantucket, had escaped the full force of this injunction, but even she found, when she attacked slavery in public, that she had invaded a world sacred to men, and she was sternly warned back. Miss Susan B. Anthony also began her public life as a teacher and a temperance reformer. It was only when she found herself helpless, in presence of the prejudices against her sex, that she turned her attention to freeing women from all purely sex limitation in public life.

When the Civil War broke out, the women were ready to do their part It is quite possible that the names of Clara Barton and Dorothea Dix may be remembered when Grant and Sherman are forgotten. With the establishing of new human values the historian of the future may consider the saving of life and the preventing of misery as more worthy of lasting record than even military genius. These women and their millions of helpers had not the resources of organized government at their disposal; but, instead, they had oftentimes to work against the jealousy of those in authority. At the close of the war, the Sanitary Commission comprised seven thousand aid societies scattered over the country, and it had raised over fifteen millions of dollars. Those women who remained at home, in the absence of fathers and sons for four years, faced all the problems of practical life. Who can estimate the value of training in cooperative work and organization which the Civil War gave to the American women?

In the Civil War, women directly served men; but in the great industrial reorganization which came afterward they served mainly women and children. Here the victories have been won in the press, in the legislative halls, and in courts of law. Working with men, or alone, they have perfected organization, agitated, raised money, printed appeals, and carried cases through the courts, until factories and stores have been made safer, excessive working hours have been cut down, young children have been exempted from labor, many sweat-shops have been closed, and women workers have begun to be organized to care for their own needs. Much has been done; more remains to be done; but the training of the women has gone steadily forward.

These, then, are the forces which have pushed women forward in America: European political and religious persecution, the forest necessities of colonial life, the American Revolution, the struggle with slavery and intemperance, the Civil War, the industrial struggle and the need to protect women and children from capitalistic exploitation. Possibly women have now reached a point in their development where they can turn to public service and to a full realization of their powers and responsibilities without the goading necessity of a great wrong. If not, there are sufficient wrongs still calling to lead them for many years. Intemperance is not yet banished; the negro is not yet freed from the effects of his slavery; working women and children are not yet fairly protected;

disease reaps needlessly large harvests; Lazarus still begs at the table of Dives; our public education leaves much to be desired; criminals are badly handled; millions of European refugees come marching into our land needing guidance. Meantime, millions of women are content, because themselves comfortable, and there are some even willing to aid the powers of obstruction.

In these later years, marvelous changes have taken place all over the world. Even in China, official attempts are now being made to leave women free to walk by abolishing the bandaging of infants' feet In Turkey, women are going out from the harem to participate in public life. In Germany, they are escaping from the exclusive service of the home. In England, they are repeating the cries of the men of 1776 and of 1789: "All men and women are born free and equal" "No taxation without representation.'' "One person, one vote." In Finland, Australia, New Zealand, Norway and Sweden, women have all the essential civic and political rights of men.

But, as in all human progress, first the ideas of a few leaders change; they shape legislation; and the new organization slowly makes over the practices and then the deep-seated mental and moral habits, which constitute popular prejudices. These old unreasoning feelings still largely dominate us, blinding us to the facts of life and blocking each new advance by which women might pass into the world of free choice and adjustment of their lives as co-workers with men. In the next chapters we must study these present-day conditions in detail.

●●

2
Women in Education

In discussing woman's relation to formal education we are really examining her ability to master and teach certain intellectual exercises, for in our modern industrial democracies our efforts are confined almost exclusively to training the mind and to stocking it with information. Each year we talk more and more about physical, moral, political, social and industrial education; but requirements for entrance into schools, promotions in them, and graduation from their courses, still rest almost entirely on information acquired; and in a less degree, on intellectual ability displayed.

Even in selecting and certifying teachers, the emphasis is all laid on intellectual equipment On the physical, moral, or social sides we at most demand that the candidates shall not be too bad; on the political side we do not demand even this, since nearly 80 per cent of our whole teaching force is declared legally unfit to vote or hold office, and is yet employed to train our future citizens. But on the intellectual side we demand positive proof of fitness. Thus it is fair to say that our modern education deals almost exclusively with knowledge.

Knowledge, in the past, has nearly always been considered much as we consider dynamite to-day. It was a dangerous force, useful to a ruling class, and hence preserved in the hands of a cult, generally a priesthood; but it was thought capable of working endless mischief in the hands of ignorant people. Through all the pages of history we find individuals, and weaker groups, driven away from the accumulated treasure; and if detected in their desire to know, especially if they sought knowledge through original investigation, they were branded with such titles of disgrace as "wizard" or "heretic;" and, as a warning to others, they were often burned in the public square or buried alive.

Women, as an inferior class, were especially restrained from learning. Knowledge would breed discontent in them; it would make them question the binding power of the conventions and beliefs which held them in their place; and it would show them how to achieve their freedom, and might even encourage them to assume leadership. Here and there, individual women gained the training necessary for leadership, as in the cases of Sappho, Aspasia or Hypatia; but the great mass of women was sternly repressed. Eve leads a long line of women martyrs who, across the ages, have paid a great price for their desire to eat of the tree of knowledge. For herself, she might have paid the price but, with subtle understanding of women, the penalty was made to involve all whom they loved; the terrors of that price have held the sex in restraint ever since. Eurydice, Pandora, Eve, Lot's wife and Bluebeard's wife have in turn served as awful warnings. After a time it came to be understood by women that they should fix their eyes on their husbands and never look forward or backward, lest they lose their Eden and drag those whom they loved after them to destruction. Of course, if women could not learn they could not teach; at least, they could not teach where it was necessary to impart knowledge; and so their share in formal education has been slight, until our own time. Young children have been considered their special charge, and the care and culture of infancy and young childhood have always rested in the hands of mothers, grandmothers, aunts and female servants. Beyond these early years, however, woman's part has been restricted to emphasizing, mainly with girls, the dogmas and practices of caste, kitchen and church.

These were the conditions which prevailed through early Oriental and Classical times. Christianity brought women some degree of intellectual freedom, but it also imposed new forms of restraint. Its fundamental teachings, based as they were on a belief in individual values, were favorable to the extension of knowledge and to the opening of opportunity for all. The Church, however, shaped under the half-civilized conditions of the Middle Ages, quickly took knowledge into her own keeping, forbade its extension, and increasingly held before woman, as her highest ideal, the negative virtues of the cloister.

The humanistic and theological changes which came with the awakening of the European mind at the close of the Middle Ages, did much to set free the accumulated treasures of knowledge. Protestantism, by exalting individual judgment and insisting on the necessity of each one reading and judging the sacred records for himself, made it possible for even women to enter into the heritage of the ages. At least, the key to learning, reading, was given into her hands. Later Protestant sects broke down the limits of sacerdotalism, until women found that they could look forward a little way without losing their Edens, or could even glance backward without being turned into pillars of reproach.

The political revolutions of the eighteenth century also affirmed in their point of view the same intellectual freedom for women as for men. It has taken a long time to make the practical adjustments, but they are now well under way. Since 1870, women have had very great freedom in their approach to knowledge; and having knowledge, they have been allowed to impart it to others.

In America, freedom for women to study has moved more rapidly than in Europe. Even in the colonial period, there were emancipated women, as we have seen; and in the last half of the eighteenth century several schools were opened for girls, which were more than polite finishing schools. Notable among these institutions were the seminary at Bethlehem, opened in 1753 by the Moravians, and the school established by the Society of Friends, in Providence, R. L., in 1784. But nearly all girl's schools before 1800 were limited to terms of a few months, where girls attended to learn needle-work, music and dancing, and to cultivate their morals and manners.

At the close of the Revolutionary War, the leaders of public opinion universally recognized that their new experiment in government would succeed only if the voters were intelligent. This statement of belief became the major premise on which all arguments for free and compulsory education were based; and while we have practically accepted a much wider justification for education, in connection with the care of defectives, industrial training, and other recent movements, we have not yet changed our formulated philosophy concerning the relation of the state to its children. Free and compulsory education is still mainly justified on the ground that it produced good citizens.

But the women had not full citizenship and hence the argument for general education did not apply to them. Had they been enfranchised after the Revolution, all educational opportunities would have been open to them at once as a matter of course; and an immense amount of struggle, futile effort, and unnecessary friction would have been saved. But this larger view of woman's rights and powers would have required an adjustment in deep-seated ideas and prejudices, concerning her proper position, too great to be undertaken by men facing a new form of government and the material problems of a new world.

But even without this change in ideas, economic conditions steadily forced the women into educational activity. There were not enough men available to teach the scattered country schools, and citizens had to be trained for the needs of the new democracy. John Adams recognized this when he wrote to Mr. Warren that their wives must "teach their sons the divine science of politics;" though he would have been one of the last to favor admitting women to full participation in public life. He did not realize that if women were to train men for citizenship, the rudiments of knowledge which they had learned in scattered schools and in their poor little academies must be greatly supplemented. Life, however, is never logical, and at this advance men balked. Necessity was forcing women into schools as teachers, and hence into larger preparation for their own lives; but public opinion, here as elsewhere, failed to recognize the forces that were compelling its action.

Thus the work of furnishing more advanced intellectual training for American women had to be started by the women themselves. This is possibly the first time in human history that a great group of people feeling itself irresistibly moving toward a social, industrial and political readjustment, little less than revolutionary in its nature, has gone deliberately to work to prepare for the change through education. The working classes of the world are doing the same thing now; but women showed them the way.

In some vague degree, American women recognized the truth which Dr. Gore recently brought before a mass of working men in England. "All this passion for justice will accomplish nothing," he declared, "unless you get knowledge. You may become strong and clamorous, you may win a victory, you may affect a revolution, but you will be trodden down again under the feet of knowledge if you leave knowledge in the hands of privilege, because knowledge will always win over ignorance."

American women were fortunate, too, in having for their leaders such women as Emma Willard, Mary Lyon and

Catherine Beecher. Emma Willard was a woman of the world; she had traveled abroad and she brought to her work a cultivated nature, wide experience of life and natural leadership. Her personality went far toward lifting the movement to a plane of respect. After trying a little academy in Vermont, she appealed to the State of New York in 1814 for help. In this appeal, she wisely adopted the prevailing view of the relation of the state to education. The state must have good citizens, she repeats, and then goes on, "The character of children will be formed by their mothers; and it is through the mothers that the government can control the character of its future citizens." The State of New York granted her articles of incorporation for her academy at Waterford, N. Y., but refused her the modest sum of five thousand dollars for which she had asked. In 1821, she established the Troy Female Seminary, where for years she trained and led the intellectual life of American women.

Miss Mary Lyon begged the money from the common people with which she opened Mount Holyoke Seminary in 1887. Those who feared the education of women were disarmed by the fact that in the new institution domestic service was emphasized to the extent of having the girls do all their own work. Another group of possible critics was won over by the fact that religious instruction received constant care. But notwithstanding the conserving influence of housework and religion, there went steadily out from Mount Holyoke during the following years a strong line of teachers demanding ever larger opportunity for themselves and for those they taught

Miss Catherine Beecher added to her work in schools for girls a general propaganda for woman's education, and she devised large plans for its development. In 1852, she organized the American Woman's Educational Association "to aid in securing to American women a liberal education, honorable position, and remunerative employment." She helped to start girls' schools in half a dozen cities, and by writing and talking she sowed in the hearts of women, especially in the Middle West, a discontent with existing conditions and a deep desire to know.

From the time of this awakening in the thirties and forties, two lines of educational activity for the advancement of woman's education steadily developed. One was the effort of women to educate themselves in distinctly women's schools; and the other was the movement by which existing institutions for boys and men were gradually opened to girls and women. These two lines of activity still remain distinct, and not always sympathetic with each other's aims.

The effort to establish distinctly women's schools was continued after the Civil War by Matthew Vassar, who founded in 1861, and opened in 1865, the first adequately endowed and organized college for women in America. Ten years later, Miss Sophie Smith founded and endowed Smith College to furnish women "with means and facilities for education equal to those that are offered in colleges for young men." The institution was opened in 1875; and in the same year Henry Durant established Wellesley College.

The last Report of the United States Commissioner of Education shows that there are now 108 institutions of higher learning to which men are not admitted; but most of them have modeled themselves so closely upon men's colleges that they have not been able to work out lines of distinctive instruction specially fitted to women. One cannot help feeling that since they do not open their doors to men they should do something more toward working out an ideal education for women than they have so far undertaken. When the Association of Intercollegiate Alumnae met in New York, in the autumn of 1911, its discussions gathered around the possibility of adding to college courses subjects of special value to women. Hygiene, biology and sociology were the subjects most favored; but the matter needs attention from women and men who stand outside the group dominated by our older college traditions. This movement to provide distinctive schools for women had brought together, in 1910, 85,714 girl students in private secondary schools and 9,082 women students in higher institutions of learning.

The second line of development, which sought to open up all existing schools to girls and women, began when Boston opened a high school for girls in 1825. New York opened a high school for girls three years later.

It was in the West, however, that this movement took strongest root and made most steady advance. The West has always led the East in opening equal opportunity to women, even equal suffrage. The forest and the frontier compel such action even in such commonwealths as Australia, New Zealand and Canada, where there has been no political revolution to hasten it Labor is scarce; the invading people are intelligent and ambitious for their children and desire them educated. The women must teach them to read and write; the girls learn with their brothers; and so the women master the mysteries of formal education.

Thus it is no accident that Oberlin, in the western forest, was the first college to open its doors to women. Antioch, under Horace Mann's direction, was, however, the first institution of higher learning to give men and women equal opportunity. The new States of the Mississippi Valley early established State universities. These institutions were little more than seminaries, but the free spirit of the frontier was so strong in them that in 1863 Wisconsin University admitted women to its privileges, and Kansas and Indiana followed shortly after.

It is the year 1870, however, that marks the beginning of a new period in the higher education of women as in so many other lines of advance. In that year, Michigan University, California University and the University of Evanston, adopted co-education. Michigan was just entering on a great career and her influence was very important There, for the first time, women could follow a university curriculum under the same conditions as men. Two years later, Andrew D. White introduced the Michigan idea at Cornell.

In the forty years since Michigan opened her doors, the advance of women under conditions of co-education has been steady and rapid. In Harvard and Columbia opportunity takes the form of annexes where women can secure almost any educational opportunities they desire. In other universities, like Pennsylvania and Johns Hopkins, women are admitted to graduate study. Most of the institutions of higher education that do not yet admit women are theological and technical schools, or small colleges like Haverford, where there are equivalents in Swarthmore and Bryn Mawr, for women who wish to attend a Friend's College. A woman can work in almost any important university in America to-day if she cares to do so. In 1910 there were conferred in the United States 12,590 A. B. degrees, and women took 44.1 per cent, of them.

Meantime, there have been no important reactions in institutions which have once opened their doors to women. In 1902, Chicago University separated men and women students, but only during the first two years of their undergraduate work. Practically this has affected only one-half of the women in the first year and a very much smaller proportion in the second year. When Leland Stanford Junior University was opened in 1891, 25.4% of the students were women. This proportion rose in successive years as follows: 1892, 29.7%; 1898, 80.4%; 1894,88.8%; 1895,85.8%; 1896,86.6%; 1897, 87.4%; 1898,40.1%. Fearing that the institution would be swamped with women, and that able men students would stay away, Mrs. Stanford ruled that there should never be more than five hundred women students in the university at one time. This limit was reached in 1902, and it was then provided that women should not be received as special students, nor in partial standing. Later, men in partial standing were cut out, though they continued to be received as special students. Women are now admitted in order of application, but preference is given to juniors and seniors. This really establishes a higher standard for women than for men, and one would expect that men would be kept away from an institution requiring a higher standard for women quite as much as from one where there were many women working on an equality with men. In 1910, Tufts College decided to separate men and women, for local reasons. The statement was made at the time that a philanthropist had promised a gift of $500,000 for a woman's college, if the sexes were separated. The doors of Wesleyan are to be closed to women after 1912, but this is due to local and financial reasons.

The movement in European universities, while not so uniform as in America, has been in the same direction. Miss Buss, Miss Beal and Miss Emily Sheriff led an early movement for higher secondary education of girls similar to that which gathered around Miss Willard in America. In 1871, Miss Clough started in English women away from colleges. Now it has become fashionable, and a woman who has been to college stands better in a community than one who has not. Add to this the freedom and romance of "going to college" and it follows that many young women, with increasing economic freedom, are tempted to go up to the universities just as well-placed young Englishmen go to Cambridge or Oxford as passmen. They have no special interest in scholarship; but they like the life. This large body of young women, and of men under similar conditions, will doubtless lower the scholarship of modern college and university life as a whole. But possibly the need of the world for all-around men and women is even greater than its need for scholars; and in that case we may find justification for both passmen and passwomen.

With the opening of knowledge to women it became possible for them to instruct children in matters intellectual; and since our school learning was almost entirely a matter of information and mental training, they early became an important part of the teaching profession in America.

Once started, all our conditions favored the rapid increase of women teachers. There were industrial openings for men on every side; and with our rapid increase in population, an army of teachers was required. Since the calling had in the past been filled by inferior members of the clergy, broken-down soldiers, or old women, there was a tradition of constant change, and young men on their way to permanent professions were steadily supplanted by young women on their way to the altar.

Co-education very materially assisted this substitution. Social, religious and economic reasons early combined to establish co-education in elementary schools in America, and now it has become a national custom. In cities like Philadelphia and Brooklyn there are some separate schools; but in 1910, only 4 per cent, of all the elementary children and only 5 per cent of the children in public high schools were in separate classes. In private schools, which care for less than 10 per cent, of the children of the country, the percentage of children in separate schools is greater.

Practically all American children are now in co-educational institutions. Had the boys been in schools by themselves it would have been more difficult to place women teachers over them, but in mixed schools the question does not arise. Even where the boys and girls were separated, however, that fact did not prevent the employment of women teachers, though it may have retarded it. Thus in Philadelphia, in 1911, there were 125 boys' classes, 174 girls' classes, and 894 mixed classes in the grammar grades; still there were but 175 men teachers employed and, of course, the girls' classes were all taught by women.

While administrative positions are less monopolized by women than teaching posts, they are being steadily filled by them. For fifteen years Idaho has had able women State superintendents elected by popular suffrage; Colorado and Montana have also given this highest educational post to women. In most of our States we have women serving as county superintendents; and in Idaho women fill nearly all these positions. Several of our largest cities, notably Chicago and Cleveland, have women superintendents; while many high schools and most of our elementary schools have women principals. In 1909, Mrs. Ella Flagg Young was elected president of the National Education Association; and in 1911, Miss Alice Dilley was elected president of the Iowa State Teachers' Association. Both of these elections were victories for women won in the face of determined opposition from many of the men.

Another feature of this monopoly of teaching by women should be emphasized. Many boards of education require a woman to resign her position if she marries, and married women are seldom appointed to teaching positions, except where they are widows or separated from their husbands. In a test case recently carried to the Supreme Court of the State of New York a decision was rendered that the Board of Education of New York City could not dismiss teachers for marrying; but by refusing leave of absence to prospective mothers the Board is still able to remove all women who dare to have children. Thus we have a modern industrial democracy being educated almost entirely by celibate women.

But why should a woman be forced to leave teaching because she marries? Would not married women do much to strengthen and broaden the calling? Are not married women better fitted than celibates to deal with boys and girls in the period of adolescence? There is doubtless a feeling that a married woman should make way for some girl who needs the position to help herself along; but schools should not be used for the needs of teachers, no matter how deserving the individual may be.

There is, too, a possibility that a married woman might have a child, and a feeling that this would shock the other teachers and the children. Surely we have grown beyond this condition; the teacher could easily be given a leave of absence for a few months, or for a few years; and nowhere else could the children better meet this fact of universal existence around which our Anglo-Saxon reticence has woven such a shameful conspiracy of silence. At least, when a woman has passed the period of childbearing she could bring to the school incalculable gifts of balanced judgment and ripe understanding of life.

Meantime all the influences which have brought about the monopoly of teaching by women are increasingly operative. Every year more able women leave our high schools, normal schools and universities, with no corresponding new lines of occupation open to them. The feeling of rivalry between men and women teachers grows stronger each year. Powerful teachers' federations, such as those in Chicago and Buffalo, composed mainly of women, are said to be using their influence to favor women. In New York City, the women teachers have compelled the city to equalize the wages of men and women, at an annual expense of $8,500,000, after a bitter fight lasting several years.

The effects of this monopoly upon the women themselves are very difficult to estimate. Some alarmists tell us that women teachers face the danger of a premature and loveless old age; that the celibate communities they form in the commonwealth are marked by pettiness and emotionalism; that the salaries paid teachers are so small that they cannot provide for sickness and old age, and that, unless pensioned by the state, some of them must one day eat the bread of charity.

On the other hand, we are told that education is the natural province of women; that teaching fits them to be good mothers and helpful citizens; that women alone can form the character of girls; and that boys are refined and perfected by the constant contact with women.

Probably neither of these statements is wholly true. It is certain that many women teachers do marry, do become the mothers of fine children, and are social forces in their communities. With advancing standards of scholarship, better salaries, old age pensions, and a popular demand for professional efficiency in teachers, it will be increasingly difficult for men to use the calling as a preparation for law and medicine, or for women to use it as a preparation for matrimony. The calling doubtless does offer a greater equivalent for marriage than most others; and many women live their mother life vicariously *tot* other people's children.

At the same time, however, when a woman has given fourteen years of her life to preparation for teaching, eight years in an elementary school, four in a high school, and from two to four in professional training, she has made an investment and formed habits which will make her hesitate before turning to matrimony. The independence and income will prove attractive during young maidenhood; and matrimony can hardly yield its best results to the woman who enters it after she is thirty. It is certainly true that women are decreasingly willing to enter the teaching profession; and in many parts of the country there is a chronic dearth of trained teachers.

Meantime, for good or ill, women have eaten, and are eating of the tree of knowledge as they will. If this has driven them out of the little paradise of the past, they are in a fair way to make the whole world into a paradise of the present. Only through training their minds could they have broken away from an outworn past. In this time of readjustment there must be many mistakes and many tragedies. The fool-killer will gather a rich harvest, but if we are open-minded and eager to see the truth, each martyr will teach her sisters, and the future generations of women will conserve the values of the past and add to them new treasures and new graces of knowledge and understanding.

It is most unfortunate that these real issues should be obscured by sex rivalry. There can be no real rivalry between a man's soul and his body, between science and religion, between man and woman. Such antagonisms rest back in the failure to realize the incompleteness of man or woman alone, for any purposes of life. And there is, too, that evil notion which still affects economics, that when two trade one must lose. The fact is that in all honest exchange buyer and seller gain alike, and all who participate become rich. It is so in all honest relations between these half-creatures we call men and women. In agreement, association, cooperation, lies strongest significant life for both. In separation, competition and antagonism lie arid, poor, mean lives, conceited and egotistic, vapid and contemptible.

3
Economic Independence of Women

Nowhere does a human being escape compulsion. Even were he alone in the world he would be forced to obey the physical laws governing gravity, heat, cold, hunger and disease. No matter what his desires might be, he would find himself limited and constrained by fixed laws, the inexorable penalties of which he could escape only by obedience. If the man were not alone, then each one of his companions would limit his freedom, and he would limit each one in the group, if they were to live together in peace and efficiency; and yet each of the man's companions would help to free him from the tyranny of physical forces, from the social pressure of others, and even from the bondage of his own nature.

Independence is thus an ideal to be achieved only through obedience. It begins in self-sub-ordination and reaches its finest realization in social subordination. Since the beginning of time men who thought have always dreamed of freedom; and for two hundred years now independence has been a word to conjure with. But in so far as independence means freedom to follow one's own unregulated desires, it is a fantastic and dangerous dream; and yet this dream of impossible independence has been among the greatest influences in furthering human development in the past.

The old-time dependence of one individual on the immediate caprices of another largely disappeared with the passing of slavery. But in place of this personal subjection has come a more complex and in some ways more compelling and crushing control through the monopoly of wealth. Property has become the medium through which the most binding of human relations are organized. Accumulated wealth has become a great reservoir of power to which some individuals gain access through rights of birth, others through carefully guarded privileges, and still others through cunning devices or through force; but the masses of the people must gain their fragments of this wealth through arduous lifelong labor. Even the earth, the original source of all wealth, is parceled out, and all of it is now owned by individuals or groups who control it in their own interests. One man may thus have thousands of acres which he cannot use, and which he will not allow others to use, while another has not where to lay his head. Laws jealously guard this wealth, which is the key to all opportunity; and public opinion, that most subtle, pervasive and compelling of all forms of law, gathers a thousand sacred initiations, rites, ceremonies, prohibitions and excommunications around it. A man who has killed his neighbor, or ruined his friend's family, may be less punished by society than one who cheats at cards.

In primitive life a man may be a man by virtue of what he is; to-day he may have all the rights and privileges of any man by virtue of what he possesses. In any community can be found strong men, honest, though misplaced or unfortunate, begging bread, wasting their lives for want of money to live decently. And beside these one sees other men of weak physique and feeble minds, who have lived as parasites on society all their lives, but who are handsomely dressed, well fed, and possessed of power to do as they will, simply because they have access to wealth. It is no wonder that if one would seek freedom to-day in America he must look for her image on a gold coin.

It is not difficult to see why property has become such a powerful instrument in civilization. Anything which a person really owns, in a psychological sense, is a home for his soul. Really owning an object, a toy, a garment, a watch or a home, means infusing one's personality into it. A man who possesses significant things has a new body through which his soul can work; this body trains his powers; and it should give him life more abundantly. A landless man must become a soulless man. Of course, we are not here speaking of legal ownership. Many people own legally things into which they have never infused themselves; sometimes they have so many things that no individual could possibly infuse himself into them.

These conditions may prevail even in primitive life, but to-day they have been vastly increased through the fact that with advancing civilization money was devised. This is a system of counters, generally coin or paper, not really valuable in themselves, but always resting back for value on the earth, or on something derived from it. In the past it was supposed that there were some things which, because of their nature, were not marketable, while others were beyond price. To-day we set values on everything, even on men's bodies; eyes, ears, legs and lives can be priced. There are, in fact, insurance companies and factories that have regular schedules of value for various parts of the body. Our courts set prices on blighted affections, damaged reputations, social advancements, impaired digestions, damaged complexions, nervous shocks and extreme humiliations. Even a woman's honor may have a price in dollars.

These property rights, like the rights of the person, have always been subject to violence. Powerful individuals and groups have always been able to overstep legal restrictions and public opinion, and seize what they desired. The land grabbing going on in North Africa and Persia to-day and the activity of great industrial monopolies at home, show us that some property rights still need to be secured by force. In this struggle, it has come about naturally that men, being stronger, freer and less scrupulous than women, have outstripped them and have so far had a pretty complete monopoly of wealth. In fact women themselves have at times become property. In such times a man who stole or bought a woman, naturally took over with her all her rights in real estate and personal property as well as her person and her services.

Only gradually did women gain power to hold property themselves. Mainly because fathers wished to preserve property in their families, the right of women to inherit became slowly established as civilization advanced. In Judea, Greece and Rome, certain rights of a woman to hold property were clearly settled. In the reversion to force under feudalism, woman's rights to outside property suffered; but they have been gradually restored during the last few centuries. To-day, in civilized lands, a woman's rights to property, inherited or definitely given her or purchased by her, are everywhere recognized, if she does not marry. In France, and other Latin countries, she may still lose control of her property if she takes a husband; but in northern and western lands, even a married woman may retain her possessions.

Woman's body, too, is increasingly looked upon as her personal property. With the raising of the age of consent; with increasing severity in laws punishing rape, and with the abrogation of judicial orders for the restitution of marital rights, it is now quite generally recognized that a woman should have the right to control her own person. Still, in many lands there is much to be done before this right is fully safeguarded.

The place where a woman has not yet achieved economic freedom is in the disposal of her labor. One must remember, however, in this connection, that not only is there no fixed standard of values in human service as yet, but that many indispensable forms of service have not even been legally recognized as valuable. In early forms of civilization, fighting and praying were considered the most important work the community received, and warriors and priests gained the big rewards. They received lands, gold, servants and dignities, while industrial workers, even the directors, were despised. Today we have reversed all this and we may pay a general only five thousand dollars a year, and a priest eight hundred dollars, while a man who develops a big industry may receive a hundred thousand dollars annually. Again, a man who invents a new gun may be given a fortune, like that of Herr Krupp, while a man who invents a surgical instrument is prevented by the ethics of his profession from even patenting it. If Pasteur had been paid for his services to France and to humanity, he would have ranked in the financial world with Mr. Rockefeller and Mr. Schwab. We pay a State superintendent of public instruction ten thousand dollars a year; but Miss Jane Addams, as instructor in ethics to the United States, receives no salary, and she must even beg the money to maintain her laboratory at Hull House. The whole question of payment for services is in a chaotic condition. Those who serve mankind most faithfully are rewarded on the principle, "From each according to his ability;" but nowhere is the remainder of the principle, "To each according to his needs," recognized. Hence our greatest servants must still beg support from our cleverest exploiters.

Domestic service is indispensable to society, but so far it has remained in the field of semi-slavery and uncertain barter; in a word, it is still in the feudal stage. The woman gives what she is and has, and nominally she gets protection and support Sometimes these fail and, on the other hand, she occasionally receives the unearned gifts supposed to befit a potentate or a shrine. As women become educated they find this condition of uncertainty and instability unbearable. They are willing to work, but they must have a chance to think and to plan their lives according to their individual needs. Some degree of economic independence is necessary to intelligent thinking and orderly living. It is not that women are demanding more property; they are demanding some definite individual property as a home for their souls; and they are coming to realize that if this property rests on some one else's feelings and caprices it is no home for the soul; it is only a tavern.

This conception is well illustrated by the case of a woman in western New York, who married about 1850, and went to live on a farm with her husband. They had small means, but she brought seven hundred dollars to the altar, which was more than he possessed in ready capital. Her part was, however, soon swallowed up in the general business, and while there was a tacit agreement, voiced at long intervals, that she had put something into the business, her part never increased, though the man with whom she worked grew well-to-do. Certain feudal rights in the butter the woman made and in the chickens she raised, yielded her small sums, which often escaped her, but which she sometimes secured and put into a few silver spoons and dishes for her table, a square of Brussels carpet, three lace curtains, a marble topped stand, and six horsehair covered chairs for her parlor. These articles were considered in a very special sense her own. The man might have sold them and used the money, but public opinion would have condemned him had he done so.

Meantime the woman cooked for the family and the hired men, scrubbed and washed and mended. She strained and skimmed the milk from a dozen cows, and churned the butter; she fed the calves; cared for the hens; dug in the garden; gathered the vegetables; did the family sewing; and stole fragments of time for her flower-beds. Her hours were from five in the morning until nine at night, three hundred and sixty-five days in the year, with no half-days or Sundays off.

Incidentally she read her Bible, maintained religious exercises in the village, provided the church with a carpet by methods of indirection and kept the church clean. She upheld a moral standard toward which men only weakly struggled; hunted down and drove away all other women who refused equal service to their lords; ministered to the neighboring sick; and doled out alms in winter-time. Her home was a social and industrial microcosm which she conducted as a feudal holding under the protection of her lord. It would be an interesting study to work out the rules of this feudal relation between husband and wife in any agricultural community. They would be found as varied, as unjust and arbitrary, and as generous, as those of the old regime in France.

A woman in a home is supposed to furnish three kinds of service. She must be a housekeeper, a wife and a mother. As housekeeper, her services can be estimated in current values running from three to twenty-five dollars a week with board and lodging. The other two kinds of service have never been reduced to monetary values.

As a wife, a woman is supposed to give her love, her person, her sympathy and inspiration; the personal care of a husband, including his clothes, attention to his relations and friends and general management of his social position and reputation. If she fills this position well, she is mistress, valet, confidential adviser and public entertainer. Possibly these services can be rated except the first, and even here the divorce courts scale alienated affections all the way from five hundred to twenty-five thousand dollars, according to the appearance of the woman and the skill of contending lawyers.

As a mother, the woman is supposed to give children a good heritage, nurse them, care for them, doctor them and train them. We have established values for these services as wet-nurse, nurse-maid, governess, doctor and teacher, but who can estimate a woman's value in giving a child a good heritage?

It is no wonder that such a difficult problem has remained thus far unsolved. Here and there a man gives his wife a household allowance, from the money they earn in common, and she struggles to save from it some fragments for her individual needs; others put their wives on a salary; and some others divide the income on a fractional basis. But the slightest study of existing conditions must convince any one that women are everywhere deeply dissatisfied with their economic relations to the family. On referring recently to this fact before an audience almost equally divided between suffragists and anti-suffragists, I found every woman present applauding the statement. Another time when I asked more than sixty of the wealthiest women in one of our cities how many were dissatisfied with their relations to the family property, explaining that I was not asking how many wanted more money but how many wanted a different relation to the family money, all the women raised their hands except three and they all had private property.

Meantime, economic changes, to be described in the next chapter, have transformed our homes and nearly eight million women have gone outside to earn money. The gladness with which they have gone shows that they were not afraid to work, though at first the money did not belong to them, but to their families. Almost everywhere in the United States the money women now earn is their own; only in Louisiana can the husband collect his wife's wages. Any one who reads Mrs. Gilman's masterly study of the evil effects accompanying woman's economic independence must feel how far-reaching are not only the discontent but also the evil influences of our present system through over-emphasizing sex and through corrupting the public thinking and feeling concerning services and wages in general.

Yet no one can seriously approach this problem in his own person without feeling that the relations of husband and wife contain elements that not only make it impossible to resolve the woman's service into money values, but that would make it useless to do so even if it could be done. The most distinctive quality of love is its desire to give. Love that seeks to get is not love. If when a woman gives herself she tries to secure individual property it will be only that she may give it to the man she loves. Marriage is a partnership of soul and body, and this includes property. It still remains true, however, that each must have in order that he may give. Besides this, there are always outside obligations, and special needs within the group, that require individual property for their realization.

In the past, the partnership of marriage has been incomplete on the property side; why not complete it? Why not reorganize our laws and our public opinion so that two people who establish a family, putting into it all they have, should pay out of the income the necessary family expenses and divide all else equally between the parties? Property acquired before marriage, and all inherited property, might well be held in individual right since it should never be a prize for prostitution, not even when it is euphemistically termed "a good home."

Under equal suffrage Idaho has passed such a law, and all property gained after marriage belongs equally to husband and wife. If the wife dies, her heirs, in absence of a will, inherit half of the family property. If the two separate, the court, in absence of an outside agreement, settles the property as it does the children. The judge may order that it be divided equally, or he may give it all to either party, according to conditions; but the woman has identical rights with the man. Surely some such solution is demanded by our present unrest. No one will ever be economically independent; but husband and wife should be economically equal.

●●

4

The Feminizing of Culture

With the weakening of sex prejudices and the removal of legal restrictions on women's freedom it was inevitable that they should invade fields of activity where formerly only men were found. Since women must eat every one knew that they must work, and the sight of a woman at work was no new experience. Even in the days when they were most secluded and protected, the number kept in ease was always very small compared with the women slaves and servants who spun, cooked and served. Hence men were used to seeing women at work; and while industrial adjustments have not been easily made, they have still been accepted as a matter of course. But who, fifty years ago, could have imagined that to-day women would be steadily monopolizing learning, teaching, literature, the fine arts, music, the church and the theater? And yet that is the condition at which we have arrived. We may scoff at the way women are doing the work, and reject the product, but that does not alter the fact that step by step women are taking over the field of liberal culture as opposed to the field of immediately productive work.

Some of the reasons for this change are so clear that it seems as though they might have been anticipated. In a comparatively few years the greater part of Western Europe and all of America has become rich, not this time through the enslavement of other peoples and the confiscating of their wealth, but through the enslaving and exploitation of the material forces of nature. This wealth is not [well distributed, but large numbers of families have received enough so that the women do not have to work constantly with their hands. At this point all historic precedent would have turned these women into luxury-loving parasites and playthings. A good many of them have taken this easiest way and entered the peripatetic harems of the rich. But several million women refused to repeat the old cycle of ruin; they knew too much. What then should they do? Faith in the value of conventual life for women had passed; industrial changes had transformed their homes so that the endless spinning, weaving, sewing and knitting were no longer there, even to be supervised. Penelope's tasks had passed to foremen, working under trades union agreements, in the factories of Fall River and Birmingham. Even the function of the lady bountiful who looked after the spiritual and family affairs of her tenants and servants and distributed doles and Christmas baskets was gone. Her tenants owned their own farms, and her chauffeur resented her interference with his personal life. What should she do?

And this movement was not confined to the rich, for those who were not yet economically free were still deeply influenced by the changes which were taking place. The Goulds, Stan-fords, Vanderbilts, Floods, Carnegies and Schwabs had all been lifted from the level of the masses to financial grandeur before the eyes of the multitude, and democratic ambitions drove parents who thought themselves in the line of financial advancement to secure culture for their girls in time. If the daughter was destined to live on Fifth Avenue, or to marry a duke, it was best to get her ready while young. In all our industrial democracies, armies of American parents have devoted themselves to labor, and even sacrificed comforts and necessities, that the daughters might get ready to live easier and fuller lives than the parents had known. If the choice had to be made between the girl and her brother, the chivalry of the father and the ambition of the mother very often gave the opportunity to the girl.

And so an emancipated army of leisure has been formed which has transformed the very-nature of the culture with which it has busied itself. Books, periodicals, musical instruments, travel became cheaper and cheaper as the demand increased. Wholesale production makes almost any luxury accessible to every one. It is also possible to find modern and agreeable forms for older academic exercises. If Greek and Latin were too full or too difficult, courses in Romanic and Germanic philology would do as well. Anglo-Saxon gave way to Old English; and Chaucer to the Lake Poets. Philosophy struggled for favor with the English novel on equal terms. The works of Raphael were photographed and lithographed until the Sistine Madonna became as commonly known as the face of any strenuous and popular statesman of the day. With the aid of these art productions, and John Addington Symonds, every woman with leisure became an art critic. If economics was not interesting, sociology was available; and it could be democratized to any degree desired. If travel was troublesome, one could leave it to Cook; buy a ticket and he would do the rest.

If these awakening hungers and corresponding opportunities had affected only the period of life formerly thought available for education, these changes would have come about much more slowly than they have. But the genetic conception of life, steadily popularized since 1870, has led us to see that education is coterminous with life. It seems strange that we should have ever thought that mental activity belongs alone to youth. Borland's study shows that in a list of four hundred fairly representative great men, only 10.25% ceased their mental activity between the ages of forty and fifty; 20.75% between fifty and sixty; 85% between sixty and seventy; 22.5% between seventy and eighty; and 6% after eighty.

The recognition of such facts as these has given us a new genetic sense of life, under the influence of which mothers and grandmothers have joined the younger women in the pursuit of culture. They have formed clubs—study clubs, current events clubs, camera clubs, art clubs, literary clubs, civic clubs. They have organized courses of university extension lectures; enrolled in Chicago University correspondence courses; and have flocked to Chautauqua by the thousand in the summer, when not abroad. It is not through the generosity of men that liberal culture has come into the possession of women; they have carried it by storm and have compelled capitulation.

Judging by the facts presented in the last chapter, women are pretty fully in possession of formal education. If we examine this monopoly a little more carefully, we shall find that while in the kindergarten and in the elementary schools boys furnish 51% of the enrollment, simply because more boys are born in civilized communities than girls, as soon as we reach the high schools, girls increasingly take the lead. In 1910, the girls formed 56.45% of the enrollment in high schools—or there were 110,249 more girls than boys. The proportion of girls increased through each of the four years of the course, and of the graduates, 60.8% were girls. In the public normal schools, 64.45% of the students were girls.

The universities, colleges and technical schools, which are massed together in our government reports, had hardly any women students in 1870; in 1880, 19.8% of the students were women; in 1890, 27%; in 1910, 80.4%. In all these institutions we had enrolled in 1910, 17,707 women. Of 602 institutions reported in 1910, 142 were for men only; 108 were for women only; and 852 were open to both sexes. But here again the influence of women increases during each of the four years for, as we have seen, the women took 41.1% of the A.B. degrees granted in 1910. It is surely not too much to say that, if present conditions continue, women will soon be in an overwhelming majority in all secondary and higher education in the United States.

If we examine the teaching force, we find this monopoly already established. In 1870, when our government records begin, 59% of the teachers were women; in 1880, 57.2% were women; in 1890, 65.5%; in 1900, 70.1%; in 1910, 78.6%. The more settled and intelligent the community the more rapid this advance has been. Thus Arkansas has 52.4% women teachers; but Massachusetts has 91.1% and Connecticut has 98%.

In cities, too, the women fill nearly all teaching positions. New York City has 89% women in its force; Boston, 89%; Philadelphia, 91.4%; Chicago, 98.8%. In many cities the proportion is even greater than this: Omaha has 97%; Wheeling, W. Va., 97.5%; Charleston, S. C, 99.8%; and in forty-six American towns of 4,000 to 8,000 inhabitants there is no man teaching. When we remember that many of the men indicated above are in high schools or in supervising posts, we are prepared for the statement in a report recently laid before the Board of Education of New York City that in half the cities of the United States there are virtually no men teaching.

In our high schools, 54% of the teachers are women; in public normal schools, 65%; and in institutions of higher learning 17.6% are women. Even in supervising positions, there are more women than men in the large centers of population. Certainly these figures justify us in saying that women have established a monopoly of education in the United States, except in the higher institutions.

In order to discuss the effects which this monopoly of education by women is having on the curriculum of the schools we must first agree on what constitutes the peculiarity of women's minds as compared with men's minds. In our first chapter, it was asserted that women are more interested in the concrete, human, personal, conserving and emotional aspects of life; while men more easily turn to the abstract, material, impersonal, creative and rational aspects. To put it broadly, women are more interested in the humanities; men more readily pursue the sciences. Let us admit at once that there are many individual exceptions to this statement Some women have reached great excellence in abstract studies; and some men are notoriously concrete and emotional; but nevertheless the general statement seems borne out by a wealth of common observations and detailed comparisons.

Personal observation must always be colored by prejudices and prepossessions, but my own have been so wide, and so uniformly in one direction, that it seems justifiable to report them.

For a quarter of a century I have been working in schools or with teachers, and my personal observations all agree with the above characterization. I have spent five years in Cornell University, New York; one year in Zurich University in Switzerland; two years in the State University of Indiana and seven years in Stanford University in California. These institutions are widely distributed; they were all fully co-educational; and they each had a wide range of elective studies. In all of them, class-rooms devoted to literature and modern languages had a large attendance of women, while lecture-rooms and laboratories devoted to abstract science were almost deserted by them. This could not have been due to commercial considerations, for many of these women were facing teaching; and during all this time the demand for women who could teach science has been much greater than for women who could teach literature.

In my work with teachers, both in the classroom and in the field, I have carried out many inductive, quantitative studies, based on measurements or returns from large numbers of children. I have never found women teachers taking up and carrying out this kind of work with any such enthusiasm as men apply to it, though it lies at the base of their professional life.

Institutional generalizations seem all to point in this same direction. For instance, the Girls' Evening High School in Philadelphia is managed by one of the best known scientific women in the country, Dr. L. L. W. Wilson, head of the biological department of the Philadelphia Normal School. With a thousand girls of high school grade, under the leadership of a scientific woman, the only science courses given in the school are those in domestic science. The reason is that the girls, most of them not being candidates for a degree, will not take up science work, though they form strong classes in literature and languages.

If, from such general facts of observation, one turns to exact comparisons, where quantities can be measured, the results are all the same. Of students enrolled in classical departments of universities, colleges and technical schools reporting to the United States Bureau of Education, in 1910, 86.5% were women, while of those enrolled in general science courses, but 17.2% were women. In 1,511 public and private high schools and seminaries, reporting to the Bureau of Education in 1909-1910, a larger percentage of boys than of girls was enrolled in algebra, geometry, trigonometry, physics, chemistry, physical geography, civil government and rhetoric, which is a scientific study of language. A larger proportion of girls enrolled in Latin, French, German, English literature and history, and there was a slightly greater enrollment of girls in botany, zoology and physiology.

In the further discussion of this subject it will then be taken for granted that in education, feminization means emphasis on languages, literature and history, as opposed to mathematics, physics, chemistry and civics. For the elementary schools we have no data capable of reduction to figures, but general observation, backed by an examination of courses of study and textbooks, will compel any one to say that in twenty years we have made wonderful progress in reading, language, stories, mythology, biography and history; while all our efforts to bring nature work into vital relation with the schools have borne little fruit. Our country schools need lessons in agriculture, and the children should gain a deep sense of country life. But how can celibate young women, longing toward the towns, give this? Any subjects well taught are sure to be increasingly taught, and it takes no extended study to see that our elementary schools are being feminized in the direction of literature. This is the more striking when we remember that these twenty years have been dominated, in the larger world, by scientific interests.

In the high schools and seminaries, we have fairly complete returns showing the number of students enrolled in certain subjects since 1890. The pupils taking Latin have increased 15%; French, 4%; German, 18%; English literature has increased in ten years 7% (there is no record for this subject before 1898); and European history, 27%. There has also been an increase of 11% in algebra and 10% in geometry, probably partly due to vocational need and to the emphasis laid on these subjects for admission to college. But physics, in the twenty years under consideration, has fallen off 7%; chemistry, 8%; physical geography, 5%; physiology, 15%; and civics, 7%. A careful study of these figures must convince any fair-minded person that our school curriculum, even in the secondary field, where women's control is least complete, is moving rapidly in the direction of what we have called feminization.

The schools, too, must increasingly do something more than train the intellect; and in all physical activity involuntary suggestion is very powerful. Playgrounds are laboratories of conduct, and they should not only give physical exercise, but should also furnish standards and ideals. There can be no doubt that women are physically more restrained, retiring, non-contesting, and graceful than men; but can dancing, marching, and gymnastics take the place of more aggressive, direct and violent contests in the training of boys? So in industries, women are more given to conserving, arranging and beautifying, more given to clerking and recording, while men are more creative, disbursing, more given to mining, agriculture and commerce. Even granting equal understanding and experience, the tradition of the race must count for much; and it would seem that at every stage of growth, boys and girls alike should feel the impulse to imitate men who have an instinct to make and unmake, to trade and carry. It is no justification of existing conditions to say that the men now in the teaching profession lack these qualities; if they do, let us get rid of them and have real men. And for purposes of political life, does it not seem strange to bring up a generation of boys and girls who are to be the future citizens of a democracy under the exclusive leadership of people who have never been encouraged to think about political life nor allowed to participate in it? Let us by all means enfranchise women; but even then they cannot hope to quickly catch up with those who have some thousands of years the start, even after allowing for the fact that girls inherit from both father and mother.

Most of these differences which we have been discussing seem to rest in the fact that women are more personal in their interests and judgments than men are. This may be due to their education for thousands of years; but that makes it no less true. Women certainly, in a great majority of cases, are more interested in a case than in a constitution; in a man than in a mission; in a poem that in a treatise; in equity than in law. In a generation when everything is tending toward great aggregations, consolidated industries, segregated wealth, and new syntheses of knowledge, both boys and girls should have such training as will fit them to play their part in these larger units.

As to the feminizing influence of exclusively women teachers on manners and morals and general attitude toward life there can be no real doubt Boys and girls cannot spend eight or twelve impressionable years of childhood and youth under the constant daily influence of women without having the ladylike attitude toward life strongly emphasized. To deny this is to repudiate the power of constant involuntary suggestion and association. Whether it is desirable or not, is another question. The change may be all in the direction of advancing civilization; but just as in the assimilation of our subject races, the philosophic mind must be distressed by the disappearance of so many varieties of speech, customs, and artistic and industrial products, so in this present assimilation, one cannot help regretting the steady disappearance of the katabolic qualities of the human male. One does not need to say that this feminized product is better or worse than what we have had, but it is certainly narrower, and less in harmony with the world's thought and work, than it formerly was.

If we turn from education to the press we have similar conditions. During these past few years, hundreds of journals have sprung up devoted to women's special interests. They are almost all of them showy, fragmentary, personal, concrete and emotional. It is difficult to find one that represents general or abstract interests. At least one of these journals which boasts a fabulous circulation is supported by its women subscribers and readers to oppose the larger interests of women in education, industry and political life. At least, if it does not oppose these interests, it does not aid them. Imagine a million German women sending the Kaiser one dollar and a half a year to induce him to tell them once a month to go back to their kitchens, churches and children!

The newspapers of America have steadily changed during the last three decades in the same direction. Editorial pages and news columns have been steadily modified in the direction of fragmentary, egoistic, personal and sensational, or at least emotional, appeals. These are the qualities of children's minds and of undeveloped minds everywhere. The change is, of course, a part of the larger democratic movement of our time, and many causes have contributed to bring it about. Had women not been so active, something of the same sort would have happened; but if women were all to forget how to read overnight, there is little doubt that the newspapers would find it advantageous to print more statesmanlike editorials and more general and abstract news.

With the weeklies and monthlies, the change taking place is the same. The new reading public, brought in by increase in population and by popular education, does not support the *Atlantic*, the *Century* and *Scribner's*, but turns to *Munsey's*, *McClure's* and *Everybody's*. The very change in names speaks of the new personal and egoistic element that has come into journalism. Of course, such changes are only in part due to the influence of women, but the change is in the direction of the qualities that characterize distinctively women's journals.

In books, the personal and romantic novel has taken precedence over every other form of literature. Many of these are written by women; their circulation, both through libraries and through sales, is much greater with women than with men; and in many of them the personal gossip is as transient as that which fills the evening papers.

In the churches, especially in the ritualistic churches, women have long been the faithful attendants. Nowhere, except in the churches which make a rationalistic and abstract appeal, and in the Ethical Societies, does one find a preponderance of men. In 1903, a careful enumeration of all attendants at places of worship was made in the city of London. The count was taken on fair Sundays in autumn, and covered both morning and evening services. Sixty-one per cent, of all adult attendants were women, 146,872 more women than men passing through the doors.

About the same time a similar census was made in the part of New York City lying on Manhattan Island. The women were in excess by 171,749, and formed 69 per cent, of all attendants. Even church service, if not entirely tied to set forms, must seek to interest those who occupy the pews; and no observer can fail to note in both England and America, a movement toward ritualism on the one hand, and on the other, toward popular, personal, concrete and sometimes sensational preaching. The same general changes are taking place in libraries, in the drama, in concerts, in all group activities connected with learning and the fine arts.

But on the other side, if emancipated women had not applied themselves, since 1870, to the direction of education, literature, religion and amusements, all these interests must have suffered serious neglect and probable deterioration through the concentrating of the interests of the ablest men in engineering, manufacturing, commerce and other fields of pure and applied science. By popularizing these interests, women have really humanized them, as all similar revolutions have done in the past. In breaking up old forms and intellectual conventions they have set free new and vital impulses. Whether the historian of the future will consider this period of democratization and feminization a time of advance may be uncertain; but it is certainly a time of liberated energy and of broadening participation in all that is best in life.

●●

5

Political Life and Women

It is a well-known fact that when words have been long and vigorously used they gather within and around themselves varied meanings. Some parts of these meanings are remnants of historic, and possibly outworn, experience; other parts are the result of more or less deliberate perversion under the stress of deep feelings aroused by opposition and fighting. This is especially the fate of words in any way associated with politics. Think how battered and useless for purposes of ordinary discussion "democrat" and "republican" or "socialist" have become in America!

In the struggle of the last fifty years over woman's suffrage, most of the words involved have undergone such transformations; and so many prejudices have become associated with them, that no one can think or speak clearly and fairly to-day in these terms. "Woman's Rights," "enfranchisement," "Votes for Women," "suffragette," "polls," "ballot," "political issues," and many other words, have gone through this destructive process.

To read some of the most popular literature on this subject one might imagine that women had all deserted home and fireside, babies and baking, and were lined up, struggling fiercely to deposit certain printed slips, called votes or ballots, dealing with esoteric mysteries understood only by men like Mr. Bryan or Mr. Roosevelt, in ballot-boxes. These receptacles are supposed to be behind, or very hear, lawless saloons, where gangs of hoodlums are waiting to assault the bearers of these mysterious tickets. Thus Miss Seawell writes in the *Atlantic Monthly* for September, 1910: "The trouble would begin with the mere attempt of women to deposit their ballots. A dozen ruffians at a single polling-place would prevent a single woman from depositing a single vote. There can be no doubt that this means would be used by the rougher element and that the polls would become a scene of preordained riot and disorder." Of course, such statements could not appear in a leading magazine, in a land where women have been voting quietly for many years, were it not for the perversity of the words which the author tries to use, but which really use her. In other periodicals, equally respectable, one learns that women, goaded on by the intolerable political tyranny of men, have agreed as one soul to advance, with ballots in their hands, and sweep graft and greed, drink and all other human wrongs, into the sea of oblivion forever. Of course, this is nonsense, or worse, and in this chapter I should like to turn away from this warfare, leaving even the battered and prejudiced-soaked words alone, as much as may be possible, and simply ask: What is political life, not as defined in books, but as actually lived by a self-respecting farmer or merchant of our acquaintance? What qualities does political life presuppose in a participant? How does its use affect him? What does it enable him to accomplish? What is the relation of a woman— not some militant or unsexed ogre, nor a female breeding animal in a harem, but our own sisters, wives and daughters as they really are—what is their relation to this mysterious process?

If one approaches the political life of our modern democracies in this simple spirit of inquiry it would seem that the first requisite for participation is the ability to form sound judgments concerning political matters; and all matters are now becoming political which affect the welfare of the community. Certainly the citizen cannot devise political machinery nor select candidates to work such machinery, much less "cast a ballot," until he knows what he wants done. What are some of the questions, then, on which he must form judgments?

First of all, he must be prepared to think intelligently about protecting his life and property. He must know something of the danger of foreign invasion, of the consequent need of a navy and standing army. He must make up his mind whether it is necessary to spend $123,-000,000 yearly on an American navy and $156,-000,000 on an American army, as we are at present doing, that we may be ready to fight England, Germany or Japan if at any time we want to do so. He must ask himself whether this money might not better be used in fighting ignorance, crime, poverty and disease.

The would-be citizen must also think about protecting himself from assault as he walks about the streets; about protecting his house from thieves as he lies asleep at night He must have thought about the careless use of cars, automobiles, firearms and explosives in general. He must consider the danger from fires, contagion, diseases, mobs; he must think intelligently about contaminated water and impure foods. All these things are necessary for the physical well-being of the community life. Of course, if either man or woman cannot think intelligently about these things, he ought not to have control of them; he should leave such matters to those who can think of them.

In the second place, the would-be citizen must have fairly sound judgments on questions of raising and spending necessary revenue. What are the effects of direct and indirect taxation? Would a heavy tax on land force unused lands, including mines and waterways, into use? Should a man with a cash income of $50,000 a year pay more to support government than one with a cash income of $500? What are the objections to an income tax? How does it work in England, where it has been fairly tried? Should a great corporation pay taxes in proportion to its wealth, and in places where the wealth is protected by the law? If so, how can it be reached? Should churches, museums, libraries and schools be taxed; if not, why not? Should taxes be laid on flour, meat and eggs, on woolen cloth, on silks, velvets, ostrich plumes and diamonds? Should taxes be laid on whiskey, wines, tobacco, cigars and race-tracks? Should taxes be devised, or continued, to protect such infant industries as now handle our kerosene oil, meat, sugar and steel? Surely no one who cannot form independent judgments on these matters should presume to direct them through voting.

But not only must a nation raise revenue in the wisest and most equitable manner possible, and spend it effectively and economically, but it must also care for its present possessions. So the would-be citizen must know about the wealth in which he wants to share. What do the national, State and municipal governments own? How should the vast domains of land, the onetime inexhaustible forests, the mines of coal and metal, the waterways and water-powers, the special privileges and franchises belonging to the people be used? Should they be thrown away, gambled away, given away as favors, rented, sold, or handled directly by the people? On what terms or under what guarantees should they be turned over to individuals or companies, if this is to be done? Those who cannot form judgments on these matters should not be entrusted with such vast responsibility, be they men or women.

Questions of our foreign relations must also occupy the thought of the citizen. Are foreign entanglements necessary or desirable? If so, with what European or Asiatic nations should we seek to strengthen our friendship? Are our interests nearly identical with those of England? If we formed a close defensive alliance with her should we be thereby aiding universal peace as much as we might by maintaining more generally friendly relations with all European powers? Would an alliance with England probably draw us into her troubles, if she has any, in Egypt or India? How would such an alliance affect our relation with England's present ally, Japan? Are we fitted by the genius of our institutions and by our experience to handle a foreign empire? If not, what should we do with the Philippines?

So, too, those who are to direct the destinies of the country must think out what our relations are to be with Latin America. In the past some statesman, a Richelieu or a Bismarck, had a policy and led his nation to it by devious paths of indirection. But now that each citizen is a king, he must have a policy for his realm. Are our republican neighbors to the south to be increasingly recognized as under our protection and direction? If so, how are we to maintain the peace and secure payment of their foreign debts? All these problems are bound up with the management of the Panama Canal. They confront us in different forms in connection with immigration, especially of Asiatics.

Our institutional life must also be regulated by the citizens, and so they must have judgments about each of its details. They must know what they think about the family, forms of legal marriage and divorce, and the care of children when the family fails. The Church must be considered and protected; possibly it should be encouraged; and possibly its unwarranted assumption should sometimes be checked. Schools must be founded, supported, directed. Art galleries, museums and clubs must be chartered, and then controlled; and so must all the other institutions of our modern society. The would-be citizen must be able to think about all this work.

Industries, on which our individual and collective well-being depend, must be encouraged by special favors, limited to the public good, protected from violence, inspected in the interest of employees. Hours must be regulated, disputes settled, conditions of labor and safety secured. Children should be protected against employers' greed; and working women must receive special consideration, if the race of strong men is to continue. Here again the citizen must have judgments, or the power to make judgments, as new needs arise.

Then, too, there is a tradition of government, established by the fathers and modified by experience, which should be understood by the citizens. It recognizes certain rights as being reserved by the individual States, and others as belonging to the national government The would-be citizen should be acquainted with this tradition so that he can determine how far it is desirable to adopt a new nationalism. He will have to pass judgment on the control of interstate commerce, national or State control of public lands, national divorce and liquor laws, national food inspection, and other practical subjects which may destroy the older balance of power so jealously guarded by our earlier statesmen. The citizen must make up his mind if this is desirable.

Newer political theories must also receive the citizens' attention. Many people believe that wealth created by the people can be enjoyed by the people only when they control the sources of supply and the means of production and distribution. The citizen should know whether these socialist tendencies should be favored or suppressed. There are others who believe that government is unnecessary, and that men and women can be happy and effective only when formal laws are abrogated. The citizen must determine whether he will allow those who hold such doctrines to express them; or whether he will suppress their meetings and forbid them to enter the country. These are but a few of the subjects concerning which the citizen must think, but they are typical and they may represent the rest.

In the last analysis, it is these judgments on political matters which govern a modern democracy, whatever the laws on the statute books may be, and whatever machinery of government may be established.

Not long since, I visited one of our States where the laws forbid any one to make or sell, as a beverage, any intoxicating liquors, within the State. At the leading hotel, in the large city where I stopped, beer and whiskey signs were displayed outside the entrance; and at an open bar, in the center of the hotel, four bartenders were dispensing all kinds of drinks, while at the tables of the hotel restaurant, liquors were openly bought and drunk. There are many indictments standing against this hotel, but in two test cases juries have refused to convict the proprietors. I am told it is the same in all of the principal hotels in the larger cities of this State. In this same State, the laws forbid the manufacture or sale of cigarettes, but they are openly displayed and sold in nearly all cigar stores. In the same State, whites and blacks live under the same laws, but blacks seldom vote; they do not use the parks, attend white people's meetings nor ride with the whites in public conveyances. And yet the city was quiet and orderly and I felt as safe in person and property as though the laws on the statute books, instead of the judgments in the public mind, were being obeyed. Since this form of public opinion is so powerful, it is well that it should be intelligent.

Granted, then, that the candidate for citizen honors is prepared to pass judgment on such matters as we have indicated, he must next be prepared to devise and control means to carry these judgments into effect. Here he approaches the problems of states craft He must have in his mind a general scheme of government, with a sense of legislative, judicial and executive functions. He must realize the value of a constitution, as a point of departure; and have a theory as to safe ways of modifying it He must have fairly clear notions of legislation, and of the kinds of laws that are desirable and effective. He should know how far representative legislative bodies can be trusted to express the will of the people; and he should have studied the working of the initiative and the referendum. It is also desirable that he should know the theory of two chambers, and should have ideas as to how the members of the second chamber, if there is to be one, should be chosen.

The candidate for citizen honors should know something of the organization of the judicial branch of government He should know something of the powers and duties of local magistrates, of county, State and national courts. He should recognize the difference between civil and criminal jurisdiction. He should have an opinion as to whether judges should be elected or appointed, and if appointed, who should select them. He should realize the grave dangers that surround a corrupt judiciary, and he should know the means by which a court is enabled to maintain its standing and authority.

So of the executive power, he should see its relation to the other powers, from the constable to the president He should know the qualities required in a good executive and should be able to distinguish them in possible candidates. He should know that when the executive is lax the best of laws fall into abeyance, and he should know how such officers can be held up, through criticism by public opinion and penalties, to the fulfilment of duties. The recall should have been considered.

In the third place, the citizen should know how to select the right kind of people to carry his political judgments into effect Possibly, under a representative form of government, this is the most necessary qualification for a good voter. Many of the matters with which modern government must deal are technical, and the citizen here, as in his private affairs, must rest on the judgment of those he employs. And yet, in general, he must know what he wants.

He must know the general laws that govern the organization of parties; and he should be somewhat acquainted with the psychology of crowds. He should know how candidates are selected under the convention or caucus system; he should have an independent judgment on direct primaries.

In selecting men, the citizen must be able to recognize general ability and intellectual fitness. It is at this point that modern democracies are most apt to go wrong. The standards by which we measure men and women are most imperfect; and we are prone to let one good or bad quality overshadow all others. Thus in an extended study on school children's attitude toward Queen Victoria in England, and toward President McKinley in America, made while these rulers were alive, we found that less than twenty per cent mentioned any kind of political ability, nor did they often mention their general ability, nor their honesty. They admired them primarily because they were "good and kind." In other words the school children of these two lands approve their rulers because, in a vague general way, they like them. The significance of the study lies in the fact that in all democracies a large number of the voters live on an intellectual plane represented by these school children.

This conclusion is borne out by the judgment of Miss Jane Addams who, writing of foreign voters about Hull House, says: "The desire of the Italian and Polish and Hungarian voters in an American city to be represented by 'a good man' is not a whit less strenuous than that of the best native stock. Only their idea of the good man is somewhat different He must be good according to their highest standard of goodness. He must be kind to the poor, not only in a general way, but with particular and unfailing attention to their every want and misfortune. Their joys he must brighten and their sorrows he must alleviate. In emergency, in catastrophe, in misunderstanding with employers and with the law, he must be their strong tower of help. Let him in all these things fill up their ideal of the "good man' and he has their votes at his absolute disposal."

To be a safe citizen one must be able to go beyond this kindly feeling and ask, Does the candidate know enough to do what I want done? Has he the honesty to resist the temptation to exploit me? Has he the leadership to command the best efforts of the subordinates in his department? Has he serious defects that may cause his failure? Is he an opportune man for the time and place?

This selection is made very difficult to-day by the misrepresentation of interested individuals and political parties; and especially by the reports in the press, which seek to discredit candidates they oppose, and to gloss over or deny defects in their chosen leaders. Thus the whole public atmosphere in the midst of a campaign is intended to confuse and bewilder the citizen who is honestly seeking the best candidate. Only ripened intelligence, experience with men and women, and ability to judge conflicting evidence, can enable the voter to select wisely.

In the last place, if the citizen knows what he wants, how to devise the governmental machinery to get it, and how to select the right men to see that it is done, he must register his desire by a vote; and then watch his servant carefully to see if he justifies the trust imposed in him. If he does not, then the citizen must criticise, threaten, and, if necessary, finally dismiss the unfaithful employee. Only one who can fulfil all these functions can be considered a desirable citizen from the point of view of a modern democracy. "Eternal vigilance is the price of liberty."

And why should one desire to undertake this arduous responsibility? In the first place, because he wants the public work well done, as he understands it; and the only way to have it done in this manner is to attend to it himself. If he does not attend to it, some one else will do so; and if the intelligent citizens do not look after it then the public business will be exploited by individuals, or groups, in their own interest; and, before the citizen realizes what is happening, he will be deprived of that political liberty to secure which millions of men and women have struggled and suffered and even given their lives in the years which lie behind us.

And yet possibly the most important value of participation in political life to-day is the byproduct of continuous education which it gives. Modern political life has probably done more to train the men involved in it than have schools or churches. Business and industries alone might claim to be its rivals. In a despotism, all the events of public life are uncertain and seemingly accidental, depending as they do on the caprice of an individual This discourages thought among the masses, paralyzes action, and breeds inertia and hopelessness. At best, it gives rise to periods of desperation and violence; at its worst, it gives us the hopeless masses of Mohammedan lands. In a free democracy, on the other hand, those who participate are in a continuous process of education, judging, selecting, willing, and always with regard to realities that affect daily life. Citizenship gives one a continuous laboratory course of training in the art of right living.

Nor can the full value of this continuous training be obtained by the onlooker, no matter how intelligent he may be. For full growth of mind and spirit one must participate; just as in athletics one must leave the spectator's bench and play the game if one would develop one's own powers. Participation means love, hate, devotion and sacrifice, and only when all these powers of the soul are brought into play, together with the judgment, is the character strengthened and life more abundantly obtained It must be evident to any one who has carefully followed this analysis that hardly any of the adult male voters in our modern democracies have the qualifications of good citizens. How, then, is good government achieved? It is not achieved. We have very bad government. Everywhere there is waste and inefficiency. Wealth is unjustly divided; great corporations seize public utilities and exploit them for private gain; enormous sums are squandered on unnecessary and dangerous battle-ships and soldiers; in building a single State Capitol, $3,500,000 was recently stolen, not only wasting public wealth, but corrupting public morals; in some parts of our land little children still drive the wheels of industry; and it is everywhere cheaper to scrap-heap men and women than machines; most of our cities are ugly and badly ruled; drunkenness, gambling and prostitution are common; life is not always secure from lawless attack; and the machinery of justice is clogged and moves slowly. Part of our intelligent adult population has no direct share in the government under which it must live. We have just such a government as we should expect where incompetent people decide such vast issues of life.

But, on the other hand, we are vastly better off than any great people has ever been before us. The mistakes are our own; they are made by us who participate in government, and we are learning from them. Those who exploit us may be called to account; and frequently they are caught and punished. Of those who stole the millions in Harrisburg, nearly a score have died disgraced, or are in prison or exile; and $1,300,000 has been returned to the treasury of the State. Even when those who betray us are not caught red-handed we learn to distrust and then to despise them. They pass their last years in exile, and when their statues are erected in our State Houses they are memorials of shame. Thus we learn the art of living, we who participate in political action.

The whole business of a modern democracy is to educate itself through doing, and we are all at school. If the bills are heavy, they are our bills; and we are steadily learning how to make them less. In the past no one learned. "The Bourbons learned nothing, and forgot nothing;" and the common people were too discouraged to think. It is on these lines that our modern democracies must be judged, not as efficient and economical political machines, but as educational institutions. Judged by this standard, we believe ourselves to be the triumph of the ages.

Nor can it be possible for people to enter political life fully prepared for its duties. Even when a young man approaches a business career we do not ask that he shall possess a knowledge of the business before beginning. If he has general preparation, and a desire to learn, he is admitted to share in its responsibilities, and then learns as he goes along. It is the same in political life; few young men at twenty-one or foreigners at the time of naturalization, have the knowledge indicated in the preceding pages. If they have general preparation and a desire to learn, we admit them to participation, and they learn through doing.

Years ago, while discussing education with an English statesman, he asked whom I considered the leaders of education in his country. Knowing his Tory instincts, I replied, "Bradlaugh, Annie Besant, William T. Stead, John Burns and Keir Hardie." He laughed contemptuously: "Why those people," he said, "are merely educating themselves in public." The statement was true and far-reaching; that is what we are all doing in our modern democracies; and that is at the same time our weakness and our glory.

WOMAN'S RELATION TO POLITICAL LIFE

In discussing woman's right to vote it is well to remember that the right to rule, which is implicit in the right to vote, has always been limited by conditions of birth, residence, wealth, morality or intelligence. Universal manhood suffrage has never yet been achieved, and probably never will be. Under the best Greek conditions, it was only the free-born citizen, residing in his native city state, who voted. In both Greece and Rome, the suffrage was limited to classes defined by social position, wealth or military service. In our modern democracies there have always been limitations of birth, which might be overcome by naturalization; of residence, which could be overcome by living for a certain time in a locality; of wealth, which was supposed to insure a stake in the communal well-being; and of morals and intelligence, which at least shut out criminals the insane and the imbeciles.

Thus the right to vote is not the same thing as the right to live; and even in a commonwealth founded on ideal justice only those having a stake in the community life, and possessing normal intelligence and morality, will be allowed to rule. In a word, equal suffrage is possible, while universal man or woman suffrage is not

All through our colonial period women had a large influence in determining community questions, and in Massachusetts, under the old Providence Charter, they voted for all elective officers for nearly a hundred years. Here and there women—like Margaret Brent, of Maryland; Abigail Adams, of Massachusetts; or Mrs. Corbin, of Virginia—put forward their right to participate in the public life around them. But, in 1776, women were not voting, and the Federal Constitution left the matter of determining electoral rights to the several States. They all decided for male suffrage.

The initial impulse to secure suffrage for American women came from Europe. After the Revolution, Frances Wright, a young Scotchwoman, came to America to lecture and write, claiming equal political rights with men. In 1886, Ernestine L. Rose came from Poland and also advocated equal political rights. All the teachings of the American Revolution had favored the idea of human equality; and, as has been pointed out, when, with established peace after the War of 1812, women engaged in anti-slavery, temperance and allied movements, they were driven by the logic of events to demand the suffrage.

In 1848, the women of the country began to organize. Mrs. Elizabeth Cady Stanton, Lucretia Mott and Martha C. Wright called together at Seneca Falls, New York, the first convention in America to further equal suffrage. No permanent organization was founded, but in 1850 a convention was held in Salem, Massachusetts, and in 1852 a Woman's Rights Convention was called in Syracuse, New York, with delegates present from eight States and Canada. Miss Susan B. Anthony had meantime joined the movement; and from this time on conventions and appeals became common.

The Civil War distracted attention from all social and political issues but one. The Equal Rights Association turned its attention mainly to the rights of negroes; and in 1869 the National Woman's Suffrage Association was organized to work exclusively for woman's rights. Backed by such women as Susan B. Anthony, Lucy Stone and Julia Ward Howe, and aided by men like Henry Ward Beecher, the association became a national power. In 1890, the two organizations were united under the name of The National American Woman's Suffrage Association. This organization still leads the movement in America.

In 1902, an international meeting was called in Washington; and in 1904 the International Suffrage Alliance was formed in Berlin with Mrs. Carrie Chapman Catt as president. Thirteen nations are now affiliated with the Alliance; and the women of the world are highly organized to further equal suffrage.

Two generations of women have given themselves to this movement, and a third still faces it To the first group belong those leaders we have already named: Emma Willard, Elizabeth Cady Stanton, Julia Ward Howe, Susan B. Anthony and their associates. It was their problem to secure woman's control of her own body and property, some share in the direction of her children, and some opportunity to train her own mind and earn an independent living. These women bore the heat and burden of a conflict in which all the blind prejudices of a fixed regime were strongly massed, presenting few promising points of attack. It is small wonder that some of these leaders gained a reputation for being hard, dogmatic, aggressive, and sometimes careless of popular sensibilities. The first generation of reformers in any field must be made of stern stuff; and their beneficiaries are apt to forget the conditions that justified means no longer necessary.

The lives of these women could not be expected to fully illustrate the type of life they hoped to see their sisters living when opportunity was finally won. Only women who participated in this struggle could fully appreciate the splendid devotion of these lives to the service of a group many of whom, being personally comfortable, were insensible to the needs of less fortunate women; and were sometimes even willing to fight back any advanced ideas which might disturb their own comfort The feeling within this group of leaders, and the failure of oncoming generations of American women to recognize the debt of obligation they owe to its efforts, was illustrated by an incident that came up in connection with the Third International Congress of Women which met in London in 1899. The session was opened in Westminster Town Hall, with seven hundred delegates present, representing the most thoughtful women of the world Lady Aberdeen was in the chair, and Mrs. Creighton, wife of the late Bishop of London, was reading a paper. In the midst of deep attention, a door at the rear of the platform was gently opened, and Miss Susan B. Anthony stepped onto the stage. She had just arrived from America. Her strong figure was bent with the weight of years; her face was squared by the conflict and partial ostracism she had met; but her glance had lost none of its stern kindliness, and her bearing none of its indomitable courage.

As she appeared, this most representative audience of women in the world sprang to its feet and burst into wild cheering. In vain did Lady Aberdeen rap for order and beg the audience to let Mrs. Creighton proceed. Not until Miss Anthony came to the front and urged the women to sit down was quiet restored. These women knew the price of a life which their champion had paid for their opportunities. A few months after this the school children of the prosperous city of Rochester, N. Y., where Miss Anthony had been a leading citizen for many years, were asked to write school compositions in which they named the person they would most wish to be like. Over three thousand girls, in the elementary grades, wrote these papers, but not one chose Miss Anthony. This first generation of women reformers could not establish the type of womanhood for the modern world; they had not the leisure, nor the freedom, nor could they see all that lay in the future. But all the more, because their lives were hard, should they be held in grateful remembrance.

To the second generation of leaders belong women like Alice Freeman Palmer, Mary Sheldon Barnes and Charlotte Perkins Gilman. They came on the scene when the first campaign had been won; they could command their own bodies and property; college doors were swinging open where they could secure the training that should fit them for the struggle to win educational, industrial, social and political opportunity for all their sisters. They were still looked upon as blue-stockings and queer; they had often to serve as the butt of ridicule; but they had education, income, a certain degree of leisure, and a social recognition which, if grudging in some quarters, was all the more generous in others.

With the rapid development of higher education, these women found themselves associated with large groups of independent women who could create a society of their own in advanced centers of population. There was still much to be done in securing opportunity for women; but they could go on establishing the type of life that free women were to live. Their problems were, however, even more complex than those which confronted their predecessors. What line of education should women pursue? What lines of work could they best undertake? How could they combine an independent professional or industrial career with the life of a home and the responsibilities of a mother? How far must older social restraints be modified in the interest of intellectual and industrial freedom? It was a time for constructive statesmanship, rather than for revolution; and each woman knew she was under criticism, and that her success or failure was vastly more than her own personal concern. In her all free women were being judged.

To the third generation belongs the host of women who are to-day filling our college halls, managing the women's clubs, teaching the state schools, and competing with men in every industrial calling. Theirs is the task of completing woman's social and political emancipation, and of educating them to meet their newfound liberties. It is possible that this present generation has a keener sense of rights than of duties; and the young women of to-day must be led to realize that the delicate adjustments still to be worked out require devotion equal to that of the earlier generations, if the toll of wasted life is not to be excessive.

What now is the relation of women to the range of political activity described in the last chapter? Have they need of the protection which government gives? Are they able to form political judgments? Have they knowledge of the working of political machinery; or, lacking it, are they prepared to obtain it? Are they able to make a wise selection of people to represent them in political action? Have they need of the training which participation in political life gives? Have they the preliminary preparation to take up that training to advantage, and can they undertake these duties without serious loss of qualities desirable in women?

Women certainly have need of protection; each has a life dear to her, and honor which is dearer to her than life. In this respect she has a greater need than men. Most women, also, have property of some kind, and we are increasingly recognizing their right to control this for themselves; hence they need property protection the same as men. We do not need to think of Mrs. Sage, Mrs. Harriman, Miss Gould or Mrs.

Green, in this connection, for in every community we now have many women who are immediately responsible for large property interests which new legislation might affect most seriously.

In matters of institutional regulation by government, women are at least as vitally interested as men. In all that touches the family, marriage, or divorce, women have more at stake than men; and there are as many wives as husbands involved. The schools are also nearer to women than to men; more girls than boys attend them; more women are teachers; and more women than men are interested parents of school children. The church is also more vital to women to-day than to men. On the side of industries, it is clear that our 8,000,000 independent wage-earning women have a desperate stake in all governmental action touching the regulation of working conditions. In whatever concerns general sanitation, safe water, and pure foods, all are equally interested who must breathe and eat to live. Surely the need of women for political protection is quite as great as that of men.

In the matter of forming political judgments, not even the wisest men are beyond improvement International affairs, monetary systems, the best way of raising taxes, and similar problems, often divide the male electorate pretty evenly into rival parties. Since both cannot be right, a great deal of poor political thinking must be done by the present body of voters. Meantime, women are showing their ability to deal intelligently with all sorts of subjects in our educational institutions, in business and in social life. Their judgments command respect in every other field; and it is hard to see why they could not apply their powers to political questions.

We must remember, too, that during these last years the field of political life has been rapidly broadening, through the awakening of social consciousness among the people. To concern one's self with politics now is to be interested in good market facilities, in rapid transit for cities, in recreation centers for children, in honest labelling of food products, in reformation of criminals, in preventing marriage among the unfit, and in a hundred similar matters.

Here women will doubtless bring us a strong addition to our political efficiency. They have long been considered the natural directors of social life and, in spite of being disfranchised, they mainly handle such matters at present. Now that these subjects are being brought into the political field, women should follow them there, as they have followed their industries from the homes into the factories. There is no reason to believe that their judgments will be less sound than those of their brothers and husbands.

Of course, women's knowledge of means and methods is much less than that of men in their own class. Not only have they not participated in political life, but they have been steadily warned away from that particular tree of knowledge. Yet the present generation of women has gone through the same preliminary education in schools with its brothers; and many women in high schools and colleges have made a more extended study of political institutional-ism. Still more important, more than a million women have been educating themselves for some years in this direction through voluntary associations of some kind; while in most States they have had some political practice through limited suffrage, and in a few States full experience.

In selecting representatives to carry out their will, women have certain obvious defects of temperament and training. Having been brought up for generations to judge men only as providers of sustenance and fathers of children, they must at first find it difficult to consider candidates impersonally. Still, their general morality and their standards of right are probably superior to those of men, and they are more intolerant of faults, and they find it harder to compromise on matters of character than do men. One can hardly believe that 1,700 women could be found among the respectable, church-going, American-born residents in any county of America, who would sell their votes, year after year, as that number of men voters has recently confessed to doing in Adams County, Ohio. In fact, Judge Blair says: "There was one class of the population which rebelled against the practice. It was the womanhood of Adams County, which had never become reconciled to the custom, and whose continual hostility has resulted finally, I hope, in its abolishment."

Of the need of women for the training which participation in political life gives there can be no doubt Their lives have always been directly dependent upon other individuals, and they are prone to think in small details. Any training which extends the horizon of their interests and enables them to deal more largely with these details will fit them better for living in a world where industrial, business and social changes are so rapidly merging details in larger wholes. Experience in selecting candidates for public office would also do much to broaden women's judgments of life, and would help to break down the pettiness which sometimes characterizes their personal relations.

In the case of women, the community has a double reason for desiring that they shall develop political judgments and become acquainted with political methods. It is not only that they may share in the general intelligence and carry their fair part of the political burdens; but they have become the teachers, both in homes and schools, of the oncoming generation of male voters. We no longer live in small communities where children can see the simple processes of government operating around them, but in a complex civilization where it must all be interpreted to them, and mainly by women. Many boys who complete our elementary schools never work a day under the direction of a man. In the homes, busy fathers increasingly turn over the training of children to their wives. How can these women train safe citizens for the future if they do not understand the processes involved well enough to use them themselves?

Meantime the old arguments against woman suffrage are too outworn to need serious attention. In the past decades our civilization has become so complex, with so many groups carrying on differentiated functions, that even if we had not the millions of educated, property-owning, wage-earning, voting women that now fill our public life, the old arguments would still be obsolete. The issues of life are no longer primarily military, and but a fraction of men voters is capable of meeting modern requirements as policemen and soldiers; in time of crisis, all men would be called into the reserves; but in such periods women have always fought in the breach, from Carthage to Paris. Still, in modern warfare, those who guard the rear and furnish supplies are as necessary as those who go to the front.

It has also long been recognized that women who rear finest sons and daughters must sometimes turn away from the cradle to refresh their lives with the touch of other interests. It has also been demonstrated a thousand times over that women do not incite the lawless element to riot about the polls; but that, instead, their presence tends to remove the polling-place from the saloon and make it safer for men to go there on election-day. The plea that women would introduce a new element of sex into politics, thereby confounding its real issues, is certainly not well grounded. Sex has always played a great part in politics, as it has in all the vital affairs of life. In the open competitions of education, business or politics, sex ceases to be as significant as it is in the drawing-room.

Nor do thoughtful people imagine to-day that if women participated in political life they would suddenly bring about a reign of universal peace and righteousness. It has taken many centuries for men to learn to play the game of politics indifferently well as they do. The first effect of woman's participation would probably be to lower the efficiency of the electorate in some directions; but they are starting much farther along than men began, and they would learn more rapidly than men have learned.

It is often claimed that women do not want to vote; and, of course, there are many who do not care to assume such arduous and often difficult duties, if they can avoid it. The same holds true of many intelligent, but selfish men who desire the advantages of good government without its burdens. All such must be urged to do their duty to the state. Those who have vision and a large sense of duty can be trusted to do their fair part in caring for the public welfare. Those who wish to enjoy the benefits of peace and settled government, participating in the advantages of education, engaging in business, and having their persons and property protected, without sharing the burdens of government, should be forced to play their part

If a woman should board a street-car to-day and, when asked for her fare, should hide her face with womanly modesty and declare that she did not wish to be involved in such public matters, but preferred that the man swinging on the strap before her should pay, she would be informed that all who use the cars must pay for their maintenance. Women in America now have more than their share of education and leisure. If they do not wish to pay their fair proportion of service, they should withdraw from the high schools and colleges, from literature and music, from offices and factories, and not crowd into places where they are unwilling to play the game. The woman who leads the movement against equal suffrage in England has made a fortune in the open market as a writer, protected by the national copyrights; she maintains a house where she is protected in person and property by the city of London, the organization and administration of which calls for the constant attention of all intelligent citizens; and yet she urges women to take what they can get, but to refrain from doing their fair share of the city and national housekeeping, lest they lose their feminine charm. Surely those who profit by government should give their share of service.

It is idle to claim that equal suffrage will make no change in women. It will certainly accentuate the changes already made by higher education and by a freer business life. Some loss there must inevitably be in any such far-reaching change. We lost something of chivalry and of the spirit of *noblesse oblige* in the transition from feudalism to democracy. In transferring causes of personal difference from the dueling field to the courts of law, we lost a degree of poetic feeling and tragic exaltation, of personal initiative and physical courage. So when women passed from slavery to serfdom we lost something of male dominance and of female submission. We shall lose something in the present transition; but one must be content to lose Louis XIV and Versailles if one thereby finds modern France; one must be satisfied to lose an institution which gave us the tragically pathetic death of Alexander Hamilton, if it increases human justice and saves fathers to their families. We must even be content to lose the languishing and weeping lady of chivalry, and the coquetting, crocheting and confiding maiden of the eighteenth century if we gain in return fair minded comrades in daily living, devoted partners in family life, and strong, intelligent mothers for the coming generations. The sex instinct needs no fostering; it has led us to our best developments in civilization; and its work has only begun.

So far we have taken the popular position, and have discussed this matter as though it were still in the period of debate. The fact is, it long ago passed from the field of theory; it is now a condition. In six of our States, women have now full participation in managing public affairs. In Wyoming, since 1869; in Colorado, since 1893; in Idaho, since 1896; in Washington, beginning in 1910; and in California, since 1911, women have been sharing the vote with men. In twenty-nine States they have school suffrage, and in many places municipal suffrage. In newer parts of the world, like New Zealand and Australia, women have complete suffrage, while in old countries, like Norway, Sweden and Finland, they have essentially all the rights of men. In England, there are 1,141 women on Boards of Guardians and 615 on Educational Committees; and they are demanding full participation in all political life. In Canada they have school and municipal suffrage. It is no longer a time for argument; it is time for adjustment

Meantime the results of woman's full participation in political life, even where they have had the suffrage for some years, are difficult to determine, because of the fact already pointed out that political life in a modern democracy is so closely bound up with all the other life about it. It is quite as difficult to estimate these effects as it would be to estimate the effects of housekeeping or of woman's special costume. And yet some results are clear enough to have a large bearing on the extension of woman's suffrage in new localities.

In 1906, the Collegiate Equal Suffrage League engaged Miss Helen Sumner to make a careful study of the actual working of equal suffrage in the State of Colorado. Miss Sumner, aided by several assistants, spent nearly two years in the investigation. She gathered and carefully analyzed written answers to an extended set of questions from 1,200 representative men and women of Colorado, some opposing and some favoring equal suffrage; and she and her assistants interviewed many more. They also made a general study of industrial conditions and of legislation for the State as a whole, and a detailed study of election records and newspaper files for representative cities and counties. Her report is a masterpiece of patient research and scientific exposition.

Equal suffrage goes back to 1898 in Colorado; and while the influence of women has been in no way revolutionary, this report shows that, on the whole, political conditions have improved and woman's intelligence and her general public spirit have increased with no appreciable loss in distinctive feminine charm. One cannot help feeling as one reads this report that it is what a disinterested observer would have to say about the effect of woman's larger educational or industrial life since 1870.

In all democracies it is difficult to bring voters to the polls unless, as in some Swiss cantons, they are fined for absence. In Colorado, Miss Sumner shows that women cast about forty per cent, of the total vote in the earlier years of their enfranchisement, though they were in a minority of the total population. In the work of the primaries they were in a much smaller minority, except when some special problem or candidate appealed to them. The more intelligent the community, the larger the woman's vote; and it is largest of all in the best residence districts of Denver, the capital city. The vote of American born women is larger than that of foreigners; and while the prostitutes of Denver have been voted in the interests of the party in power, public opinion is steadily making this more difficult In Idaho, all residents of the red light district have been disfranchised by statute; and practically they do not vote.

There is no appreciable tendency on the part of women to form a new party, nor to favor their own sex. They are more inclined than men to scratch the ticket and, as illustrated in the case of Judge Lindsey, they sometimes rally efficiently around an independent candidate, especially on a moral issue. On the whole, women vote with their husbands, just as sons vote with their fathers; but the strength of the family vote, as compared with the vote of unsettled people, is certainly desirable.

Since the beginning of equal suffrage, Colorado has fully held her own with other States in advanced legislation, especially in social and educational lines. Women have suffered no insult at the polls, and on the whole polling-places have improved; but how far this is due to women's presence no one can say. Women have occasionally held legislative and executive offices; but they have especially distinguished themselves as State and county superintendents of schools.

When it comes to estimating the effect of voting on the women themselves, it is still harder to form an opinion. A large majority of those reporting to Miss Sumner think that women have become more intelligent and more public-spirited, but some doubt it Morally, they have shown themselves less corrupt than men; but a considerable number think women as a whole have suffered some deterioration. This is a question bound up with our deepest feelings and our most conservative ideals; and it is inevitable that some observers should find any change for the worse. On the whole, belief in equal suffrage seems to have increased in Colorado during the twelve years under survey. Probably the results are much what they would be if one were to study a group of the most intelligent and refined men in the same community.

During the summer of 1911, I spent a month in the State of Idaho; and as I had long been interested in the problem of equal suffrage, both in England and America, I seized eagerly on the opportunity to study its practical workings at first hand. On the streets and in the tram-cars, in hotel lobbies and in lecture halls, when dining out or when making a call, few people escaped inquisition. I interviewed working men and women, men of affairs, ranchers, sheep raisers and miners, doctors, lawyers, teachers, ministers and practical politicians, both men and women.

The thing that first impresses one who has been intimately in touch with the excited and turbulent condition of mind among the English suffragettes, and the sustained and often impassioned feeling of Eastern suffrage leaders, is the absence of any burning interest in the subject on the part of men or women in Idaho. In London or New York, a suffrage inquirer would constantly strike "live wires;" in Idaho, every one is insulated. The subject is no more an issue than civil service reform or state versus national control of banking systems. Most people have even forgotten the passage of the constitutional amendment conferring equal suffrage, in 1896. Since then, men and women have gone on voting and holding office until the woman's right has become as commonplace as, and no more interesting or questionable than, the vote of any busy citizen in New Jersey.

The first question that one raises, is naturally whether women do actually vote and hold office in Idaho. To answer this question, there is no body of statistics available. Every one, however, declares that they pretty generally vote. On account of long distances in the country side, they poll less votes than men, especially if the weather is bad. Probably about three-quarters as many women as men go to the polls. Often I met women who said that they did not care for the vote, and sometimes one who said she thought women ought not to vote; but these same women often added that since they had the responsibility they felt it their duty to cast a ballot; and no woman told me that she did not fulfil the obligation.

In the first legislature which met after the granting of equal suffrage, that of 1898, three women were seated, Mrs. Hattie F. Noble, Clara L. Cambell, and Mary A. Wright; Mrs. Wright afterward became chief clerk of the House. In 1908, another woman, Mrs. Lottie J. Mc Fadden, was returned; but there was no woman in the last legislature, and so far as I can learn, only these four have taken part in law-making. When asked why, after the first ardor of emancipation, women have taken so little part in legislation, most people said it was because they had found the work and conditions surrounding it unsuited to them. It seems generally agreed, however, that a woman could be elected to the legislature at any time if she represented a cause which needed to be brought before the people through that body.

Theorists have always insisted that equal suffrage would greatly improve the material conditions which surround the polls on election day. One of the prominent political leaders in Idaho, who has been intimately in touch with conditions for a quarter of a century, said that of course there had been great improvement in the last fifteen years. "Things would have improved any way," he said, "but I am sure that the women have had a large influence. No woman has ever been insulted at the polls in Idaho and she runs no more danger of annoyance than she would in buying her ticket at a railway window. Men are not always sober in either place; but if a man made a remark to a woman that was not polite, or used annoying language in her presence, he would be mobbed by the men even in the roughest mining camp in the State." Doubtless women have helped to break the connection between the saloon and the polling-place, but no one claims that women have made voting into a drawing-room ceremony. On the contrary, women are very persistent workers at the polls, seeking to direct doubtful voters.

Advocates of equal suffrage have pretty generally held the belief that if women were given the ballot their superior moral standards would lead to a marked change in the handling of such problems as the liquor traffic and the control of red light districts. Of woman's superior moral standards there can be no doubt; of the actual effect of her vote upon these questions there is a great deal of doubt While I was in Idaho, the question of local option came up before the voters of Salt Lake City, in the neighboring equal suffrage State of Utah, and the "wets" won by a vote of 14,775 to 9,162. Thousands of women must have voted for license to bring about this result In April, 1911, the question of license or no license was voted on in Boise.

In this case again the "wets" won by a considerable majority.

Take another case. For several years in Boise, until 1909, the red light district was segregated in two alleys in the heart of the city. In the municipal election of that year this issue came fairly before the voters, and the democratic nominee for mayor, who was pledged to break up the system, was elected by a considerable majority, though the city is strongly republican. This result was undoubtedly due to the women's vote. After two years, the issue came up again; and the republican nominee, who was opposed to the scattering policy though not pledged to segregation, was elected; and this result must again have been due to the woman's vote. Prominent women of the city told me that during the two years when the scattering policy prevailed, the evil was very conspicuous, and women going about alone felt far less comfortable than under the older system.

There are two ways to explain the fact that, after fifteen years of political experience, the women of Boise voted in large numbers for license and for a policy in handling the red light district which they knew would mean a return to police control. In the first place, it may be said that fifteen years of steady contact with political life had blunted the sensibilities of women and dulled their moral feeling. On the other hand, it may be held that practical experience, under the steady pressure of responsibility, had made them realize the difficulties involved in the handling of these great social problems and had made them feel that a law which could command the support of public opinion, even though it regulated these difficulties, was better than a law which they might consider ideal, but which was incapable of execution.

In Idaho, as in Colorado, the payment of women political workers seems to have become a rather wide-spread abuse. Under the conditions of the State, with many new settlers constantly arriving, it has long been thought necessary to employ paid workers to register voters, get them out on election-day and influence those who are uncertain. After 1896, women were often hired to do this work, and were paid from three to five dollars a day. With their weak sense of party affiliation, it is claimed that they will work for the party that pays best. A candidate with plenty of money may hire so many workers that it becomes a system of wholesale bribery. It is universally conceded that this is an abuse, and that many women look upon election service as a source of pin money to a degree that is undesirable. Meantime, practical politicians assured me that it was a system the women found in operation when they came in; that far more men than women were paid; and that the abuse could be corrected by proper legislation.

To summarize the matter, we may say that equal suffrage in Idaho has simply accentuated the movement toward setting women free to live their individual lives which general education and participation in industrial life has already carried so far all over the country. Equal suffrage is accepted there, as the higher education of women is accepted in Massachusetts, and the results in the two cases have been much the same.

Surely these reports carry the matter beyond the experimental stage. Conditions in Colorado and Idaho are not identical with those in the East, but they are similar enough to make the experience of these States amount to a demonstration. Meantime the new obligation resting on women is profound. They must learn to "sweat their tempers and learn to know their man." They must become students of public affairs and of institutional life. Old issues are past; and equal suffrage will soon prevail everywhere. Women, like men, have more "rights" in our modern democracies than they can use. Woman's Rights are largely realized; from now on we must front Woman's Duties.

6

Women in Industry

In all the animal world one can hardly find a place where orderly effort, planned to secure some future advantage, does not appear. Getting food, defending life, and caring for offspring have all combined to drive not only the descendants of Adam, but his ancestors as well, to sweat-producing effort. Of course this is not definitely planned; getting food often waits on appetite; defense is sometimes merely running away; and the young are frequently left to feed themselves or die. But the fact remains that in digging burrows, building nests, laying up honey and nuts, and in protecting and providing for the young, a vast deal of effort is put forth in forest and field which is not immediately productive of pleasure.

This work is seldom equally shared by all the members of the group. With bees, the drones and the queen are alike exempt from work, and an asexual group has been developed to feed and protect them. Some ants compel others to do their work; and everywhere there seem to be individuals who are constitutionally lazy and others who, because of strength or sex attractiveness, are able to get more than their share of food and protection with less than their share of effort.

From the first, some division of work between male and female grows almost inevitably out of their different relations to reproduction. Following conception, the male can always run away and leave the female to feed and fight for herself and her offspring, and he is very prone to do so. Even when he stays by and shares in the joy of the newly born he generally leaves the female to get ready the nest, and largely she protects and provisions it.

Among domesticated animals, where their working possibilities have been very highly developed, females are much more desirable workers than males. The maternal function partly explains this, as in the case of cows and hens which give us milk and eggs; and even with mares and sheep the offspring adds to the general working value. Still, it seems to be true that even for purposes of draught, the males are of less value than the females, unless reduced to the non-sexual condition of geldings and oxen. The stallion, bull or ram is too katabolic, too much of a consuming, distributing, destroying force to be very valuable in the daily routine of agriculture or commerce* While the female is generally smaller and less powerful than the male, she is quiet, easily enslaved; and, as we have said, her maternal functions can be diverted to our daily use. She produces more workers, and her flesh is more palatable, because less distinctive, than that of the male. Hence, among domesticated animals, selection, based on considerations of work, multiplies females and keeps males only for breeding purposes.

As a quadruped, the female suffers very little handicap from the functions peculiar to her sex, except when actually carrying her young or nursing them. When she stands erect, however, the support for the special organs of reproduction is far from ideal; heavy lifting, or long-continued standing, often leads to disaster, and the periodic functions, even in the healthiest conditions, must always place women at a working disadvantage as compared with men. Add to this the fact that women are smaller, less agile, and far less strong, than men, and, even when not encumbered with young, it is clear that a woman, when confronting physical work in competition with men, needs something more than a fair field and free competition. Idealists and travelers among primitive people love to tell us how easily women meet their special functions, carrying burdens equal to those carried by men when on the march, and dropping out from the caravan for only a few hours to give birth to a child; but the fact remains that women in all primitive societies age quickly and that those who are spoiled are thrown aside and forgotten. Woman's handicap as a working animal in competition with man is too obvious and too deep-seated to be idealized away.

In all savage societies labor is clearly specialized between the sexes. The man, because of his superior strength and mobility, fights, hunts and makes weapons of the chase. The woman fetches and carries, digs and delves, cures the meat, makes the rude huts, clothing and pottery. Gradually she changes wild grasses to domesticated plants, and rears the young animals brought home from the chase, till they follow and serve their human masters. She is truly the mother of industries, and it in no way detracts from her credit that her motherhood is here, as elsewhere, mainly unthinking.

With the exhaustion of the supply of wild animals, man is forced to turn his attention to the world of vegetàtion and he takes over the direction of the plants and animals which woman has largely domesticated. In his career as fighter and hunter he has learned to cooperate with his fellows to a degree which aids him greatly in dividing the arable land, protecting his crops, and using grazing lands in common with the tribe. He has also learned to make stone hatchets, spears and bows and arrows. Woman has not felt the same necessity to invent in her work; such new tools as she has devised have been helpful, but men who could not invent have been wiped out by those who learned to make stronger spears or better arrow-heads.

It is the same difference in adaptability which one observes to-day between the farmers on the western frontier of America and those who remain in their peasant homes in Europe. The peasant has even greater need of inventing than has his expatriated countryman in Colorado, but he lacks the driving impulse. It was the same with women and men under the conditions of savage life. Thus it came about that man's greater strength and mobility, backed by power of cooperation and invention, gave him the leadership in such primitive life as we find depicted in the pages of Homer or in the epic of the Jews. True, woman was his first lieutenant, but he spoke for her in most of the larger matters of the industrial life.

With settled conditions and accumulation of wealth, the most desirable women were almost entirely freed from physical labor and gradually became luxury-loving parasites and playthings, as we pointed out in the second chapter of this volume. Meantime slaves were multiplying, male and female and, while the most desirable women passed to the harem, the mass of them became drudges in house and field. It is hard for us to realize that it is exactly in those times when a few women are surrounded with great luxury that most of the sex are reduced to heavy labor and wretchedness.

During the early Christian ages, a tradition was gradually formed concerning woman's place in industry, or rather three traditions were formed. The working woman of the lower classes was to be the housekeeper, which meant that she was to care for food, cook, spin, weave, sew and mend, scrub and wash, bear children and nurse and tend them. If she were of the middle class, she was to be a mother, to supervise this range of work, look after dependents, conserve social conditions and be the lady bountiful of her district. The second ideal was the woman of religion, who was to subdue her passions, observe set prayers and other religious exercises etc.

As 1870 marks the beginning of higher education for women, so it also marks the beginning of her industrial self-consciousness. The perfecting of such inventions as the typewriter, the telegraph and the telephone, and the creation of a great variety of office appliances, together with the perfecting of highly elaborate means of distribution, like the departmental store, called for thousands of cheap workers possessed of some slight intelligence but not necessarily having any serious preliminary training. Our elementary schools and high schools have increasingly turned out a multitude of girls who could meet these requirements. The increased cost of living, the lessened labor demands of the home, and the attractions of the pay envelope, have called millions to work in industrial plants. In 1890, there were 4,005,582 wage-earning women in the United States; in 1900, 5,819,-897; while in 1910, we have probably nearly 8,000,000.

Like most other great changes in civilization, this industrial transformation was neither preceded nor accompanied by any general consciousness of what was happening. Daily necessities were offset by weekly pay envelopes, or the failures fell out of sight, and so the next week and the years followed. Country populations moved away; cities grew enormously, leading to congestion in living which, combined with the daily absence of women, has often transformed the old time homes into communal tiers of tenements occupied, during working hours, only by the young and the infirm.

The children of all ages after a while followed their mothers into the factories; but the evil effects of child labor were so apparent that repressive legislative measures have increasingly raised the age of their admission until now, in the more advanced communities, they must stay outside the factory doors until they are twelve or fourteen years old. Some growing self-consciousness, largely of a police nature, has led us to institute measures for the protection of the children who are not allowed to work. Schools, playgrounds, day nurseries, institutional churches, college settlements and public social centers now bid against the streets and vacant lots, the nickel shows and the dancing halls, for the children's patronage.

Education, however, true to its origin as the assistant of theology, refuses to recognize in any large way the new world into which we have come, and where the next generation of children must follow. Manual training has, here and there, quieted the fears of some who had disturbing visions; and we go on employing an army of unenfranchised, celibate women, with little or no industrial experience, to teach ten million boys how to be good citizens of a republic, and how to serve in a modern industrial army; and ten million girls how to work in shops and factories, and how to live without homes. As a consequence, girls come up to the factories from their schools with ideals, so far as the school has shaped them, founded on unmarried school mistresses and George Washington; and they pass, by way of the altar, into cheerless tenements which the school still thinks of as places where children are cared for, family clothing is made and the family baking is done.

Practically, of course, most education is given outside the schools, and there the evils of an unregulated time of transition are multiplied through imitation.

The wealth and material comfort produced for the fortunate classes by these segregated industries have blinded us to their effects on human life, and we have all been bribed to silence concerning everything which could discourage enterprise or frighten capital. Like most bribes, however, these have largely stopped in the pockets of the exploiters of public opinion.

In the opening years of this new century, public consciousness has had a wonderful awakening. The popular mind, quickened by universal education, and freed from a burden of fixed beliefs, is turning restlessly to inquire about everything that affects human life. Work could not escape this inquisition, and so we are asking not only for a fairer division of the profits of work, but we are also inquiring what occupations are unfit for women, with their special limitations and obligations. When the work is reasonable, how long should a woman work daily? Should she work at night and overtime? Should she work with dangerous machinery? Should she handle substances that endanger health? Should she be required to stand through hours of continuous work? Should she work in bad air, due to dust, moisture, or excessive heat or cold? Should she have a decent retiring-room? Some daring inquirers are even asking whether industrial efficiency, gained through specialization and keying up, may not be purchased at too high a price of mental monotony and nervous strain. Most people are content to learn that the effects are not immediately destructive to the girls and women involved; but some day we shall demand that the barons of industry shall not be allowed to squander the heritage of the unborn generations.

Women have themselves done much to quicken this public consciousness. Enrolled in labor unions, they have shown power to stand together and make sacrifice, as in the shirt-waist makers' strike in New York in 1908, which commanded the admiration of all fair-minded observers. The more fortunately placed women have aided these movements toward self-betterment; and, through such organizations as the National Consumers' League, they have compelled manufacturers and shopkeepers to observe more reasonable hours, pay better wages, and furnish decent material conditions for their employees.

The solution of woman's present industrial problem is not an easy task, but out of the present unsettlement certain facts are emerging with a good deal of clearness. The efficiency in production, secured by concentration and specialization, make it certain that the old-time home with its multiplied industries will not return, but that more and more even of its present lessened activities will be transferred to factories and to their equivalents. It is also certain that women are not going to be supported in indolence by men, because when deprived of the dis-receive constant and intelligent attention. In the first place, we should realize that we are not fitting women for drawing-rooms nor for convents, but for a working world; therefore well graded and interesting manual training should run through all these years and should furnish a well-developed base for later special industrial preparation of some kind. In the second place, the girls should be taught by men and women, married and unmarried, and fine ideals of actual womanhood, not alone in shops and factories, in school-rooms, and in professions—but also in homes, should be constantly held before them. Our present education leaves this training mainly to the homes, and neither the parasitic rich nor our eight million wage-earning women, when mothers, can or will attend to it.

After the girl reaches the age of fourteen, she should have at least two years of further education in which she could master the details of some necessary work which would enable her to look the world in the face and offer fair payment for her living. With most girls, this work would be connected with children and the service of the home; for domestic service, no matter how organized, must always occupy a multitude of women. All girls should have at least rudimentary training in these matters.

During the period of transition from schools to their own family life, the girls might well give a half dozen years to work in factories and stores where the conditions should be as good, and as well guarded, as in our best school buildings—in factories, in a word, where the employers would be willing that their own daughters should work. This is surely a fair standard. Work which is not safe or fit for me to do, is not fit for me to hire done. If this principle fails, then democracy is but a dream.

But during all this period of preparation we should never forget that, as Madame Gnauck-Kuhne so admirably points out, "women's work has to a large extent an episodic character." All women confront romantic love, marriage and children; and any woman who misses them misses the crowning joy and glory of her life. Vicarious realization may save the soul, but it can never fill the place of reality. The man fronts these same experiences, but they are not related to his work as they are related to the work of women. Surely there can be no doubt that the ideal solution, in this period, is a man and woman so deeply bound together by love that there is no question of self-protection, either in terms of work or money; and the man being freed from the burdens of maternity, should mainly earn the income. We shall discuss the new type of home and family in a later chapter, but in any home where there are children there is need of an intelligent mother's very constant care.

If a happy home were the universal destiny of women, our problem would be greatly simplified; but this is far from being the case. Not more than one-half of all women over fifteen are married at any one moment. From the ages of twenty to thirty-five, one-half are married; but it is only from thirty-five to fifty-five that as many as three-fourths are married; over fifty-five there are less than one-half married, and most of the others are widows. Most of these women who are not married must work outside the home, and no girl, rich or poor, should be allowed to reach maturity without being prepared to face this possibility. Work is not a curse but a blessing; it is an indispensable part of every well-ordered life; and without it, the individual and the group will certainly degenerate. Rich and foolish parents, who cannot realize this basal fact, should nevertheless see that, even as insurance, their daughters must be able to pay their way in life, if need comes, without selling themselves either in marriage or out. Even if the woman marries happily, she is never sure that she may not some day have to face self-support, and possibly for more mouths than her own.

But the woman who marries during her adolescent period, between the ages of twenty-five and fifty, must also work, and here we meet the hardest problem of all. More money is often needed than the man can earn; the wife may bring an industrial or professional equipment which is too valuable to discard; often the demands of the home, especially where there are no children, do not call forth the best energies of the woman, and she needs the larger life of outside work. Hencc many married women must continue to work away from the home. In any of these cases, the problem is difficult. Bearing and rearing a child should retire a mother from fixed outside occupation for at least a year. Arguments born out of conflict cannot change this primitive fact Women should not do shop or factory work during the last months of pregnancy, and babies should be nursed from seven to nine months. A baby should be nursed for twenty minutes, every two or three hours of its waking time; and since it does not always waken regularly, the nursing mother is debarred from most continuous work, even if it does not interfere with her effectiveness as a milk producer.

The question of maternal care for children after they are weaned is more difficult to settle, but notwithstanding certain statistics gathered in Birmingham, in February, 1910, which showed that the infant mortality among working mothers was one hundred and ninety per thousand, while, among those not industrially employed, it was two hundred and seventy per thousand, it seems sure that infant mortality is extremely high in foundling asylums and in factory homes. In Fall River, where out of every one hundred women, forty-five are at work outside the home, three hundred and five babies, out of every one thousand born, die before they are a year old; while even in New York City, but one hundred and eighty-nine out of a thousand die. The natural location of Fall River should make it a very healthy city. One remembers, too, the classic statement that deaths among little children fell off steadily in Paris during the siege of 1870. Little children seem better off even in time of war, with the mothers at home, than in time of peace with their mothers in the factory.

A few years ago, we turned to sanitary day nurseries, and to pasteurized milk and other prepared baby foods, as the solution for neglected or unhygienic feeding. To-day we know that even a dirty and ill-conditioned mother secretes better milk for her baby than can be prepared in any laboratory. We must wash the mother and feed her the milk, and then let her give it to her baby, instinct with her own life. It is quite possible that our recent talk of ignorant mother love and of the necessary substitution of sanitary nurseries, canned care and pre-digested affection must all go the same way. We shall probably get our best results by cleaning up the home, enlightening the mother, and then letting her love her child into the full possession of its human qualities.

Economically, too, at least with factory workers, it is questionable if their wages will support sanitary day-nurseries, with intelligent nurses for small groups of children, and at the same time pay some one to cook and scrub at home. If the mother must still cook and care for her house, in addition to her factory work, the burden is too great; and if money for nurses must come from the state, or from charity, then we all know the danger of such subsidies to industry, in its effect on wages.

Surely the ideal toward which we must work is for the mother, during the period when she is bearing and rearing children, to be supported by the father of her children. Let her do the work meantime which will best care for her children, and at the same time conserve and strengthen her powers for the third period of her life.

This period, from fifty to seventy-five years, is now more shamefully wasted than any other of our national resources. If one attends a State federation of women's clubs one will find nearly every delegate of this age. They are women of mature understanding and of ripe judgment, still possessing abundant health and strength, and where relieved by economic conditions from the necessity of manual work, they have to live such irregular and uncertain relations to life as can be maintained by mothers-in-law, grandmothers, club secretaries, and presidents of town improvement societies. Remove all restrictions on woman's activity, and these strong matrons would vitalize our schools, give us decent municipal housekeeping, supervise the conditions under which girls and women work in shops and factories, and do much to clean up our politics. Debarred from direct power as they are, they are still making us decent in spite of ourselves.

For the future, then, it seems that we must accept working women in every path of life. We must remove all disabilities under which they labor, and at the same time protect them by special legislation as future wives and mothers. All girls must master some line of self-supporting work; and, except in the cases of those who have very special tastes and gifts, they should select work which can be interrupted, without too great loss, by some years of motherhood. During this time, the mother must be supported so that she can largely care for her own child, though she must also maintain outside interests through work, which will keep her in touch with the moving current of her time. Industries must be humanized and made fit for women. The last third of a woman's life must be freed from legal limitations and popular prejudices, so that we may secure these best years of her life for private and public service.

And meantime, it is well to remember that every step we take in making this a fit world for woman to work in, makes it a fit world for her father, her brothers, her lover and her husband to work beside her.

●●

7

The Modern Family

The most powerful influence in shaping our lives to-day is the sexual impulse which has created the institution we call the family. Few of us, at least in our modern democracies, live in daily fear that our neighbors will attack and kill us, or carry us off into slavery. Even the hunger for food, that once forced men into action, plays little direct part in the shaping of the lives of most of us. None of those who read these pages would starve if they never did any more work. If they tried to starve, they would be arrested and sent to jail; and if they persisted, they would be fed by force.

Meantime it is sex hunger, manifesting itself in a hundred forms of beauty and ugliness, courtesy and insult, cultivated conversation and ribald jest, beautiful dancing and suggestive indecencies, honor and dishonor, self-repression and prostitution, love and lust, children of gladness and children of shame, that lifts us to such heights as we attain, or plunges us into the hells we create for ourselves. If one could insure one good thing in life for the child one loves, one would ask, not money nor fame, but a continuously happy marriage.

In the past, women have always looked upon marriage and family life as a career; and the majority of men have found their most significant life in the building up of the family institution. To-day, however, family life as a career is everywhere called in question. Many women claim to prefer educational opportunity, professional recognition or an independent bank account to husband and children. Social service is exalted; domestic service is debased. Why is it so much nobler to care for other people's children in a social settlement, or in a school, than to care for one's own in a home? Why should women mass themselves together in vast groups as industrial workers, as teachers, as suffragettes? We hear of women's work, of women's careers, of women's clubs, associations and parties, of women's interests, movements, causes. In November, 1911, two hundred and twenty women were arrested in London for assaulting the English government in the supposed interest of women. Why do women prefer social to domestic service?

Two reasons spring at once to the mind of any intelligent observer of the life about him. The first is the complexity of our modern life; the second is the nature of the institution of marriage.

A man or woman wishes to live with the one he or she loves. Sexual love is in its very nature restricted, circumscribed, monopolistic— in a word, monogamic. As has been said repeatedly in this volume, the human unit is neither a man nor a woman; it is a man and a woman united in a new personality through the unifying and blending power of love. To say that this unit is exclusive and monogamic is simply saying that it respects its own personality. It can no longer act simply as a man or a woman; it is a family and it must act as such in order to satisfy its own demands. A man can no more act independently of the woman he loves than the heart can act independently of the lungs. The man and woman who compose the new unit are not only flesh of one flesh, but they are one soul, one life; they are a complete organism. And the life of this organism must be persistent to realize its own aims. In all the higher forms of existence, processes move slowly. For nine months a woman carries her baby as a part of her own body; then for three years the father and mother carry the child in their arms; for a score of years they must support, protect and train it before they let it go to seek its own. Hence sexual love must be persistent as well as monogamic.

From all this it follows that each half of the human unit must find the major part of its adult life in devotion to the one it has chosen as its complement This is no hardship; it is divine opportunity, if love binds the lives in harmonious unity. If love is lacking, then there is na new organism; and such a case falls outside this discussion.

Under the simpler forms of civilization that have prevailed in the past, it was comparatively easy to find the complement for any particular man or woman. With physical sympathy and desire, little more was needed than common race and the same general social position. With simple personalities even the marriage of convenience was apt to prove happy.

But, to-day, not only have men become infinitely more complex and self-conscious than formerly, but women have ceased to be a general class; and, in becoming individuals, they have developed wide ranges of individual needs. Instead of fitting at the two or three points of physical desire, race and social position, a man or woman, to live strongly and well in this close union of body and soul, must fit each other at many points. To the older sympathies must be added a common attitude toward religion, education, artistic tastes, social ambitions, industrial aptitudes, and a score of other living sympathies, if the days are to pass in happiness, and each is to maintain his fair share of the life of the new unit Physical desire still remains the paramount thing, but these other sympathies tend to strengthen it, or their absence may weaken and ultimately destroy it It is comparatively easy for a person to find a complement to two or three of his, or her, qualities; it is very difficult for a person to find fulfilment for a score of his personal needs in another personality.

In earlier times, too, the individual reached such maturity as he or she was to attain much earlier than now, when education has become a life-long process. Once united, there was comparatively little danger that passing years would develop latent tastes that might prove dissimilar. To-day, complete union at twenty may mean many oppositions at forty, if each half of the unit goes on developing its powers. And we must add to this individual complexity and slower development of the present-day men and women the intense self-consciousness of modern times which makes it impossible for us to forget our conditions and go on living in a world once significant and true but now empty or false.

A second cause for the unrest of the present is doubtless to be found in the inflexibility of the institution of the family, under which lovers are allowed to live together and bring into existence the children of their love. The family, as we have it, was shaped under the stress of mediaeval disorder. In such a time men are willing to pay any price for peace and quiet And so the barbarian invaders, living among the broken fragments of Greek and Roman civilization, gradually shaped feudalism, culminating in absolute monarchy, which gave them political security. They shaped the Holy Roman Catholic Church that they might worship in peace. They shaped the guilds that they might work quietly, and enjoy the fruits of their labors. The family, with its civil and ecclesiastical sanctions, was formed to protect the personal lives of men and women who wished to live together and rear children.

But with peace, life grew stronger and more intense; and the bonds which the people had shaped, and which had given them security, reached their limits of growth, became painful, and threatened to prevent all further development. The rising cities bought their freedom from feudal lords; even the serfs won better conditions; and the rising national units beat down the older political institutions with their swords. Finally the movements that gather around the French Revolution opened the way for us into the democratic freedom and security which we enjoy to-day. The guilds were broken up and a measure of freedom was secured, though the industrial institution which shall give us freedom and security in our work is yet to be formed. The Protestant Revolution led us by devious ways into religious freedom where men can worship as they will

Of all these older institutions, shaped under iron necessity, the only one that remains practically unchanged is the family. Dealing with the most powerful of all our human hungers, as it does, we have not dared to make it fit our modern life. Not only is this true, but the forces of the older state and church which survived, fastened themselves upon this institution and strengthened its resisting power. The church increasingly made marriage into a holy sacrament, so that it not only protected lovers, but became a subtle, inviolable and indissoluble mystery. The state sanctioned the family, and made it an instrument for regulating political and property rights. Formal society proclaimed the family and made it the standard for respectability.

Two centuries hence, our family, with its sacramental significances, its lack of a eugenic conscience, its financial subordination of women, its frequent lack of love and sympathy, its primogeniture, and its determining power over social opportunity, will be as incomprehensible to students of institutional forms as the Holy Roman Empire is to us to-day. Who will then understand how church and state could have licensed and consummated marriages between young and inexperienced people, marriages which were to be binding on their thought, feeling and action for life without requiring some time, however brief, between the application for a license and the final binding of vows? Who will be able to understand how church and state could have sanctioned marriage between a broken-down old noble and a young and inexperienced girl of seventeen? How will the future student explain the fact that in New Jersey state and church combined to sanction and bless the marriage of an imbecile woman and of her offspring until they had produced 148 feeble-minded children to curse the state.

Who will then understand why a man and woman who had not only ceased to love each other but had come to feel a deep repugnance for each other should have been compelled to share bed and board, even when there were no children, until even murder seemed preferable to such slavery of soul and body? How can this student understand woman's economic dependence, her uncertain income, her insecure rights in property for which she toiled side by side with her husband? Who will then believe that in the year 1911 an English citizen could go before a court and secure an order for legalized rape, under the name of restitution of marital rights?

Meantime every issue of the daily press counts as its choicest items stories of the shameful and soul-destroying ways in which men and women are trying to live their lives in spite of this mediaeval institution. So far-reaching is the unrest, that at each new revelation of marital heresy, society feels constrained to rush forward and frantically denounce the heretic in order to prove its own orthodoxy.

Our own attitude toward marriage as a sacrament to be directed by a church, or as a pleasure to be exploited by individuals, must be changed if the life of the family is to be re-established as the great vocation of earnest men and women. Intelligence must be turned upon this problem as upon all others that vitally affect our lives. What President Eliot has called "the conspiracy of silence touching matters of sex" must be broken, and when it is, I believe honest men will agree with Ellen Key that "In love humanity has found the form of selection most conducive to the ennoblement of the species."

In this field, at least, a eugenic conscience must take the place of the older theological conscience. We must recognize the infamy of knowingly bringing defective children into existence. We must agree that under no conditions should people tainted with syphilis be allowed to marry ; and that those subject to imbecility or insanity should not be allowed to live together unless they are unsexed. Justice to future generations, and protection of the state, demands at least this much.

Whether alcoholics, those suffering from congenital sense defects, and near relatives, should be allowed to marry may still be an open question; but it should be recognized that the state has the right and the duty to inquire into these conditions and to impose restrictions. Society must come to feel that it is at least as shameful for a broken old noble to live with a young girl under the forms of marriage as for two young lovers to live together outside them.

As to what the personal, social and industrial relation of man and wife should be, we have widely different views and practices. Thc older view, still embodied in the practice of most nations, and best seen in Germany and England, is that the woman's duty is to complement the husband. He does what he wishes, so far as he can, and the wife rounds out the whole. It is the old ideal of later savagery, that the man should provide and protect, and the woman should breed children, care for the home, pray and wait.

This is really the same ideal that dominated our political life until a hundred and fifty years ago. It was the duty of the lords to direct and fight; the peasants should work and wait In politics there gradually grew up a middle class which combined with the peasants to overthrow the older privileges; and now all classes direct, fight, wait and watch together. Whether this democratic idea is finally to prevail, we may not know; but it is well worth trying, and the results so far are full of promise.

In the same way, in the family, a great middle class of wives has grown up, largely since 1870, through education and industry, as the burgers did in political life, and these emancipated women are insisting that the peasant of the family, the *Hausfrau,* shall join with them and dethrone the husband so that all shall share life's responsibilities together as free and equal partners. In fact, in America, the revolution has already come; and, as in the earlier stages of political revolutions, those deposed are having a hard time to maintain even their equal share of opportunity.

But the parallel between political and domestic life is not complete, and if pushed too far the analogy is mischievous. The assumption of physical, intellectual and social superiority on the side of political lords and domestic lords was the same. It is possible, however, rightly or wrongly, to reduce all the people to the same political level and set them all at work doing the same things. But between men and women there was not only the assumption of physical and mental difference, but there was and must always be the infinite difference of In domestic life, the women cannot live without men nor the men without women. Not only would the generations fail, but the present generation would lose its deepest meaning, if either sex were banished or debased.

In their reactions against old abuses, writers like Mrs. Gilman or Olive Schreiner try to create a world for women alone, on the political analogy. Men might be tolerated as fathers; but, to secure political freedom, these leaders would turn to that nebulous creation of social reformers, the state; and it should subsidize the mothers in their periods of need. But there are only two ingredients out of which a nation can be formed: one is women; the other is men. Shall woman in her time of need turn to a state made up of other women, or to a state made up of men? Obviously it must be to both; and if woman is to depend on men, she might as well depend on man. No, in the political revolutions we broke up artificial, outworn and unjust combinations; but in this domestic revolution we are breaking up and must readjust the fundamental unit of life.

Men and women must live and work together in the domestic unit, and they cannot do the same things. Nature has specialized their functions and each must supplement the other. Even in Germany, the *Hausfrau* is not going back to an exclusive service of children, cooking and church; nor in America will man continue to be merely the breadwinner and the father of children. With the enlightenment that is on the way, we shall see that husband and wife can have no antagonistic differences. Each profits in all that really benefits the other; and slowly we shall shape a new institution based on absolute equality, and at the same time on complementary service.

In this adjustment, legal forms can help or hinder; but they cannot prevent nor compel the final action of human beings. Sex instinct is stronger than any human law. The law can, however, help us in regulating conditions of marriage, in settling disputes about common property and children, and in determining how the contract may be set aside when that becomes necessary.

The right of the church to sanction or regulate the family, rests in a belief that marriage involves spiritual changes and obligations that make it a sacrament, in its nature inviolable, and to be administered only by the church, like the sacrament of baptism. This is a belief resting not in eugenic considerations, nor in the human needs of the persons involved, but in theological dogmas with which this chapter cannot deal. Hence we shall maintain that the church has no more right to control matters of marriage than it has to interfere in business or political relations.

The state, on the other hand, meaning by the state the whole community, must concern itself with the marriage of its individuals. The commonwealth must have future citizens, and these should be strong and intelligent; hence it must prevent the breeding of the unfit If parents die, or fail in obligations, the community must care for the children. In case of disagreement between married people, the courts of the community must settle disputes about children and property; hence the state must know when a man and woman determine to live together. The regulation of marriage certainly belongs to the state, that is, to all of us.

Marriage should therefore always be a matter of definite and open record in the archives of the community. It should also be advertised, through the public record, for a considerable time, preferably six months or a year, before consummation, that the past experiences of contracting parties may be looked up by interested friends or officials, and the marriage of the unfit prevented; and so that mere caprice and passion shall have time to realize their mistake and turn away. The form which the final ceremony of marriage will take can well be left to the tastes and traditions of the contracting parties.

The question of rights in children, or in property acquired after marriage, should be settled by the state; and it is hard to see how it can ever be settled satisfactorily except on a basis of equal partnership. No man should be contented with a woman to bear and train his children, and create a social atmosphere for his home, who is not worth half of what he makes; and the same holds true of a woman. So with regard to children, while one parent or the other may, under certain conditions, be given the direction of the child's life, it is hard to imagine any circumstances that would justify society in refusing either father or mother the right frequently to see his child.

Since marriages must be contracted in youth and since inexperienced people must make mistakes and the wisest must sometimes change, it will sometimes happen that men and women must face the possibility of separation. The problem of divorce is very difficult. In less than twenty years, from 1887 to 1906, 945,625 divorces were granted in the United States; so that probably to-day there are nearly one million divorced people in this country. Generally speaking, the divorce rate increases as one goes westward. In 1900, the State of Washington led the country with 184 divorces for each 100,-000 of population. For the whole country we averaged 73 per 100,000 of population. Japan alone leads us with 215, while England and Wales had only 2. England grants divorce only for infidelity; and on the man's side it must be accompanied by cruelty; all divorce cases must be tried in London, and the expense, never less than two hundred dollars, is prohibitive for the poor. Meantime, England grants many separation orders; and it seems sure that the Royal Commission, which has been taking evidence for the past three years, will favor a freer system of divorce.

While divorce is increasing steadily all over the world, and most rapidly in the most intelligent and progressive sections, the subject is so bound up with our most deep-seated prejudices that it is difficult to secure any intelligent thinking on the subject Thus, most people think Sioux Falls, in South Dakota, and Reno, Nevada, are places of free divorce, but the fact is that twenty-one other States have a higher divorce rate than South Dakota; and fourteen have a higher rate than Nevada. So, too, the impression that divorces spring from hasty action is certainly wrong, for in 46.5 per cent of those for which we have records there had been a separation of more than three years before the divorce was granted. The idea that people generally seek divorces that they may marry some one else seems also unfounded, since in the cases for which we have records, less than forty per cent remarry within a year.

There are three main objections which one hears urged against free divorce. The first is that organized society rests on the family, and with free divorce anarchy would ensue. In reply, it is pointed out that the same argument was used to support kings, aristocracies and a universal church. All these have been set aside, in many parts of the earth, and society seems even more stable than before. The love of men and women is probably more powerful and less in need of adventitious support than either patriotism or religion.

In the second place, it is claimed that children will suffer when parents separate. It is replied that this is true, but they were already suffering when parents had ceased to love each other. The fact that children are involved in only two out of five divorces seems to indicate that children hold parents together when the opposition is not too strong; and when a separation occurs, those who favor divorce claim that a child is better off with either father or mother alone than with both if love is absent. In the third place, it is pointed out that often only one desires the divorce and that this brings tragedy to the other life. In reply it is claimed that many of the tragedies of life have always gathered around the love of men and women, that when marriage is declined tragedy often follows, and that compelling a person to live with some one whom he does not love, and may even dislike, is more tragic than any separation.

In conclusion, advocates of free divorce claim that their proposals are profoundly conservative, that they are seeking to bring marriage back to its eternally binding realities. They say that under our present conditions of restricted divorce, we have wide-spread prostitution, constant irregularities that are tolerated and condoned, and a million divorced people, some prevented from remarrying and all socially ostracized, so that the whole group is a dangerous element in our midst. These advocates claim that with free divorce, granted some months after the determination to separate had been registered in the public records, the love of men and women and their mutual love for their children would be free to bind families together in permanent trust and open honesty; and that with all excuse for irregularity absent, the unfaithful man or woman would sink to the level of unfaithfulness in business or political life. With freedom to readjust their lives, if they preferred to keep what they had and get what they could, they would simply take their place among thieves and liars, and most of them would disappear.

All transitions are hard, and this one in which we are involved is most difficult of all; but no one can study the conditions around him without seeing that change is inevitable and that we are not going back to our earlier ideals. At the same time, no one can read the singularly scholarly and fair-minded presentations of Ellen Key without feeling that she has a vision of the future.

With regard to the nature of the material plant in which the family should live, there are also two widely different ideals struggling for favor in the public mind, and for realization in practice. The one ideal, while recognizing the changes necessitated by modern conditions, would still seek to retain those features which have been supposed to make for family privacy, the kitchen, the nursery, and the garden. The other would frankly accept our changed conditions, and pass on to the larger groups of socialized buildings, with common kitchens, day nurseries, and parks.

This question has been discussed in the chapter on industry, and it will be considered again in the following chapter. Meantime there can be no doubt that love is reticent so far as the outside world is concerned; and domesticity must always demand a large measure of privacy. It still remains to be proved that this can be secured, in the absence of a private kitchen, nursery and garden. Children, too, seem to need the personal care and constant love of mothers, and women seem to need a long period of loving and caring for a family to round out a deeply significant life.

To summarize this chapter we may say that the realization of romantic love, under conditions of domesticity, is necessary for men and women, and for the well-being of the race. Our present marriage system is defective, and needs to be corrected through the creation of a eugenic conscience. It should be taken out of the hands of the church and made more difficult by the state. Women's property rights should be defined and safeguarded, and men and women should never live together when they are repugnant to each other.

FAMILY LIFE AS A VOCATION

The greatest of all wisdom is that which leads men and women to see the real significance of their lives while they are still living. Life's values, like the manna in the wilderness, must be gathered daily. If not nourished day by day the power to live atrophies and dies; and no one can live well today on the shrunken memories of yesterday. A full and significant life is its own justification; and in a last analysis philosophies and theologies offer us only the life more abundantly which the great Teacher said he came into the world to bring. Buddhism offers us eternal peaceful existence in Nirvana; Epicureanism offers pleasure, which is but an intensification of life; Stoicism offers us life freed from disturbing forces; and the great lure which Christianity has always held before humanity is life eternal. Life is its own justification.

We have maintained throughout this volume that complete self-realization is impossible for the half-units which we call men and women, when either lives alone. On every side of their natures they are complementary; and the unit of human life must be found in the family composed of a man and woman who love each other and the children born of their love. "There are two worlds below, the home and outside of it" It is in this unit, under the stress of sexual passion and maternal love, that all the finer forces of our civilization have had their origin. Unselfishness, devotion, pity and the higher altruisms all hark back to the home as their source.

But, meantime, evil counsels prevail and one hears everywhere of the antagonistic interests of men and women. There can be no real rivalry between a man's soul and his body, between science and religion, between man and woman. The trouble all rests back in the failure to realize the incompleteness of man or woman alone for any of the purposes of life. And there is that evil notion which still afflicts economics that when two trade one must lose. The fact is that, in all honest trade, buyer and seller gain alike; and fair exchange makes all who participate in it rich. It is so in all real relations between these half-creatures we call men and women. In agreement, association and cooperation lies strong and significant life for both. In antagonism, separation and competition lie arid, poor, mean lives, egotistic and conceited, vapid and fickle.

In primitive life, the family furnished a full and adequate career for men and women alike. The political life was the family life; each family was a religious group; families mustered for war; and each family maintained within itself a wide range of industrial activity. But, because this unit was so basal, because all later special developments of state, church and industry came from it, it was steadily perverted. Warped from its original purpose, it has served in turn, as we have seen, to define and secure all our later institutions until it has become the servant of state, church, social ambition, property and industrial advance. Marriage and the birthrate are seldom discussed to-day from the point of view of individual needs; but are almost always considered from the point of view of national and industrial efficiencies.

To-day men and women are confronted by two tempters which constantly lure them away from the complete living of the family; one is work, and the other is comfort. With the majority of people in our modern industrial democracies work uses up the hours and the energy of life. We have passed into a time when our habitual material needs are great, and the products of work are shamelessly diverted to the excessive uses of comparatively few individuals and groups. Hence millions of workers march along the narrow dark roads that lead through factories and farms to the grave. Only little patches of their nervous systems are ever used, but all their energy flows through these sections day after day, leaving their lives dull and empty.

Marriage for these workers means decreased earning power for the woman, with increased needs for the family, especially when the children come. As one watches the procession of young factory and shop women, with Sunday finery and some leisure, passing over into draggled factory mothers, with no finery and no leisure, one marvels at the strength of the forces with which nature drives them to their destiny. And yet, even with these hopeless workers, marriage and children mark the heights of life.

With others, who are economically freer, work has become an obsession. A Charles Darwin or a Herbert Spencer turns all of life's forces to shaping facts into science; our industrial leaders mint their hours into dollars; our reformers give up their lives that social conditions may be changed; our society leaders trade life for triumphs. Meantime we all know, or would know if we stopped to consider, that we are here to live life fully and significantly day by day. But domesticity takes time and effort, and so the hurrying specialist follows the narrow line of success until he or she becomes a machine for manufacturing generalizations, for painting pictures, for performing surgical operations or for merely getting money.

The richest woman in America said with approval recently that her son was too busy to fall in love.

As industry drives the mass of workers and specialists away from life's deepest realizations, so the desire to become comfortable, physically and mentally, through avoiding the deeper experiences of life, robs many of those who have a large measure of economic freedom. In all periods of great wealth this disease of ease has afflicted mankind. Life more abundantly comes only at the price of vigorous living; and love travels always in company with anxiety. It would be well, says Cicero, to have children, were it not for the fear of losing them. Let a man apply this principle to wife, friends, possessions and enthusiasm in general and life sinks into utter worthlessness.

The love of ease among women is in a measure independent of the emancipation movement, but the entry of great numbers of young women into lines of independent livelihood has placed them in a condition where the ideals of a materialistic and commercial civilization appeal to them with great force. Many of them have been liberally educated and are living lives of independence. They lodge in flats or boarding houses where they have no responsibilities for the routine work connected with daily living. They carry their own latch-keys; and no one interferes with their friendships or their pleasures. They read the books they like, attend the theaters that appeal to them, and avoid people who bore them. One can easily understand why these young women hesitate before abandoning their easy conditions for the uncertain economic position of wife and mother, with a man whose career lies in the future. And yet here, as everywhere, one must lose one's life to gain it

What then does daily association of a man and woman who belong together do for them? It gives gladness and peace, and these are fundamental conditions for all good and healthful living. It gives incentive to effort, for a man or woman dares not fail before the one he or she loves; but, in case of failure, it gives comfort and support, for love understands and credits intent and effort as highly as achievement. It complements the powers, for it gives four eyes, four hands and two minds with but one aim. And in this it does not simply multiply by two, but the blended powers are far more than two times one. It calls into activity all the gracious, artistic and altruistic powers of the soul Surely these are gifts for which we may well forego some material comforts, may well work, and even face anxieties unafraid.

Each part of the human unit must educate the other to a realization of the fulness of life. This education is not entirely dependent on physical intimacy. It is the development of soul and spirit. It polishes the manners, cultivates the voice, broadens the judgments, sharpens the wit. It makes conversation an art and discussion significant. A woman-hating man or a man-hating woman is an unpolished and half-alive creature, whether he be a mediaeval saint, or she a militant suffragette, or they both be simply commonplace egoists.

Because married life is so perfect when it finds its highest levels, it is capable of sinking to any form of vulgarity, base betrayal and cynicism when realization fails. The God to whom noblest souls aspire in hours of deepest exaltation, is the God invoked by the ribald drunkard when he curses his comrade. The family life we are discussing is the subject of most of the vulgar and indecent jokes of the disappointed and the unfit. The earth which nourishes the nations, merely soils the boots of the boor who unthinkingly lives on her bounty. On the working side the life of the family has an evil record for pettiness and monotony, but much of this is due to wrong comparisons. A woman who does her own housework would presumably have to work in any case. Is the work of the family more petty or monotonous than the work of the factory, shop or office? Surely the woman who spends her days looking after the details of furnishing a house and keeping it clean, of providing and serving meals, of looking after clothing and caring for children, has a world of self-expression compared with which factory and shop work is infinitely petty and mean. In the social life of friends, neighborhood, school and church she is at least as well placed as the factory worker. If the woman has the preparation required for teaching or independent business, she will find ways to use her powers that will relieve the routine of housework. And if the family has means to hire help, the wife has a position from which she can exercise social and political power superior to that of the foot-loose celibate.

Meantime, the housework grows steadily-simpler and less exacting, even with the growing complexity of our modern life. Most of the primitive industries have left the home, and products come from the factory ready to use. Furnace heating, hot and cold water, improved cooking conditions and many domestic inventions of our day are keeping housework well abreast of other unspecialized work in attractiveness.

The fact that domestic servants are scarce and unwilling to do general housework, in no way disproves the soundness of these conclusions. The wife, if she is a real wife, and we are discussing no others, is working for those she loves, under conditions of free initiative. The general servant is working for those who will not even admit her right to participate in their social life, and instead of freedom in her industrial life, she must generally adjust her efforts to the caprices of an untrained mistress. Well-trained mistresses, who know how to work themselves and who have a democratic sense of human values, seldom have trouble in securing able servants, even in this transition time when the shops and factories are calling so loudly to working girls.

No intelligence which a woman may possess needs remain unused in the handling of a family. Women spend most of the household money to-day, at least in lower and middle-class homes. To use wisely the family pay-envelope requires knowledge and judgment of a high order. Problems in economics, sanitation, food-values and aesthetics confront the housewife at every turn of the day's work. "Even a slave need not work as a slave;" and a woman living with the man she loves is the freest woman on earth, so far as mind and spirit are concerned.

But the factory girl, or the teacher, or the professional woman who seeks the fulfilment of all of life in the factory, the school or the consulting-room, will soon tire and clamor for relief. The housewife, or the mistress of a home, must likewise seek life away from her work if she is to love it and wake each morning with a desire to continue it. Luckily we have reached a place where working women in the home are seeking supplementary life outside, and they seem to be quite as successful in their search as are factory girls or teachers.

To the man, family life, of the kind we are considering, brings a vital connection with the past and the future. Reputation, possessions, friends, all become deeply significant when a man becomes a link in the generations of men. In establishing his material home, and modifying it to the changing conditions of the family; in building up a social setting for the group; in projecting his work and his service into the future, he is held to highest standards by the fact that he is working with the partner of his choice, and for interests that are in harmony with the constitution of the universe.

Of the greater physical health of married people there can be no doubt. Statistics all show the greater longevity of married people, and insurance companies recognize it. The celibate type of physical degeneration is so well differentiated that it can generally be recognized even among strangers, at least after forty. On the moral side, too, very few criminals are found among married people.

If children come to bless these homes of men and women, then even intellectual life may shift to a higher level than was before possible. With advancing years intellectual interests tend to become specialized. The man or woman gives up singing, ceases to be interested in plant life, stops reading poetry. One activity after another is cut off and interests concentrate in some comparatively small field of work or pleasure. But when a child comes, the parents are forced to start over the round of human interests and thought once more. Before, they lived it as children; now, they live the cycle as grown men and women.

No matter how completely a woman has given up music, she will some day find herself singing when she holds her baby in her arms. As she recites Mother Goose and the fairy and folk-lore tales, she moves through the path of man's upward progress, led by a child, but with the life and understanding of adult years. As she walks with her child in the garden and in the fields, she is driven to a new interpretation of the world of nature. Few things can so broaden, quicken and enrich the intellectual life as growing up with one's children.

On the social side, a parent who has children is forced to live in all the social world around him. The water-supply, the sewage, pure foods, vacant lots, paving, fast driving in the streets, police protection, undesirable residents, saloons and churches, schools and libraries—everything that touches the social well-being—touches him vitally and imperatively. The foot-loose celibate can always go away. The parent finds it difficult to leave the place where he has planted his roof-tree. Of course, there are many unmarried people, and people who are childless, who live this domestic life vicariously through friends or other people's children. One cannot but be grateful that life is so organized that no woman can be entirely shut off, unless she wills it, from the fructifying life that knits together the generations of the old and the young.

Ideals are very powerful in determining conduct, and the ideals of extreme individualism, now so constantly presented by certain leaders among emancipated women, must bear bitter fruit for an army of women in the future. While the women are young, ambition and the charm of freedom bear them gaily along. Generally better educated than the men of their own class, habituated to a personal expenditure which would correspond with a large family expenditure, their intelligence prevents their falling desperately in love with the men whom they might marry. But in the thirties they have visions of the future which are deeply disturbing; and in the forties they face the tragedy of a lonely old age. Some men and women there must always be whose lives lack the fulfilment of family life because of ill health or the accidents of personal relations. But most women, if they are willing to pay the same price for a significant family life that they so gladly pay for professional success, will find the way open to live all of life. Why is it that women count it an honor to work and starve for an art, but dishonor to undergo privations for their children? All that is here said of women may be said of men, but the man's period of family life is longer than woman's, and the tragedy of lonely old age with him seems less overwhelming.

The old plea that we must have an army of Celibate women because in civilized countries there is a preponderance of females does not hold at present in the United States. The census of 1910 shows an excess of 2,691,678 males in this country. Nor is this entirely due to immigration. More boys than girls are always born in civilized lands; and of native white people born of native parents in the United States there were, in 1910, 25,229,294 males and 24,259,147 females, a difference obviously due to natural causes. New England alone in America has a preponderance of females; and the excess there, as also in England and Germany, is needed all along the frontiers of civilization. With the industrial and social freeing of women now going on, we may reasonably hope that the communities of old maids left behind, through the emigration of young men, will be broken up.

Of course, it will be pointed out that many men and women who do marry fail to realize the ideal presented in these pages. Every form of living is dangerous and not every one can hope to be a successful husband and father or wife and mother. Even devotion to religion furnishes many inmates for insane asylums; athletic contests leave a line of cripples behind them; and railroad disasters fill thousands of graves annually. The institution of marriage has had no such intelligence applied to its improvement during the past years as has been given to perfecting railroads; and since founding a family is a more difficult undertaking than making a journey, one need not be astonished at the number of fatalities. Even if the institution of marriage were as intelligently and carefully brought up to date as railroad systems are, it would still remain dangerous to live either in or out of marriage.

And yet the danger could be greatly reduced by proper education of youth. At present we are educating 10,000,000 girls in the state schools of America, and as many boys. They are spending eight to twelve years, under the direction of celibate women teachers, sharpening their intelligence. Their most important work in life is to be the making of homes, but they are supposed to master this art through imitating the homes in which they grow up. Many of these are unworthy of imitation, and they are all in process of transition.

Every girl should be thoroughly trained in handling an income and in spending money wisely. She should have a general knowledge of household sanitation, of water-supply and sewage, of foods and their preparation. She should know; about clothes, their cost, wearing qualities and decorative values. She should have a sense of the family and its significance in life; of at least the social relations that husband and wife must maintain toward each other if their partnership is to be happy and effective. She should have the beginnings of a eugenic conscience established in her, and she should know something of the care of infancy. All this should be given in the school, if it is not definitely given in the home, and no girl who goes through the eighth grade should escape it Before the girl is married, she should have wise counsel from mature women who have lived and learned the art of living. Boys should, of course, also be trained in comparable directions for this great part of their lives.

Something is already being done in this direction through the establishing of special courses in domestic science, and allied branches in our schools. The fact that educational leaders are awake to the need was shown by the applause that followed Superintendent Harvey's plea for this training in his paper on the education of girls at the Superintendents' Association in St. Louis in February, 1912. The leading educators of the country greeted his plea with an enthusiasm called out by no other paper of the session.

Every woman, then, and every man, not debarred by disease or accident and not specially dedicated to a work which precludes marriage, should spend his life in a family group, not that the state may have more soldiers, or factory employees, but that he may realize the deepest significance of his life. In this life the woman should be as free as the man, an equal financial partner, and should share in all the social and political opportunities of the community. When she bears children, she should have special protection, support and reverence; and support human relations have been involved in this time of readjustment Instead of talking of unquiet women today, we should talk of an unquiet world.

In the midst of this confusion, most of those who have sought to secure a truer relation of women to the life around them have worked on the lines of minimizing sex differences. It has been felt that the educational, industrial, social and political limitations under which women rested were due to the desire of men to exploit them. Men, being free, had developed for themselves an ideal world of thought and work; and if women wished to be free and happy, they needed only to break down the barriers separating them from this man's world.

Most of these barriers are now down; but the women who study in universities, teach in the schools, maintain offices as doctors or lawyers, collect news for the press, tend spindles in a factory or sell ribbons at a counter have found that the man's world is far from ideal and that by entering it they have not escaped the special limitations of their sex. Everywhere the feeling is abroad that, instead of having arrived at a destination, women have embarked on a journey fraught with many uncertainties.

This volume has been written in the belief that men and women alike will achieve greatest freedom and happiness, not by minimizing sex differences, but by frankly recognizing them and using them. If we could reduce men and women to sameness, we should destroy at least half the values of human life. They are not alike; but they are perfectly supplementary. The unit can never be a man nor a woman; it must always be a man and a woman. This means that in all the activities essential to human development men and women must carefully study to find what each can best provide.

Thus we must some day have a Church, not composed exclusively of male priests and women worshipers, not confined to rationalistic appeal nor to ritualistic observance, but expressing the whole range of human aspiration toward the unknown. Rational men and women of feeling must combine with reverent men and intelligent women to create a belief and a service which will express all the longings of humanity toward perfection.

So in government, we must have a state which will be not only just but merciful; which will concern itself not only with militant economics but also with human well-being. If men are more capable in expressing the katabolic needs of aggression and protection, women must furnish the anabolic products of care and conservation. If women must help pay the bills and nurse the wounded, they must first have a voice in determining whether there shall be a war. Men and women must join their qualities in building and caring for cities, and in shaping nations, where they can both live their largest lives.

In education, we must devise institutions which will provide for the special needs of women; and we must have the combined qualities of men and women brought to bear on children of both sexes, and at all ages. The foster parents of the nation's children must be both men and women. The present attempt to exploit our twenty millions of boys and girls in the interest of a sex will be a crime against humanity when we are intelligent enough to see its real meaning.

The specialization going on in industry means infinite variety if we look at the whole field of activity. Some parts of the world's work are specially fitted for men; other parts to women. No intelligent division of labor has been attempted in the period since all work was transformed by our modern inventions. Possibly men should do most of the dressmaking, and women should make men's clothing, but no intelligent man or woman can doubt that most work falls naturally into the hands of one sex or the other. Some day we shall know enough so that there will be little or no industrial competition between men and women.

It is, however, in the family that both men and women must find their deepest supplementary values. Sex antagonism can do much to impoverish and ruin individual lives; but the monogamic and persistent union of lovers, surrounded by their children, will easily survive all the mistakes of a time of transition. In the meantime, those who would uphold the finest family ideals of the past have less cause to fear the militant agitator than they have to fear the idle, parasitic wife, who relies on her legal rights to give her luxuries without labor, position without leadership, and wifehood without the care and responsibility of children.

From the point of view of this book, all the efforts to open the doors of opportunity, through which women can pass into the man's world, are but preparations for the beginning of a journey. The sooner all such doors are opened the better, for then a great source of dangerous sex antagonism will pass away; and the energy of reformers will be set free to work out the difficult problem of supplementary sex adjustments.

And meantime, sex remains the greatest mystery and the most powerful thing in human life. Its deeper values are lost sight of when men and women are warring over work, wages, and votes, just as the meaning of religion has been lost when priests and laity sought to advance their meanly selfish interests. But in the crises of life it always comes back. When a great ship founders in midocean, and but a third of the people can be saved, there is then no question of woman's rights. In the darkness of early morning, eager men's hands place their women in the life-boats and push them off.

The poorest peasant woman takes precedence over any man. Almost every woman there would prefer to stay and die with her man; would glory in staying and dying if he might thus be saved; but in her keeping are the generations of the future, and she is weak, therefore the strong gladly stand back and go down to death. The solution of woman's place in the society of the future must be based on a recognition of the supplementary forces that send women to undesired safety while men die.

●●

8
Parasitism

In that clamor which has arisen in the modern world, where now this, and then that, is demanded for and by large bodies of modern women, he who listens carefully may detect as a keynote, beneath all the clamor, a demand which may be embodied in such a cry as this: *Give us Labour and the training which fits for Labour! We demand this, not for ourselves alone, but for the race.*

If this demand be logically expanded, it will take such form as this: Give us Labour! for countless ages, for thousands, millions it may be, we have Laboured. When first man wandered, the naked, newly-erected savage, and hunted, and fought, we wandered with him: each step of his was ours. Within our bodies we bore the race, on our shoulders we carried it; we sought the roots and plants for its food; and, when man's barbed arrow or hook brought the game, our hands dressed it. Side by side, the savage man and the savage woman, we wandered free together and Laboured free together. And we were contented!

Then a Change Came

We ceased from our wanderings, and, camping upon one spot of earth, again the Labours of life were divided between us. While man went forth to hunt, or to battle with the foe who would have dispossessed us of all, we Laboured on the land. We hoed the earth, we reaped the grain, we shaped the dwellings, we wove the clothing, we modeled the earthen vessels and drew the lines upon them, which were humanity's first attempt at domestic art; we studied the properties and uses of plants, and our old women were the first physicians of the race, as often, its first priests and prophets.

We fed the race at our breast, we bore it on our shoulders; through us it was shaped, fed, and clothed. Labour more toilsome and unending than that of man was ours; yet did we never cry out that it was too heavy for us. While savage man lay in the sunshine on his skins, resting, that he might be fitted for war or the chase, or while he shaped his weapons of death, he ate and drank that which our hands had provided for him; and while we knelt over our grindstone, or hoed in the fields, with one child in our womb, perhaps, and one on our back, toiling till the young body was old before its time—did *we* ever cry out that the Labour allotted to us was too hard for us? Did we not know that the woman who threw down her burden was as a man who cast away his shield in battle—a coward and a traitor to his race? Man fought—that was his work; we fed and nurtured the race—that was ours. We knew that upon our Labours, even as upon man's, depended the life and well-being of the people whom we bore. We endured our toil, as man bore his wounds, silently; and we were content.

Then again a Change Came

Ages passed, and time was when it was no longer necessary that all men should go to the hunt or the field of war; and when only one in five, or one in ten, or but one in twenty, was needed continually for these Labours. Then our fellow-man, having no longer full occupation in his old fields of Labour, began to take his share in ours. He too began to cultivate the field, to build the house, to grind the corn (or make his male slaves do it); and the hoe, and the potter's tools, and the thatching-needle, and at last even the grindstones which we first had picked up and smoothed to grind the food for our children, began to pass from our hands into his. The old, sweet life of the open fields was ours no more; we moved within the gates, where the time passes more slowly and the world is sadder than in the air outside; but we had our own work still, and were content.

If, indeed, we might no longer grow the food for our people, we were still its dressers; if we did not always plant and prepare the flax and hemp, we still wove the garments for our race; if we did no longer raise the house walls, the tapestries that covered them were the work of our hands; we brewed the ale, and the simples which were used as medicines we distilled and prescribed} and, close about our feet, from birth to manhood, grew up the children whom we had borne; their voices were always in our ears. At the doors of our houses we sat with our spinning-wheels, and we looked out across the fields that were once ours to Labour in—and were contented. Lord's wife, peasant's, or burgher's, we all still had our work to do!

A thousand years ago, had one gone to some great dame, questioning her why she did not go out a-hunting or a-fighting, or enter the great hall to dispense justice and confer upon the making of laws, she would have answered: "Am I a fool that you put to me such questions? Have I not a hundred maidens to keep at work at spinning-wheels and needles? With my own hands daily do I not dispense bread to over a hundred folk? In the great hall go and see the tapestries I with my maidens have created by the Labours of years, and which we shall Labour over for twenty more, that my children's children may see recorded the great deeds of their forefathers. In my store-room are there not salves and simples, that my own hands have prepared for the healing of my household and the sick in the country round? Ill would it go indeed, if when the folk came home from war and the chase of wild beasts, weary or wounded, they found all the womenfolk gone out a-hunting and a-fighting, and none there to dress their wounds, or prepare their meat, or guide and rule the household! Better far might my lord and his followers come and help us with our work, than that we should go to help them I You are surely bereft of all wit. What becomes of the country if the women forsake their toil?"

And the burgher's wife, asked why she did not go to Labour in her husband's workshop, or away into the market-place, or go a-trading to foreign countries, would certainly have answered: "I am too busy to speak with such as you! The bread is in the oven (already I smell it a-burning), the winter is coming on, and my children lack good woolen hose and my husband needs a warm coat. I have six vats of ale all a-brewing, and I have daughters whom I must teach to spin and sew, and the babies are clinging round my knees. And you ask *me* why *I* do not go abroad to seek for new Labours! God-sooth ! Would you have me to leave my household to starve in summer and die of cold in winter, and my children to go untrained, while I gad about to seek for other work? A man must have his belly full and his back covered before all things in life. Who, think you, would spin and bake and brew, and rear and train my babes, if I went abroad? New Labour, indeed, when the days are not long enough, and I have to toil far into the night! I have no time to talk with fools I Who will rear and shape the nation if I do not?"

And the young maiden at the cottage door, beside her wheel, asked why she was content and did not seek new fields of Labour, would surely have answered: "Go away, I have no time to listen to you. Do you not see that I am spinning here that I too may have a home of my own? I am weaving the linen garments that shall clothe my household in the long years to come! I cannot marry till the chest upstairs be full. *You* cannot hear it, but as I sit here alone, spinning, far off across the hum of my spinning-wheel I hear the voices of my little unborn children calling to me—'O mother, mother, make haste, that we may be!'—and sometimes, when I seem to be looking out across my wheel into the sunshine, it is the blaze of my own fireside that I see, and the light shines on the faces round it; and I spin on the faster and the steadier when I think of what shall come. Do you ask *me* why I do not go out and Labour in the fields with the lad whom I have chosen? Is his work, then, indeed more needed than mine for the raising of that home that shall be ours? Oh, very hard I will Labour, for him and for my children, in the long years to come. But I cannot stop to talk to you now. Far off, over the hum of my spinning-wheel, I hear the voices of my children calling, and I must hurry on. Do you ask me why I do not seek for Labour whose hands are full to bursting? Who will give folk to the nation if I do not?"

Such would have been our answer in Europe in the ages of the past, if asked the question why we were contented with our field of Labour and sought no other. Man had his work; we had ours. We knew that we upbore our world on our shoulders; and that through the Labour of our hands it was sustained and strengthened—and we were contented.

But now, again a change has come.

Something that is entirely new has entered into the field of human Labour, and left nothing as it was.

In man's fields of toil, change has accomplished, and is yet more quickly accomplishing, itself.

On lands where once fifty men and youths toiled with their cattle, to-day one steam-plough, guided by but two pair of hands, passes swiftly; and an automatic reaper in one day reaps and binds and prepares for the garner the produce of fields it would have taken a hundred strong male arms to harvest in the past. The iron tools and weapons, only one of which it took an ancient father of our race long months of stern exertion to extract from ore and bring to shape and temper, are now poured forth by steam-driven machinery as a mill-pond pours forth its water; and even in war, the male's ancient and especial field of Labour, a complete reversal of the ancient order has taken place. Time was when the size and strength of the muscles in a man's legs and arms, and the strength and size of his body, largely determined his fighting powers, and an Achilles or a Richard Coeur de Lion, armed only with his spear or battle-ax, made a host fly before him; to-day the puniest manikin behind a modern Maxim gun may mow down in perfect safety a phalanx of heroes whose legs and arms and physical powers a Greek god might have envied, but who, having not the modern machinery of war, fall powerless. The day of the primary import to humanity of the strength in man's extensor and flexor muscles, whether in Labours of war or of peace, is gone by forever; and the day of the all-importance of the culture and activity of man's brain and nerve has already come.

The brain of one consumptive German chemist, who in his Laboratory compounds a new explosive, has more effect upon the wars of the modern peoples than ten thousand soldierly legs and arms and the man who invents one new Labour-saving machine may, through the cerebration of a few days, have performed the Labour it would otherwise have taken hundreds of thousands of his lusty fellows decades to accomplish.

Year by year, month by month, and almost hour by hour, this change is increasingly showing itself in the field of modern Labour; and crude muscular force, whether in man or beast, sinks continually in its value in the world of human toil; while intellectual power, virility, and activity, and that culture which leads to the mastery of the inanimate forces of nature, to the invention of machinery, and to that delicate manipulative skill often required in guiding it, becomes ever of greater and greater importance to the race. Already to-day we tremble on the verge of a discovery, which may come tomorrow or the next day, when, through the attainment of a simple and cheap method of controlling some widely diffused, everywhere accessible, natural force (such, for instance, as the force of the great tidal wave) there will at once and for ever pass away even that comparatively small value which still, in our present stage of material civilization, clings to the expenditure of mere crude, mechanical, human energy; and the creature, however physically powerful, who can merely pull, push, and lift, much after the manner of a machine, will have no further value in the field of human Labour.

Therefore, even to-day, we find that wherever that condition which we call modern civilization prevails, and in proportion as it tends to prevail—wherever steam-power, electricity, or the forces of wind and water, are compelled by man's intellectual activity to act as the motor-powers in the accomplishment of human toil, wherever the delicate adaptations of scientifically constructed machinery are taking the place of the simple manipulation of the human hand—there has arisen, all the world over, a large body of males who find that their ancient fields of Labour have slipped or are slipping from them, and who discover that the modern world has no place or need for them. At the gates of our dockyards, in our streets, and in our fields, are to be found everywhere, in proportion as modern civilization is really dominant, men whose bulk and mere animal strength would have made them as warriors invaluable members of any primitive community, and who would have been valuable even in any simpler civilization than our own as machines of toil; but who, owing to lack of intellectual power or delicate manual training, have now no form of Labour to offer society which it stands really in need of, and who therefore tend to form our *Great Male Unemployed*—a body which finds the only powers it possesses so little needed by its fellows that, in return for its intensest physical Labour, it hardly earns the poorest sustenance. The material conditions of life have been rapidly modified, and the man has not been modified with them; machinery has largely filled his place in his old field of Labour, and he has found no new one.

It is from these men, who, viewed from the broad humanitarian standpoint, are of the most lovable and interesting type, and who might in a simpler state of society have been the heroes, leaders, and chiefs of their people, that there arises in the modern world thc bitter cry of the male unemployed: "Give us Labour or we die!"

Yet it is only upon one, and a comparatively small, section of the males of the modern civilized world that these changes in the material conditions of life have told in such fashion as to take all useful occupation from them and render them wholly or partly worthless to society. If the modern man's field of Labour has contracted at one end (the physical), at the other (the intellectual) it has immeasurably expanded! If machinery and the command of inanimate motor-forces have rendered of comparatively little value the male's mere physical motor-power, the demand upon his intellectual faculties, the call for the expenditure of nervous energy, and the exercise of delicate manipulative skill in the Labour of human life, have immeasurably increased.

In a million new directions forms of honored and remunerative social Labour are opening up before the feet of the modern man, which his ancestors never dreamed of; and day by day they yet increase in numbers and importance. The steamship, the hydraulic lift, the patent road-maker, the railway-train, the electric tram-car, the steam-driven mill, the Maxim gun and the torpedo boat, once made, may perform their Labours with the guidance and assistance of comparatively few hands; but a whole army of men of science, engineers, clerks, and highly-trained workmen is necessary for their invention, construction, and maintenance. In the domains of art, of science, of literature, and above all in the field of politics and government, an almost infinite extension has taken place in the fields of male Labour. Where in primitive times woman was often the only builder, and patterns she daubed on her hut walls or traced on her earthen vessels the only attempts at domestic art; and where later but an individual here and there was required to design a king's palace or a god's temple or to ornament it with statues or paintings, to-day a mighty army of men, a million strong, is employed in producing plastic art alone, both high and low, from the traceries on wallpaper and the illustrations in penny journals, to the production of the pictures and statues which adorn the national collections, and a mighty new field of toil has opened before the anciently hunting and fighting male. Where once one ancient witch-doc-tress may have been the only creature in a whole district who studied the nature of herbs and earths, or a solitary wizard experimenting on poisons was the only individual in a whole territory interrogating nature; and where later, a few score of alchemists and astrologers only were engaged in examining the natures of substances or the movement of planets, to-day hundreds of thousands of men in every civilized community are Labouring to unravel the mysteries of nature, and the practical chemist, the physician, the anatomist, the engineer, the astronomer, the mathematician, the electrician, form a mighty and always increasingly important army of male Labourers. Where once an isolated bard supplied a nation with its literature, or where later a few thousand priests and men of letters wrote and transcribed for the few to read, today literature gives Labour to a multitude of males almost as countless as a swarm of locusts. From the penny-a-liner to the artist and thinker, the demand for their Labour continually increases. Where one town-crier with stout legs and lusty lungs was once all-sufficient to spread the town and country news, a score of men now sit daily pen in hand, preparing the columns of the morning's paper, and far into the night a hundred compositors are engaged in a Labour which requires a higher culture of brain and finger than most ancient kings and rulers possessed. Even in the Labours of war, the most brutal and primitive of the occupations lingering on into civilized life from the savage state, the new demand for Labour of an intellectual kind is enormous. The invention, construction, and working of one Krupp gun, though its mere discharge hardly demands more crude muscular exertion than a savage expends in throwing his boomerang, yet represents an infinitude of intellectual care and thought, far greater than that which went to the shaping of all the weapons of a primitive army. Above all, in the domain of politics and government, where once a king or queen, aided by a handful of councilors, was alone practically concerned in the Labours of national guidance or legislation; to-day, owing to the rapid means of intercommunication, printing, and the consequent diffusion of political and social information throughout a territory, it has become possible, for the first time, for all adults in a large community to keep themselves closely informed on all national affairs; and in every highly-civilized state the ordinary male has been almost compelled to take his share, however small, in the duties and Labours of legislation and government. Thus there has opened before the mass of men a vast new sphere of Labour undreamed of by their ancestors. In every direction the change which material civilization has wrought, while it has militated against that comparatively small section of males who have nothing to offer society but the expenditure of their untrained muscular energy (inflicting much and often completely unmerited suffering upon them), has immeasurably extended the field of male Labour as a whole. Never before in the history of the earth has the man's field of remunerative toil been so wide, so interesting, so complex, and in its results so all-important to society; never before has the male sex, taken as a whole, been so fully and strenuously employed.

So much is this the case, that, exactly as in the earlier conditions of society an excessive and almost crushing amount of the most important social Labour generally devolved upon the female, so under modern civilized conditions among the wealthier and fully civilized classes, an unduly excessive share of Labour tends to devolve upon the male. That almost entirely modern, morbid condition, affecting brain and nervous system, and shortening the lives of thousands in modern civilized societies, which is vulgarly known as "overwork" or "nervous breakdown," is but one evidence of the even excessive share of mental Labour devolving upon the modern male of the cultured classes, who, in addition to maintaining himself, has frequently dependent upon him a larger or smaller number of entirely parasitic females. But, whatever the result of the changes of modern civilization may be with regard to the male, he certainly cannot complain that they have as a whole robbed him of his fields of Labour, diminished his share in the conduct of life, or reduced him to a condition of morbid inactivity.

In our woman's field of Labour, matters have tended to shape themselves wholly otherwise ! The changes which have taken place during the last centuries, and which we sum up under the compendious term "modern civilization," have tended to rob woman, not merely in part but almost wholly, of the more valuable part of her ancient domain of productive and social Labour; and, where there has not been a determined and conscious resistance on her part, have nowhere spontaneously tended to open out to her new and compensatory fields.

It is this fact which constitutes our modern "Woman's Labour Problem."

Our spinning-wheels are all broken; in a thousand huge buildings steam-driven looms, guided by a few hundred thousands of hands (often those of men), produce the clothings of half the world; and we dare no longer say, proudly, as of old, that we and we alone clothe our peoples.

Our hoes and our grindstones passed from us long ago, when the plowman and the miller took our place but for a time we kept fast possession of the kneading-trough and the brewing-vat. To-day, steam often shapes our bread, and the loaves are set down at our very door—it may be by a man-driven motor-car. The history of our household drinks we know no longer; we merely see them set before us at our tables. Day by day machine-prepared and factory-produced viands take a larger and larger place in the dietary of rich and poor, till the working man's wife places before her household little that is of her own preparation; while among the wealthier classes, so far has domestic change gone that men are not infrequently found Labouring in our houses and kitchens, and even standing behind our chairs ready to do all but actually place the morsels of food between our feminine lips. The army of rosy milkmaids has passed away for ever, to give place to the cream-separator and the, largely, male-and-machinery-manipulated butter pat. In every direction the ancient saw, that it was exclusively the woman's sphere to prepare viands of her household, has become, in proportion as civilization has perfected itself, an antiquated lie.

Even the minor domestic operations are tending to pass out of the circle of woman's Labour. In modern cities our carpets are beaten, our windows cleaned, our floors polished, by machinery, or extra domestic, and often male Labour. Change has gone much farther than to the mere taking from us of the preparation of the materials from which the clothing is formed. Already the domestic sewing-machine, which has supplanted almost entirely the ancient needle, begins to become antiquated, and a thousand machines driven in factories by central engines are supplying not only the husband and son, but the woman herself, with almost every article of clothing from vest to jacket; while among the wealthy classes, the male dress-designer with his hundred male-milliners and dress-makers is helping finally to explode the ancient myth, that it is woman's exclusive sphere, and a part of her domestic toil, to cut and shape the garments she or her household wear.

Year by year, day by day, there is a silently working but determined tendency for the sphere of woman's domestic Labours to contract itself; and the contraction is marked exactly in proportion as that complex condition which we term "modern civilization" is advanced.

It manifests itself more in England and America than in Italy and Spain, more in great cities than in country places, more among the wealthier classes than the poorer, and is an unfailing indication of advancing modern civilization.

But it is not only, nor even mainly, in the sphere of woman's material domestic Labours that change has touched her and shrunk her ancient field of Labour.

Time was, when the woman kept her children about her knees till adult years were reached. Hers was the training and influence which shaped them. From the moment when the infant first lay on her breast, till her daughters left her for marriage and her sons went to take share in man's Labour, they were continually under the mother's influence. To-day so complex have become even the technical and simpler branches of education, 6o mighty and inexorable are the demands which modern civilization makes for specialized instruction and training for all individuals who are to survive and retain their usefulness under modern conditions, that, from the earliest years of its life, the child is of necessity largely removed from the hands of the mother, and placed in those of the specialized instructor. Among the wealthier classes, scarcely is the infant born when it passes into the hands of the trained nurse, and from hers on into the hands of the qualified teacher; till, at nine or ten, the son in certain countries of-ten leaves his home forever for the public school, to pass on to the college and university; while the daughter, in the hands of trained instructors and dependents, owes in the majority of cases hardly more of her education or formation to maternal toil.

Even among our poorer classes, the infant school, and the public school, and later on the necessity for manual training, take the son and often the daughter as completely, and always increasingly as civilization advances, from the mother's control. So marked has this change in woman's ancient field of Labour become, that a woman of almost any class may have borne many children and yet at middle age be found sitting alone in an empty house, all her offspring gone from her to receive training and instruction at the hands of others. The ancient statement that the training and education of her offspring is exclusively the duty of the mother, however true it may have been with regard to a remote past, has become an absolute misstatement; and the woman who should at the present day insist on entirely educating her own offspring would, in nine cases out of ten, inflict an irreparable injury on them, because she is incompetent.

But, if possible, yet more deeply and radically have the changes of modern civilization touched our ancient field of Labour in another direction—in that very portion of the field of human Labour which is peculiarly and organically ours, and which can never be wholly taken from us. Here the shrinkage has been larger than in any other direction, and touches us as women more vitally.

Time was, and still is, among almost all primitive and savage folk, when the first and all-important duty of the female to her society was to bear, to bear much, and to bear unceasingly! On her adequate and persistent performance of this passive form of Labour, and on her successful feeding of her young from her own breast, depended, not merely the welfare, but often the very existence, of her tribe or nation. Where, as is the case among almost all barbarous peoples, the rate of infant mortality is high; where the unceasing casualties resulting from war, the chase, and acts of personal violence tend continually to reduce the number of adult males; where, surgical knowledge being still in its infancy, most wounds are fatal; where, above all, recurrent pestilence and famine, unfailing if of irregular recurrence, decimated the people, it has been all important that woman should employ her creative power to its very uttermost limits if the race were not at once to dwindle and die out, "May thy wife's womb never cease from bearing," is still to-day the highest expression of good will on the part of a native African chief to his departing guest. For, not only does the prolific woman in the primitive state contribute to the wealth and strength of her nation as a whole, but to that of her own male companion and of her family.

Where the social conditions of life are so simple that, in addition to bearing and suckling the child, it is reared and nourished through childhood almost entirely through the Labour and care of the mother, requiring no expenditure of tribal or family wealth on its training or education, its value as an adult enormously outweighs, both to the state and the male, the trouble and expense of rearing it, which falls almost entirely on the individual woman who bears it. The man who has twenty children to become warriors and Labourers is by so much the richer and the more powerful than he who has but one; while the state whose women are prolific and Labour for and rear their children stands so far insured against destruction. Incessant and persistent child-bearing is thus truly the highest duty and the most socially esteemed occupation of the primitive woman, equalling fully in social importance the Labour of the man as hunter and warrior.

Even under those conditions of civilization which have existed in the centuries dividing primitive savagery from high civilization, the demand for continuous unbroken child-bearing on the part of the woman as her loftiest social duty has generally been hardly less imperious. Throughout the Middle Ages of Europe, and down almost to our own day, the rate of infant mortality was almost as large as in a savage state; medical ignorance destroyed innumerable lives; antiseptic surgery being unknown, serious wounds were still almost always fatal; in the low state of sanitary science, plagues, such as those which in the reign of Justinian swept across the civilized world from India to Northern Europe, well nigh depopulating the globe, or the Black Death of 1349, which in England alone swept away more than half the population of the island, were but extreme forms of the destruction of population going on continually as the result of zymotic disease; while wars were not merely far more common but, owing to the famines which almost invariably followed them, were far more destructive to human life than in our own days, and deaths by violence, whether at the hands of the state or as the result of personal enmity, were of daily occurrence in all lands. Under these conditions abstinence on the part of woman from incessant child-bearing might have led to almost the same serious diminution, or even extinction of her people, as in the savage state; while the very existence of her civilization depended on the production of an immense number of individuals as beasts of burden, without the expenditure of whose crude muscular force in physical Labour of agriculture and manufacture, those intermediate civilizations would, in the absence of machinery, have been impossible. Twenty men had to be born, fed at the breast, and reared by women to perform the crude brute Labour which is performed to-day by one small, well-adjusted steam crane; and the demand for large masses of human creatures as mere reservoirs of motor force for accomplishing the simplest processes was imperative. So strong, indeed, was the consciousness of the importance to society of continuous child-bearing on the part of woman, that as late as the middle of the sixteenth century Martin Luther wrote: "If a woman becomes weary or at last dead from bearing, that matters not; let her only die from bearing, she is there to do it"; and he doubtless gave expression, in a crude and somewhat brutal form, to a conviction common to the bulk of his contemporaries, both male and female.

To-day, this condition has almost completely reversed itself.

The advance of science and the amelioration of the physical conditions of life tend rapidly toward a diminution of human mortality. The infant death-rate among the upper classes in modern civilizations has fallen by more than one-half; while among poorer classes it is already, though slowly, falling: the increased knowledge of the laws of sanitation has made among all highly civilized peoples the depopulation by plague a thing of the past, and the discoveries of the next twenty or thirty years will probably do away for ever with the danger to man of zymotic disease. Famines of the old desolating type have become an impossibility where rapid means of transportation convey the superfluity of one land to supply the lack of another; and war and deeds of violence, though still lingering among us, have already become episode in the lives of nations as of individuals; while the vast advances in antiseptic surgery have caused even the effects of wounds and dismemberments to become only very partially fatal to human life. All these changes have tended to diminish human mortality and protract human life; and they have to-day already made it possible for a race not only to maintain its numbers, but even to increase them, with a comparatively small expenditure of woman's vitality in the passive Labour of child-bearing. But yet more seriously has the demand for woman's Labour as child-bearer been diminished by change in another direction.

Every mechanical invention which lessens the necessity for rough, untrained, muscular, human Labour, diminishes also the social demand upon woman as the producer in large masses of such Labourers. Already throughout the modern civilized world we have reached a point at which the social demand is not merely for human creatures in the bulk for use as beasts of burden, but, rather, and only, for such human creatures as shall be so trained and cultured as to be fitted for the performance of the more complex duties of modern life. Not, now, merely for many men, but, rather, for few men, and those few, well-born and well-instructed, is the modern demand. And the woman who to-day merely produces twelve children and suckles them, and then turns them loose on her society and family, is regarded, and rightly so, as a curse and down-draft, and not the productive Labourer, of her community. Indeed, so difficult and expensive has become in the modern world the rearing and training of even one individual, in a manner suited to fit it for coping with the complexities and difficulties of civilized life, that, to the family as well as to the state, unlimited fecundity on the part of the female has already, in most cases, become an irremediable evil. It is thus in the case of the artisan, who at the cost of immense self-sacrifice must support and train his children till their twelfth or fourteenth year, if they are ever to become even skilled manual Labourers, and who if his family be large often sinks beneath the burden, allowing his offspring, untaught and untrained, to become waste products of human life. So with the professional man, who by his mental toil is compelled to support and educate, at immense expense, his sons till they are twenty or older, and to sustain his daughters, often throughout their whole lives should they not marry, and to whom a large family proves often no less disastrous; while the state whose women produce recklessly large masses of individuals in excess of those for whom they can provide instruction and nourishment is a state, in so far, tending toward deterioration. The commandment to the modern woman is now not simply "Thou shalt bear," but rather, "Thou shalt not bear in excess of thy power to rear and train satisfairily"; and the woman who should to-day appear at the door of a workhouse or the tribunal of the poor-law guardians followed by her twelve infants, demanding honorable sustenance for them and herself in return for the Labour she had undergone in producing them, would meet with but short shrift. And the modern man who on his wedding-day should be greeted with the ancient good wish, that he might become the father of twenty sons and twenty daughters, would regard it as a malediction rather than a blessing. It is certain that the time is now rapidly approaching when child-bearing will be regarded rather as a lofty privilege, permissible only to those who have shown their power rightly to train and provide for their offspring, than a Labour which in itself, and under whatever conditions performed, is beneficial to society.

Further, owing partly to the diminished demand for child-bearing, rising from the extreme difficulty and expense of rearing and education, and to many other complex social causes, to which we shall return later, millions of women in our modern societies are so placed as to be absolutely compelled to go through life not merely childless, but without sex relationship in any form whatever; while another mighty army of women is reduced by the dislocations of our civilization to accepting sexual relationships which almost negate child-bearing, and whose only product is physical and moral disease.

Thus, it has come to pass that vast numbers of us are, by modern social conditions, prohibited from child-bearing at all, and that even those among us who are child-bearers are required, in proportion as the class or race to which we belong stands high in the scale of civilization, to produce in most cases a limited number of offspring; so that, even for these of us, child-bearing and suckling, instead of filling the entire circle of female life from the first appearance of puberty to the end of middle age, becomes an episodal occupation, employing from three or four to ten or twenty of the threescore-and-ten-years which are allotted to human life. In such societies the statement (so profoundly true when made with regard to most savage societies, and even largely true with regard to those in the intermediate stages of civilization) that the main and continuous occupation of all women from puberty to age is the bearing and suckling of children, and that this occupation must fully satisfy all her needs for social Labour and activity, becomes an antiquated and unmitigated misstatement.

Not only are millions of our women precluded from ever bearing a child, but for those of us who do bear the demand is ever increasingly in civilized societies coupled with the condition that if we would act socially we must restrict our powers, Looking round, then, with the uttermost impartiality we can command, on the entire field of woman's ancient and traditional Labours, we find that *fully three-fourths of it have shrunk away for ever, and that the remaining fourth still tends to shrink.*

It is this great fact, so often and so completely overlooked, which lies as the propelling force behind that vast and restless "Woman's Movement" which marks our day. It is *this* fact, whether clearly and intellectually grasped, or, as is more often the case, vaguely and painfully *felt,* which awakes in the hearts of the ablest modern European women their passionate, and at times it would seem almost incoherent, cry for new forms of Labour and new fields for the exercise of their powers.

Thrown into strict logical form, our demand is this: We do not ask that the wheels of time should reverse themselves, or the stream of life flow backward. We do not ask that our ancient spinning-wheels be again resuscitated and placed in our hands; we do not demand that our old grindstones and hoes be returned to us, or that man should again be-take himself entirely to his ancient province of war and the chase, leaving to us all domestic and civil Labour. We do not even demand that society shall immediately so reconstruct itself that every woman may be again a child-bearer (deep and overmastering as lies the hunger for motherhood in every virile woman's heart!); neither do we demand that the children whom we bear shall again be put exclusively into our hands to train. This, we know, cannot be. The past material conditions of life have gone for ever; no will of man can recall them, but *this* is our demand: We demand that, in that strange new world that is arising alike upon the man and the woman, where nothing is as it was, and all things are assuming new shapes and relations, that in this new world we also shall have our share of honored and socially useful human toil, our full half of the Labour of the Children of Woman. We demand nothing more than this, and we will take nothing less. *This is our* "Woman's Right!"

●●

9
Women and Labour Problems

Is it to be, that, in the future, machinery and the captive motor-forces of nature are largely to take the place of human hand and foot in the Labour of clothing and feeding the nations; are these branches of industry to be no longer domestic Labours?—then, we demand that in the factory, the warehouse, and the field, wherever machinery has usurped our ancient Labour-ground, we also should have our place, as guiders, controllers, and possessors. Is child-bearing to become the Labour of but a portion of our sex?—then we demand for those among us who are allowed to take no share in it, compensatory and equally honorable and; important fields of social toil. Is the training of human creatures to become a yet more and more onerous and Labourious occupation, their education and culture to become increasingly a high art, complex and scientific?—if so, then, we demand that high and complex culture and training which shall fit us for instructing the race which we bring into the world. Is the demand for child-bearing to become so diminished that, even in the lives of those among us who are child-bearers, it shall fill no more than half a dozen years out of the three-score-and-ten of human life?—then we demand that an additional outlet be ours which shall fill up with dignity and value the tale of the years not so employed. Is intellectual Labour to take ever and increasingly the place of crude muscular exertion in the Labour of life?—then we demand for ourselves that culture and the freedom of action which alone can yield us the knowledge of life and the intellectual vigor and strength which will enable us to undertake the same share of mental which we have borne in the past in physical Labours of life. Are the rulers of the race to be no more its kings and queens, but the mass of the peoples?—then we, one-half of the nations, demand our full queens' share in the duties and Labours of government and legislation. *Slowly but determinately, as the old fields of Labour close up and are submerged be-hind us, we demand entrance into the new.*

We make this demand, not for our own sake alone, but for the succor of the race.

A horseman, riding along on a dark night in an unknown land, may chance to feel his horse start beneath him; rearing, it may almost hurl him to the earth: in the darkness he may curse his beast, and believe its aim is simply to cast him off, and free itself for ever of its burden. But when the morning dawns and lights the hills and valleys he has traveled, looking backward, he may perceive that the spot where his beast reared, planting its feet into the earth, and where it refused to move farther on the old road, was indeed the edge of a mighty precipice, down which one step more would have precipitated both horse and rider. And he may then see that it was an instinct wiser than his own which led his creature, though in the dark, to leap backward, seeking a new path along which both might travel.

In the confusion and darkness of the present, it may well seem to some that woman, in her desire to seek for new paths of Labour and employment, is guided only by an irresponsible impulse; or that she seeks selfishly only her own good, at the cost of that of the race, which she has so long and faithfully borne onward. But, when a clearer future shall have arisen and the obscuring mists of the present have been dissipated, may it not then be clearly manifest that not for herself alone, but for her entire race, has woman sought her new paths?

For let it be noted exactly what our position is, who to-day, as women, are demanding new fields of Labour and a reconstruction of our relationship with life.

It is often said that the Labour problem before the modern woman and that before the unemployed or partially or almost uselessly employed male, are absolutely identical; and that therefore, when the male Labour problem of our age solves itself, that of the woman will of necessity have met its solution also.

This statement, with a certain specious semblance of truth, is yet, we believe, radically and fundamentally false. It is true that both the male and the female problems of our age have taken their rise largely in the same rapid material changes which during the last centuries, and more especially the last ninety years, have altered the face of the human world. Both men and women have been robbed by those changes of their ancient remunerative fields of social work: here the resemblance stops. The male, from whom the changes of modern civilization have taken his ancient field of Labour, has but one choice before him: he must find new fields of Labour, or he must perish. Society will not ultimately support him in an absolutely quiescent and almost useless condition. If he does not vigorously exert himself in some direction or other (the direction may even be predatory) he must ultimately be annihilated. Individual drones, both among the wealthiest and the poorest classes (millionaires' sons, dukes, or tramps), may in isolated cases be preserved, and allowed to reproduce themselves without any exertion or activity of mind or body, but a vast body of males who, having lost their old forms of social employment, should refuse in any way to exert themselves or seek for new, would at no great length of time become extinct.

There never has been, and as far as can be seen, there never will be, a time when the majority of the males in any society will be supported by the rest of the males in a condition of perfect mental and physical inactivity. *"Find Labour or die,"* is the choice ultimately put before the human male to-day, as in the past; and *this* constitutes his Labour problem. The Labour of the man may not always be useful in the highest sense to his society, or it may even be distinctly harmful and antisocial, as in the case of the robber-barons of the Middle Ages, who lived by capturing and despoiling all who passed by their castles; or as in the case of the share speculators, stockjobbers, ring-and-corner capitalists, and monopolists of the present day, who feed upon the productive Labours of society without contributing anything to its welfare. But even males so occupied are compelled to expend a vast amount of energy and even a low intelligence in their callings; and, however injurious to their societies, they rim no personal risk of handing down effete and enervated constitutions to their race. Whether beneficially or unbeneficially, the human male must, generally speaking, employ his intellect, or his muscle, or die.

The position of the unemployed modern female is one wholly different. The choice before her, as her ancient fields of domestic Labour slip from her, is not generally or often at the present day the choice between finding new fields of Labour, or death; but one far more serious in its ultimate reaction on humanity as a whole—it is the choice between finding new forms of Labour or sinking slowly into a condition of more or less complete and passive *sex-parasitism!*

Again and again in the history of the past, when among human creatures a certain stage of material civilization has been reached, a curious tendency has manifested itself for the human female to become more or less parasitic; social conditions tend to rob her of all forms of active conscious social Labour, and to reduce her, like the field-bug, to the passive exercise of her sex functions alone, And the result of this parasitism has invariably been the decay in vitality and intelligence of the female, followed after a longer or shorter period by that of her male descendants and her entire society.

Nevertheless, in the history of the past the dangers of the sex-parasitism have never threatened more than a small section of the females of the human race, those exclusively of some dominant race or class; the mass of women beneath them being still compiled to assume many forms of strenuous activity. It is at the present day, and under the peculiar conditions of our modern civilization, that for the first time sex-parasitism has become a danger, more or less remote, to the mass of civilized women, perhaps ultimately to all.

In the very early stages of human growth, the sexual parasitism and degeneration of the female formed no possible source of social danger. Where the conditions of life rendered it inevitable that all the Labour of a community should be performed by the members of that community for themselves, without the assistance of slaves or machinery, the tendency has always been rather to throw an excessive amount of social Labour on the female. Under no conditions, at no time, in no place, in the history of the world have the males of any period, of any nation, or of any class, shown the slightest inclination to allow their own females to become inactive or parasitic, so long as the actual muscular Labour of feeding and clothing them would in that case have devolved upon *themselves!* The parasitism of the human female becomes a possibility only when a point in civilization is reached (such as that which was attained in the ancient civilizations of Greece, Home, Persia, Assyria, India, and such as to-day exists in many of the civilizations of the East, such as those of China and Turkey), when, owing to the extensive employment of the Labour of slaves, or of subject races or classes, the dominant race or class has become so liberally supplied with the material goods of life that mere physical toil on the part of its own female members has become unnecessary. It is when this point has been reached, and never before, that the symptoms of female parasitism have in the past almost invariably tended to manifest themselves, and have become a social danger. The males of the dominant class have almost always contrived to absorb to themselves the new intellectual occupations, which the absence of necessity for the old forms of physical toil made possible in their societies; and the females of the dominant class or race, for whose muscular Labours there was how also no longer any need, not succeeding in grasping or attaining to these new forms of Labour, have sunk into a state in which, performing no species of active social duty, they have existed through the passive performance of sexual functions alone, with how much or how little of discontent will now never be known, since no literary record has been made by the woman of the past, of her desires or sorrows. Than in place of the active Labouring woman, upholding society by her toil, has come the effete wife, concubine or prostitute, clad in fine raiment, the work of others' fingers; fed on luxurious viands, the result of others' toil, waited on and tended by the Labour of others. The need for her physical Labour having gone, and mental industry not having taken its place, she bedecked and scented her person, or had it bedecked and scented for her, she lay upon her sofa, or drove or was carried out in her vehicle, and, loaded with jewels, she sought by dissipations and amusements to fill up the inordinate blank left by the lack of productive activity. And the hand whitened and frame softened, till, at last, the very duties of motherhood, which were all the constitution of her life left her, became distasteful, and, from the instant when her infant came damp from her womb, it passed into the hands of others, to he tended and reared by them; and from youth to age her offspring often owed nothing to her personal toil. In many cases so complete was her enervation, that at last the very joy of giving life, the glory and beatitude of a virile womanhood, became distasteful; and she sought to evade it not because of its interference with more imperious duties to those already born of her, or to her society, but because her existence of inactivity had robbed her of all joy in strenuous exertion and endurance in any form. Finely clad, tender housed, life became for her merely the gratification of her own physical and sexual appetites, and the appetites of the male, through the stimulation of which she could maintain herself. And, whether as kept wife, kept mistress, or prostitute, she contributed nothing to the active and sustaining Labours of her society. She had attained to the full development of that type which, whether in modern Paris or New York or London, or in ancient Greece, Assyria, or Rome, is essentially one in its features, its nature, and its results. She was the "fine lady," the human female parasite— the most deadly microbe which can make its appearance on the surface of any social organism.

Wherever in the history of the past this type has reached its full development and has comprised the bulk of the females belonging to any dominant class or race, it has heralded its decay. In Assyria, Greece, Rome, Persia, as in Turkey to-day, the same material conditions have produced the same social disease among wealthy and dominant races; and again and again when the nation so affected has come into contact with nations more healthily constituted, this diseased condition has contributed to its destruction.

In ancient Greece, in its superb and virile youth, its womanhood was richly and even heavily endowed with duties and occupations. Not the mass of the women alone, but the king's wife and the prince's daughter do we find going to the well to bear water, cleansing the household linen in the streams, feeding and doctoring their households, manufacturing the clothing of their race, and performing even a share of the highest social functions as priestesses and prophetesses. It was from the bodies of such women as these that sprang that race of heroes, thinkers, and artists who laid the foundations of Grecian greatness. These females underlay their society as the solid and deeply buried foundations underlay the more visible and ornate portions of a great temple, making its structure and persistence possible. In Greece, after a certain lapse of time, these virile Labouring women in the upper classes were to be found no more. The accumulated wealth of the dominant race, gathered through the Labour of slaves and subject people, had so immensely increased that there was no longer a call for physical Labour on the part of the dominant womanhood; immured within the walls of their houses as wives or mistresses, waited on by slaves and dependents, they no longer sustained by their exertion either their own life or the life of their people. The males absorbed the intellectual Labours of life; slaves and dependents the physical. For a moment, at the end of the fifth and beginning of the fourth century, when the womanhood of Greece had already internally decayed, there was indeed a brilliant intellectual efflorescence among her males, like to the gorgeous colors in the sunset sky when the sun is already sinking; but the heart of Greece was already rotting and her vigor failing. Increasingly, division and dissimilarity arose between male and female, as the male advanced in culture and entered upon new fields of intellectual toil while the female sank passively backward and lower in the scale of life, and thus was made ultimately a chasm which even sexual love could not bridge. The abnormal institution of avowed inter-male sexual relations upon the highest plane was one and the most serious result of this severance. The inevitable and invincible desire of all highly developed human natures, to blend with their sexual relationships their highest intellectual interests and sympathies, could find no satisfaction or response in the relationship between the immured, comparatively ignorant, and helpless females of the upper classes, in Greece, and the brilliant, cultured, and many-sided males who formed its dominant class in the fifth and fourth centuries. Man turned towards man; and parenthood, the divine gift of imparting human life, was severed from the loftiest and profoundest phases of human emotion: Xanthippe fretted out her ignorant and miserable little life between the walls of her house, and Socrates lay in the Agora, discussing philosophy and morals with Alcibiades; and the race decayed at its core. Here and there an Aspasia, or earlier still a Sappho, burst through the confining bonds of woman's environment, and with the force of irresistible genius broke triumphantly into new fields of action and powerful mental activity, standing side by side with the male; but their cases were exceptional. Had they, or such as they, been able to tread down a pathway, along which the mass of Grecian women might have followed them; had it been possible for the bulk of the women of the dominant race in Greece at the end of the fifth century to rise from their condition of supine inaction and ignorance and to have taken their share in the intellectual Labours and stern activities of their race, Greece would never have fallen, as she fell at the end of the fourth century, instantaneously and completely, as a rotten puff-ball falls in at the touch of a healthy finger; first, before the briberies of Philip, and then yet more completely before the arms of his yet more warlike son, who was also the son of the fierce, virile, and indomitable Olympia. Nor could she have been swept clean, a few hundred years later, from Thessaly to Sparta, from Corinth to Ephesus, her temples destroyed, her effete women captured by the hordes of the Goths—a people less skilfully armed and less civilized than the descendants of the race of Pericles and Leonidas, but who were a branch of that great Teutonic folk whose monogamous domestic life was sound at the core, and whose fearless, Labouring, and resolute women yet bore for the men they followed to the ends of the earth, what Spartan women once said they alone bore—men.

In Rome, in the days of her virtue and vigor, the Roman matron Laboured mightily, and bore on her shoulders her full half of the social burden, though her sphere of Labour and influence was ever somewhat smaller than that of the Teutonic sisterhood whose descendants were finally to supplant her own. From the vestal virgin to the matron, the Roman woman in the days of the nation's health and growth fulfilled lofty functions and bore the whole weight of domestic toil. From the days of Lucretia, the great Roman dame whom we find spinning with her handmaidens deep into the night, and whose personal dignity was so dear to her that, violated, she sought only death, to those of the mother of the Gracchi, one of the last of the great line, we find everywhere, erect, Labouring, and resolute, the Roman woman who gave birth to the men who built up Roman greatness. A few centuries later, and Rome also had reached that dangerous spot in the order of social change which Greece had reached centuries before her. Slave Labour and the enjoyment of the unlimited spoils of subject races had done away forever with the demand for physical Labour on the part of the members of the dominant race. Then came the period when the male still occupied himself with the duties of war and government, of legislation and self-culture; but the Roman matron had already ceased forever from her toils. Decked in jewels and fine clothing, brought at the cost of infinite human Labour from the ends of the earth, nourished on delicate victuals prepared by others' hands, she sought now only with amusement to pass away a life that no longer offered her the excitement and joy of active productive exertion. She frequented theaters or baths, or reclined on her sofa, or drove in her chariot; and, like more modern counterparts, painted herself, wore patches, affected an artistic walk, and a handshake with the elbow raised and the fingers hanging down. Her children were reared by dependents; and in the intellectual Labour and government of her age she took small part, and was fit to take none. There were not wanting writers and thinkers who saw clearly the end to which the enervation of the female was tending, and who were not sparing in their denunciations. "Time was," cries one Roman writer of that age, "when the matron turned the spindle with the hand and kept at the same time the pot in her eye that the pottage might not be singed, but now," he adds bitterly, "when the wife, loaded with jewels, reposes among pillows, or seeks the dissipation of baths and theaters, all things go downward and the state decays." Yet neither he nor that large body of writers and thinkers who saw the condition towards which the parasitism of woman was tending to reduce society, preached any adequate remedy.

Thoughtful men sighed over the present and yearned for the past, nor seem to have perceived that it was irrevocably gone; that the Roman lady who, with a hundred servants standing idle about her, should, in imitation of her ancestress, have gone out with her pitcher on her head to draw water from the well, while in all her own court-yards pipe-led streams gushed forth, would have acted the part of the pretender; that had she insisted on resuscitating her loom and had she sat up all night to spin, she could never have produced those fabrics which alone her household demanded, and would have been but a puerile actor; that it was not by attempting to return to the ancient and forever closed fields of toil, but by entering upon new, that she could alone serve her race and retain her own dignity and virility. That not by bearing water and weaving linen, but by so training and disciplining herself that she should be fitted to bear her share in the Labour necessary to the just and wise guidance of a great empire, and be capable of training a race of man adequate to expense an enlightened, merciful, and beneficent rule, over the vast masses of subject people—that so, and so only, could she fulfil her duty toward the new society about her, and bear its burden together with man, as her ancestresses of bygone generations had borne the burden of theirs.

That in this direction, and this alone, lay the only possible remedy for the evils of woman's condition, was a conception apparently grasped by none; and the female sank lower and lower, till the image of the parasitic woman of Rome (with a rag of the old Roman intensity left even in her degradation!)— seeking madly by pursuit of pleasure and sensuality to fill the void left by the lack of honorable activity; accepting lust in the place of love, ease in the place of exertion, and an unlimited consumption in the place of production; too enervated at last to care even to produce offspring, and shrinking from every form of endurance—remains, even to the present day, the most perfect, and therefore the most appalling picture of the parasite female that earth has produced—a picture only less terrible than it is pathetic.

We recognize that it was inevitable that this womanhood—born it would seem from its elevation to guide and enlighten a world, and in place thereof feeding on it—should at last have given birth to a manhood as effete as itself and that both should in the end have been swept away before the march of those Teutonic folk, whose women were virile and could give birth to men; a folk among whom the woman received on the morning of her marriage, from the man who was to be her companion through life, no contemptible trinket to hang about her throat or limbs, but a shield, a spear, a sword, and a yoke of oxen, while she bestowed on him in return a suit of armor, in token that they two were henceforth to be one in toil and in the facing of danger; that she too should dare with him in war and suffer with him in peace. Of this folk another writer tells us that their women not only bore the race and fed it at their breasts without the help of others' hands, but that they undertook the whole management of house and lands, leaving the males free for war and chase; of them Suetonius tells us that when Augustus Caesar demanded hostages from a tribe, he took women, not men, because he found by experience that the women were more regarded than men; and of them Strabo says that so highly did the Germanic races value the intellect of their women that they regarded them as inspired, and entered into no war or great undertaking without their advice and counsel. Among the Cimbrian women who accompanied their husbands in the invasion of Italy were certain who marched barefooted in the midst of the lines, distinguished by their white hair and milk-white robes, and who were regarded as inspired, and of whom Floras, describing an early Roman victory, says, "The conflict was not less fierce and obstinate with the wives of the vanquished; in their carts and wagons they formed a line of battle, and from their elevated situation, as from so many turrets, annoyed the Romans with their poles and lances. Their death was as glorious as their martial spirit. Finding that all was lost, they strangled their children, and either destroyed themselves in one scene of mutual slaughter, or with the sashes that bound up their hair suspended themselves by the neck to the boughs of trees or the tops of their wagons." It is of these women that Valerius Maximus says that, "If the gods on the day of battle had inspired the men with equal fortitude, Marius would never have boasted of his Teutonic victory"; and of whom Tacitus, speaking of those women who accompanied their husbands to war, remarks, "These are the darling witnesses of his conduct, the applauders of his valor, at once beloved and valued. The wounded seek their mothers and their wives; undismayed at the sight, the women count each honorable scar and suck the gushing blood. They are even hardy enough to mix with the combatants, administering refreshment and exhorting them to deeds of valor," and adds moreover that, "To be contented with one wife was peculiar to the Germans; while the woman was contented with one husband; as with one life, one mind, one body."

It was inevitable that, before the sons of women such as these, the sons of the parasitic Roman should be swept from existence, as the offspring of the caged canary would fall in conflict with the offspring of the free.

Again and again with wearisome reiteration, the same story repeats itself. Among the Jews in the days of their health and growth, we find their women bearing the major weight of agricultural and domestic toil, full always of Labour and care—from Rachel, whom Jacob met and loved as she watered her father's flocks, to Ruth, the ancestress of a line of kings and heroes whom her Boas noted Labouring in the harvest-fields; from Sarah, kneading and baking cakes for Abraham's prophetic visitors, to Miriam, prophetess and singer, and Deborah, who judged Israel from beneath her palm-tree, "and the land had rest for forty years." Everywhere the ancient Jewish woman appears an active sustaining power among her people; and perhaps the noblest picture of the Labouring woman to be found in any literature is contained in the Jewish writings, indicted possibly at the very time when the Labouring woman was for the first time tending among a section of the Jews to become a thing of the past; when already Solomon, with his seven hundred parasitic wives and three hundred parasitic concubines, loomed large on the horizon of the national life, to take the place of flock-tending Rachel and gleaning Ruth, and to produce amid their palaces of cedar and gold, among them all, no Joseph or David, but in the way of descendant only a Rehoboam, under whose hand the kingdom was to totter to its fall.

In the East to-day the same story has wearisomely written itself: in China, where the present vitality and power of the most ancient of existing civilizations may be measured accurately by the length of its women's shoes; in Turkish harems, where one of the noblest dominant Aryan races the world has yet produced is being slowly suffocated in the arms of a parasite womanhood, and might, indeed, long ago have been obliterated, had not a certain virility and strength been continually re-infused into it through the persons of purchased wives, who in early childhood and youth had been themselves active Labouring peasants. Everywhere, in the past as in the present, the parasitism of the female heralds the decay of a nation or class, and as invariably indicates disease as the pustules of smallpox upon the skin indicate the existence of a purulent virus in the system.

We are, indeed, far from asserting that the civilizations of the past which have decayed, have decayed alone through the parasitism of their females. Vast, far-reaching social phenomena have invariably causes and reactions immeasurably too complex to be summed up under one so simple a term. Behind the phenomenon of female parasitism has always lain another and yet larger social phenomenon; it has invariably been preceded, as we have seen, by the subjugation of large bodies of other human creatures, either as slaves, subject races, or classes; and as the result of the excessive Labours of those classes there has always been an accumulation of unearned wealth in the hands of the dominant class or race. *It has invariably been by feeding on this wealth, the result of forced or ill-paid la- bar,* that the female of the dominant race or class has in the past lost her activity and has come to exist purely through the passive performance of her sexual functions. Without slaves or subject classes to perform the crude physical Labours of life and produce superfluous wealth, the parasitism of the female would, in the past, have been an impossibility.

There is, therefore, a profound truth in that universal saw which states that the decay of the great nations and civilizations of the past has resulted from the enervation caused by excessive wealth and luxury; and there is a further, and if possible more profound, truth underlying the statement that their destruction has ultimately been the result of the enervation of the entire race, male and female.

But when we come further to inquire how, exactly, this process of decay took place, we shall find that the part which the parasitism of the female has played has been fundamental.

The mere use of any of the material products of Labour, which we term wealth, can never in itself produce that decay, physical or mental, which precedes the downfall of great civilized nations. The eating of salmon at ten shillings a pound can in itself no more debilitate and corrupt the moral, intellectual, and physical constitution of the man consuming it, than it could enervate his naked forefathers who speared it in their rivers for food; the fact that an individual wears a robe made from the filaments of a worm can no more deteriorate his spiritual or physical fiber than were it made of sheep's wool; an entire race, housed in marble palaces, faring delicately, and clad in silks, and surrounded by the noblest products of literature and plastic art, so those palaces, viands, garments, and products of art were the result of their own Labours, could never be enervated by them. The debilitating effect of wealth sets in at that point exactly (and never before) at which the supply of material necessaries and comforts, and of esthetic enjoyments, clogs the individuality, causing it to rest satisfied in the mere passive possession of the results of the *Labour of others,* without feeling any necessity or desire for further productive activity of its own.

The exact material condition at which this point will be reached will vary, not only with the race and the age, but with the individual. A Marcus Aurelius in a palace of gold and marble was able to retain his simplicity and virility as completely as though he had lived in a cow-herd's hut; while, on the other hand, it is quite possible for the wife of a savage chief, who has but four slaves to bring her corn and milk and spread her skins in the sun, to become almost as purely parasitic as the most delicately pampered female of fashion in ancient Rome, or modern Paris, London, or New York; while the exact amount of unearned material wealth which will emasculate individuals in the same society will vary exactly as their intellectual and moral fiber and natural activity are strong or weak.

The debilitating effect of unLaboured-for wealth lies, then, not in the nature of any material adjunct to life in itself, but in the power it may possess of robbing the individual of all incentive to exertion, thus destroying the intellectual, the physical, and finally, the moral fiber.

In all civilizations of the past examination will show that almost invariably it has been the female who has tended first to reach this point, and we think examination will show that it has almost invariably been from the woman to the man that enervation and decay have spread.

Why this should be so is obvious. Firstly, it is in the sphere of domestic Labour that slave or hired Labour most easily and insidiously penetrates. The force of blows or hireling gold can far more easily supply Labourers as the preparers of food and clothing, and even as the bearers of children, than it can supply Labourers fitted to be entrusted with the toils of war and government, which have in the past been the especial sphere of male toil. The Roman woman had for generations been supplanted in the sphere of her domestic Labours and in the toil of rearing and educating her offspring, and had long become abjectly parasitic, before the Roman male had been able to substitute the Labour of the hireling and barbarian for his own, in the army, and in the drudgeries of governmental toil.

Secondly, the female having one all-important though passive function which cannot be taken from her, and which is peculiarly connected with her own person, in the act of child-bearing, and her mere sexual attributes being an object of desire and cupidity to the male, she is liable in a peculiarly insidious and gradual manner to become dependent on this one sexual function alone for her support. So much is this the case, that even when she does not in any way perform this function there is a curious tendency for the kudos of the function still to hang about her, and *for her mere potentiality* in the direction of a duty which she may never fulfil to be confused in her own estimation and that of society with the actual fulfilment of that function. Under the mighty egis of the woman who bears and rears offspring and in other directions Labours actively for her race, creeps in gradually and unnoticed the woman who does none of these things. From the mighty Labouring woman who bears human creatures to the full extent of her power, rears her offspring unaided, and performs at the same time severe social Labour in other directions (and who is undoubtedly, wherever found, the most productive toiler known to the race); it is but one step, though a long one, from this woman, to the woman who produces offspring freely but does not herself rear them, and performs no compensatory social Labour. From this woman, again, to the one who bears few or no children, and per- forms no productive social Labour, but who, whether as a wife or mistress, lives by the exercise of her sex function alone, the step is short. There is but one step farther to the prostitute, who affects ho form of productive Labour, and who, in place of life, is recognized as producing disease and death but who exists parasitically through her sexual attribute. Enormous as is the distance between the women at the two extremes of this series, and sharply opposed as their relation to the world is, there is yet, in actual life, no sharp, clear, sudden-drawn line dividing the women of the one type from those of the other. They shade off into each other by delicate and insensible degrees. And it is down this inclined plane that the women of civilized races are peculiarly tempted, unconsciously, to slip from the noble height of a condition of the most strenuous social activity, into a condition of complete, helpless, and inactive parasitism, without being clearly aware of the fact themselves, and without society's becoming so—the woman who has ceased to rear her own offspring, or who has ceased to bear offspring at all, and who performs no other productive social function, yet shields the fact from her own eyes by dwelling on the fact that she is a woman, in whom the capacity is at least latent.

These peculiarities in her condition have in all civilized societies laid the female more early and seriously open to the attacks of parasitism than the male. And while the accumulation of wealth has always been the antecedent condition, and the degeneracy and effeteness of the male the final and obvious cause of the decay of the great dominant races of the past; yet, between these two has always lain, as a great middle term, the parasitism of the female, without which the first would have been inoperative and the last impossible.

Not slavery, nor the most vast accumulations of wealth, could destroy a nation by enervation, whose women remained active, virile, and Labourious.

The conception which again and again appears to have haunted successive societies, that it was a possibility for the human male to advance in physical power and intellectual vigor, while his companion female became stationary and inactive, taking no share in the Labours of society beyond the passive fulfilment of sexual functions, has always been negated. It has ended as would end the experiment of a man seeking to raise a breed of winning racehorses out of unexercised, short-winded, knock-kneed mares. No, more disastrously! For while the female animal transmits herself to her descendant only or mainly by means of germinal inheritance, and through the influence she may exert over it during gestation, the human female, by producing the intellectual and moral atmosphere in which the early infant years of life are passed, impresses herself far more indelibly on her descendants. Only an able and Labouring womanhood can permanently produce an able and Labouring manhood; only an effete and inactive male can ultimately be produced by an effete and inactive womanhood. The curled darling, scented and languid, with his drawl, his delicate apparel, his devotion to the rarity and variety of his viands, whose severest Labour is the search after pleasure, and for whom even the chase, which was for his remote ancestor an invigorating and manly toil essential for the meat and life of his people, becomes a luxurious and farcical amusement;—this male, whether found in the later Roman Empire, the Turkish harem of to-day, or in our Northern civilizations, is possible only because generations of parasitic women have preceded him. More repulsive than the parasite female herself, because a yet further product of decay, it is yet only the scent of his mother's boudoir that we smell in his hair. He is like to the bald patches and rotten wool on the back of a scabby sheep; which indeed indicate that, deep beneath the surface, a parasite insect is eating its way into the flesh, but which are not so much the cause of disease as its final manifestation.

As we have said, it is the power of the human female to impress herself on her descendants, male and female, through germinal inheritance, through influence during the period of gestation, and above all by producing the mental atmosphere in which the impressionable infant years of life are passed, which makes the condition of the child-bearing female one of paramount interest to the race. It is this fact which causes even prostitution (in many respects the most repulsive form of female parasitism which afflicts humanity) to be, probably, not more adverse to the advance and even to the conservation of a healthy and powerful society than the parasitism of its child-bearing woman. For the prostitute, heavily as she weights society for her support, returning disease and mental and emotional disintegration for what she consumes, does not yet so immediately affect the next generation as the kept wife, or kept mistress, who impresses her effete image indelibly on the generations succeeding.

●●

10

Female Parasitism

We have seen that, in the past, no such thing as the parasitism of the entire body or large majority of the females inhabiting any territory was possible. Beneath that body oft women of the dominant class or race, who did not Labour either mentally or physically, there has always been of necessity a far more vast body of females who not only performed the crude physical toil essential to the existence oft society before the introduction of mechanical? methods of production, but who were compelled to Labour the more intensely because there was a parasite class above them to be maintained by their physical toil. The more the female parasite flourished of old, in one class or race, the more certainly all women of other classes or races were compelled to Labour only too excessively; and ultimately these females and their descendants were apt to supplant the more enervated class or race. In the absence of machinery and of a vast employment of the motor forces of nature, parasitism could only threaten a comparatively small section of any community, and a minute section of the human race as a whole. Female parasitism in the past resembled gout—a disease dangerous only to the over-fed, pampered, and few, never to the population of any society as a whole.

At the present day, so enormous has been the advance made in the substitution of mechanical force for crude, physical, human exertion (mechanical force being employed today even in the shaping of feeding-bottles and the creation of artificial foods as substitutes for mother's milk!) that it is now possible not only for a small and wealthy section of women in each civilized community to be maintained without performing any of the ancient, crude, physical Labours of their sex, and without depending on the slavery of, or any vast increase in the Labour of, other classes of females; but this condition has already been reached, or is tending to be reached, by that large mass of women in civilized societies who form the intermediate class between poor and rich. During the next fifty years, so rapid will undoubtedly be the spread of the material conditions of civilization, both in the societies at present civilized and in the societies at present unpermeated by our material civilization, that the ancient forms of female, domestic, physical Labour of even the women of the poorest classes will be little required, their place being taken, not by other females, but by always increasingly perfected Labour-saving machinery.

Thus, female parasitism, which in the past threatened only a minute section of earth's women, under existing conditions threatens vast masses, and may, under future conditions, threaten the entire body.

If woman is content to leave to the male all Labour in the new and all-important fields which are rapidly opening before the human race; if, as the old forms of domestic Labour slip from her for ever and inevitably, she does not grasp the new, it is inevitable, that, ultimately, not merely a class, but the whole bodies of females in civilized societies, must sink into a state of more or less absolute dependence on their sexual functions alone.

As new forms of natural force are mastered and mechanical appliances perfected, it will be quite possible for the male half of all civilized races (and therefore ultimately of all) to absorb the entire fields of intellectual and highly trained manual Labour; and it would be entirely possible for the female half of the race, whether as prostitutes, as kept mistresses, or as kept wives, to cease *from* all forms of active toil, and, as the passive tools of sexual 'reproduction, or, more decadently still, as the mere instruments of sexual indulgence, to sink into a condition of complete and helpless sex-parasitism.

Sex-parasitism, therefore, presents itself at the end of the nineteenth century and beginning of the twentieth in a guise which it has never before worn. We, the women of the civilization of the nineteenth and twentieth centuries, stand therefore in a position the gravity and importance of which was not equaled by that of any of our forerunners in the ancient civilization. As we master and rise above, or fall and are conquered by, the difficulties of our position, so also will be the future, not merely of our own class, or even of our own race alone, but also of those vast masses who are following on in the wake of our civilization. The decision we are called on to make is a decision for the race; behind us comes on the tread of incalculable millions of feet.

There is thus no truth in the assertion so often made, even by thoughtful persons, that the male Labour question and the woman's question of our day are completely one, and that, would the women of the European race of to-day but wait peacefully till the males alone had solved their problem, they would find that their own had been solved at the same time.

Were the entire male Labour problem of this age satisfactorily settled to-morrow; were all the unemployed or uselessly employed males at both ends of societies, whom the changes of modern civilization have robbed of their ancient forms of Labour, so educated and trained that they were perfectly fitted for the new conditions of life; and were the material benefit and intellectual possibilities, which the substitution of mechanical for human Labour now makes possible to humanity, no longer absorbed by the few but dispersed among the whole mass of males in return for their trained Labour, yet the woman's problem might be further from satisfactory solution than it is to-day; and, if it were affected at all, might be affected for the worse. It is wholly untrue that fifty pounds, or two thousand, earned by the male as the result of his physical or mental toil, if part of it be spent by him in supporting non-Labouring females, whether as prostitutes, wives, or mistresses, is the same thing to the female or to the race as though that sum had been earned by her own exertion, either directly as wages or indirectly by toiling for the man whose wages supported her. For the moment, truly, the woman so tended lies softer and warmer than had she been compelled to exert herself; ultimately, intellectually, morally, and even physically, the difference in the effect upon her as an individual and on the race is the difference between advance and degradation between life and death. The increased wealth of the male no more of necessity benefits and raises the female upon whom he expends it than the increased wealth of his mistress necessarily benefits mentally or physically a poodle because she can give him a down cushion in place of one of feathers, and chicken in place of beef. The wealthier the males of a society become, the greater the temptation, both to themselves and to the females connected with them, to drift toward female parasitism.

The readjustment of the position of the male worker, if it led to a more equitable distribution of wealth among males, might indeed diminish slightly the accompanying tendency to parasitism in the very wealthiest female class; but it would, on the other hand, open up exactly those conditions which make parasitism possible to millions of women to-day leading healthy and active lives.

That the two problems are not identical is shown, if indeed evidence were needed, by the fact that those males most actively employed in attempting to readjust the relations of the mass of Labouring males to the new conditions of life, are sometimes precisely those males who are most bitterly opposed to woman in her attempt to readjust her own position. Not by the members of those professions generally regarded as the strongholds of obstructionism and prejudice has a more short-sighted opposition often been made to the attempts of woman to enter new fields of Labour, than have again and again been made by male handworkers, whether as isolated individuals or in their corporate capacity as trade unions. They have, at least in some certain instances, endeavored to exclude women, not merely from new fields of intellectual and social Labour, but even from those ancient fields of textile manufacture and handicraft, which have through all generations of the past been woman's. The patent and undeniable fact that where the male Labour movement flourishes the woman's movement also flourishes rises not from the fact that they are identical, but that the same healthy and virile condition in a race or society gives rise to both.

As two streams rising from one fountain-head and running a parallel course through long reaches may yet remain wholly distinct, one finding its way satisfactorily to the sea, while the other loses itself in sand or becomes a stagnant marsh, so our modern male and female movements, taking their rise from the same material conditions in modern civilization, and presenting endless and close analogies with one another in their cause of development yet remain fundamentally "distinct. "By both movements the future of the race must be profoundly modified for good or evil; both touch the race in a manner absolutely vital; but both will have to be fought out on their own ground, and independently, and it will be only by determined, conscious, and persistent action on the part of woman that the solution of her own Labour problems will proceed. co-extensively with that of the other.—

How distinct, though similar, is the underlying motive of the two movements, is manifested most clearly by this fact, that, while the male Labour movement takes its rise mainly among the poor and hand-Labouring classes, where the material pressure of the modern conditions of life fall heaviest, and where the danger of physical suffering and even extinction under that pressure is most felt; the woman's Labour movement has taken its rise almost as exclusively among the wealthy, cultured, and brain-Labouring classes, where alone at the present day the danger of enervation through non-employment, and of degeneration through dependence on the sex function exists.

The female Labour movement is, in its ultimate essence, an endeavor on the part of a section of the race to save itself from inactivity and degeneration, and this even at the immediate cost of most heavy loss in material comfort and ease to the individuals composing it. The male Labour movement is, directly and in the first place, material: *ana'*, at least superficially, more or less self-seeking, though its ultimate reaction on society by saving the poorer members from degradation and dependency and want is undoubtedly wholly social and absolutely essential for the health and continued development of the human race. In the woman's Labour movement of our day, which has essentially taken its rise among women of the more cultured and wealthy classes, and which consists mainly in a demand to have the doors leading to professional, political, and highly skilled Labour thrown open to them, the ultimate end can only be attained at the cost of more or less intense, immediate, personal suffering and renunciation, though eventually, if brought to a satisfactory conclusion, it will undoubtedly tend to the material and physical well-being of woman herself, as well as to that of her male companions and descendants.

The coming half-century will be a time of peculiar strain, as mankind seeks rapidly to adjust moral ideals and social relationships and the general ordering of life to the new and continually unfolding material conditions. If these two great movements of our age, having this as their object, can be brought into close harmony and co-operation, the readjustment will be the sooner and more painlessly accomplished; but, for the moment, the two movements alike in their origin and alike in many of their methods of procedure, remain distinct.

It is this fact, the Consciousness on the part of the women taking their share in the woman's movement of our age. that their efforts are not and cannot be, of immediate advantage to themselves, but that they almost of necessity and immediately lead to loss and renunciation, which gives to this movement its very peculiar tone; setting it apart from the large mass of economic movements, placing it rather in a line with those vast religious developments which at the interval of ages have swept across humanity, irresistibly modifying and reorganizing it.

It is the perception of this fact, that, not for herself, nor even for fellow women alone, but for the benefit of humanity at large, she must seek to readjust herself to life, which fiends to the woman's most superficial and seemingly trivial attempt at readjustment a certain dignity and importance.

It is this profound hidden conviction which removes from the sphere of the ridiculous the attitude of even the feeblest woman who waves her poor little "woman's rights" flag on the edge of a platform, and which causes us to forgive even the passionate denunciations, not always wisely thought out, in which she would represent the evils of woman's condition as wrongs intentionally inflicted upon her, where they are merely the inevitable results of ages of social movement.

It is this over-shadowing consciousness of a large impersonal obligation which removes from the sphere of the wholly contemptible and insignificant even the action of the individual young girl, who leaves a home of comfort or luxury for a city garret, where in solitude, and under that stern pressure which is felt by all individuals in arms against the trend of their environment, she seeks to acquire the knowledge necessary for entering on a new form of Labour. It is this profound consciousness which makes not less than heroic the figure of the little half-starved student, battling against gigantic odds to take her place beside man in the fields of modern intellectual toil, and which, whether she succeed or fail, makes her a landmark in the course of our human evolution. It is this consciousness of large impersonal ends to be attained, and to the attainment of which each individual is bound to play her part, however small, which removes from the domain of the unnecessary, and raises to importance, the action of each woman who resists the tyranny of fashions in dress or bearing, or custom which impedes her in her strife towards the new adjustment.

It is this consciousness which renders almost of solemn import the efforts of the individual female after physical or mental self-culture and expansion; this which fills with a lofty enthusiasm the heart of the young girl, who, it may be, in some solitary farmhouse, in some distant wild of Africa or America, deep into the night bends over her books with the passion and fervor with which an early Christian may have bent over the pages of his Scriptures; feeling that, it may; be, she fits herself by each increase of knowledge for she knows not what duties towards the world, in the years to come.

It is this consciousness of great impersonal ends, to be brought, even if slowly and imperceptibly, a little nearer by her action, which gives to many a woman strength for renunciation, when she puts from her the lower type of sexual relationship, even if bound up with all the external honor a legal marriage can confer, if it offers her only enervation and parasitism. This consciousness enables her often to accept poverty, toil, and sexual isolation (an isolation more terrible to her than to any male), and renunciation of motherhood, that crowning beatitude of the woman's existence, which, and which alone, fully compensates her for the organic sufferings of womanhood in the conviction that, by so doing, she makes more possible a fuller and higher attainment of motherhood and wifehood to the women who will follow her.

It is this consciousness which makes of solemn importance the knock of the humblest woman at the closed door which shuts off a new field of Labour, physical or mental: she is convinced that, not for herself, hut in the service of the whole race, she knocks.

It is this abiding consciousness of an end to be attained, reaching beyond her personal life and individual interests, which constitutes the religious element of the woman's movement of our day, and binds with the common bond of an impersonal enthusiasm into one solid body the women of whatsoever race, class, and nation who are struggling after the readjustment of woman to life.

This it is also, which in spite of defects and failures on the part of individuals, yet makes the body which these women compose, as a whole, one of the most impressive and irresistible of modern forces. The private soldier of the great victorious army is not always an imposing object as he walks down the village street, cap on side of head and sword dangling between his legs, nor is he always impressive even when he burnishes up his accoutrements or cleans his pannikins; but it is of individuals such as these that the great army is made, which to-morrow, when it is gathered together, may shake the world with its tread.

Possibly not one woman in ten, or even one woman in twenty thousand among those taking part in this struggle, could draw up a clear and succinct account of the causes which have led to the disco-ordination in woman's present position, or give a full account of the benefits to flow from readjustment; as probably not one private soldier in an army of ten or even of twenty thousand, though he is willing to give his life for his land, would yet be able to draw up a clear and succinct account of his land's history in the past and of the conditions which have made war inevitable; and almost as little can he often paint an exact and detailed picture of the benefits to flow from his efforts. He knows his land has need of him; he knows his own small place and work.

It is possible that not one woman in ten thousand has grasped with scientific exactitude, and still less could express with verbal sharpness, the great central conditions which yet compel and animate her into action.

Even the great, central fact, that with each generation the entire race passes through the body of its womanhood as through a mold, reappearing with the indelible marks of that mold upon it, that as the *os cervix* of woman, through which the head of the human infant passes at birth, forms a ring, determining for ever the size at birth of the human head, a size which could only increase if in the course of ages the *os cervix* of woman should itself slowly expand; and that so exactly the intellectual capacity, the physical vigor, the emotional depth of woman, forms also an un-transcendable circle, circumscribing with each successive generation the limits of the expansion of the human race;—even this fact she may not so clearly have grasped intellectually as to be able to throw it into the form of a logical statement. The profound truth, that the continued development of the human race on earth (a development which, as the old myths and dreams of a narrow personal heaven fade from our view, becomes increasingly for many of us the spiritual hope by light of which we continue to live), a development which we hope shall make the humanity of a distant future as much higher in intellectual power and wider in social sympathy than the highest human units of our day, as that is higher than the first primeval ancestor who with quivering limb strove to walk upright and shape his lips to the expression of a word, is possible only if the male and female halves of humanity progress together, expanding side by side in the future as they have done in the past, even this truth it is possible few women have exactly and logically grasped as the basis of their action. The truth that, as the first primitive human males and females, unable to count farther than their fingers, or grasp an abstract idea, or feel the controlling power of social emotion, could only develop into the Sapphos, Aristotles, and Shelleys of a more expanded civilization, if side by side, and line by line, male and female forms have expanded together, if, as the convolutions of his brain increased in complexity, so increased the convolutions in hers; if, as her forehead grew higher, so developed his; and that, if the long upward march of the future is ever to be accomplished by the race, male and female must march side by side, acting and reacting on each other through inheritance; or progress is impossible. The truth that, as the existence of even the male Bushman would be impossible without the existence of the analogous Bush-woman, with the same gifts, and that races which can produce among their males a William Kingdon Clifford, a Tolstoy, or a Robert Browning, would be inconceivable and impossible, unless among its females it could also produce a Sophia Kovalevsky, a George Eliot, or a Louise Michel, so, in the future, that higher and more socialized human race we dream of can only come into existence, because both the sex forms have evolved together, now this sex and then that, so to speak, catching up the ball of life and throwing it back to the other, slightly if imperceptibly enlarging and beautifying it as it passes! through their hands. The fact that without the reaction of interevolution between the sexes, there can be no real and permanent human advance; without the enlarged deep-thinking Eve to bear him, no enlarged Adam; without the enlarged widely sympathizing Adam to beget her, no enlarged widely comprehending Eve; without an enlarged Adam and an enlarged Eve, no enlarged generation of mankind on earth; an arrest in one form is an arrest in both, and in the upward march of the whole human family. The truth that, if at the present day, woman, after her long upward march side by side with man, developing with him through the ages by means of endless exercise of the faculties of mind and body, has now, at last, reached her ultimate limit of growth, and can progress no farther; that, then, here also, to-day, the growth of the human spirit is to be stayed; that here, on the spot of woman's arrest, is the standard of the race to be finally planted, to move forward no more, forever:—that, if the parasite woman on her couch, loaded with gewgaws, the plaything and amusement of man, be the permanent and final manifestation of female human life on the globe, then that couch is also the deathbed of human evolution. These profound underlying truths, perhaps, not one woman in twenty thousand of those actively engaged in the struggle for readjustment has so closely and keenly grasped that she can readily throw them into the form of exact language; and yet, probably, not the feeblest woman taking share in our endeavor toward readjustment and expansion fails to be animated by a vague but profound consciousness of their existence. Beyond the small evils, which she seeks by her immediate, personal action to remedy, lie, she feels, large ills of which they form but an off-shoot; beyond the small good which she seeks to effect, lies, she believes, a great and universal beatitude to be attained; beyond the little struggle of to-day, lies the larger struggle of the centuries, in which neither she alone nor her sex alone are concerned, but all mankind.

That such should be the mental attitude of the average woman taking part in the readjustive sexual movement of to-day, that so often on the public platform and in literature she adduces merely secondary arguments, and is wholly unable logically to give an account of the great propelling conditions behind it, is sometimes taken as an indication of the inefficiency, and probably the ultimate failure, of the movement in which she takes part. But in truth, that is not so. It is rather an indication which shows how healthy, and deeply implanted in the substance of human life, are the roots of this movement; and it places it in a line with all those vast controlling movements which have in the course of the ages reorganized human life.

For those great movements which have permanently modified the condition of humanity have never taken their rise amid the chopped logic of schools; they have never drawn their vitality from a series of purely intellectual and abstract inductions. They have arisen always through the action of widely spread material and spiritual conditions, creating widespread human needs; which, pressing upon the isolated individuals, awakens at last continuous, if often vague and uncertain, social movement in a given direction. Mere intellectual comprehension may guide, retard, or accelerate the great human movements; it has never created them. It may even be questioned whether those very leaders, who have superficially appeared to create and organize great and successful social movements, have themselves, in most cases, if in any, fully understood in all their complexity the movements they themselves have appeared to rule. They have been, rather, themselves permeated by the great common need; and being possessed of more will, passion, intensity, or intellect, they have been able to give voice to that which in others was dumb, and conscious direction to that which in others was unconscious desire; they have been but the foremost crest of a great wave of human necessity: they have not created the wave which bears themselves, and humanity, onwards. The artificial social movements which have had their origin in the arbitrary will of individuals, guided with however much determination and reason, have of necessity proved ephemeral and abortive. An Alexander might will to weld a Greece and an Asia into one; a Napoleon might resolve to create of a diversified Europe one consolidated state; and by dint of skill and determination they might for a moment appear to be accomplishing that which they desired; but the constraining individual will being withdrawn, the object of their toils has melted away, as the little heap of damp sand gathered under the palm of a child's hand on the sea-shore melts away, scattered by the wind and washed out by the waves, the moment the hand that shaped it is withdrawn; while the small, soft, indefinite, watery fragment of jelly-fish lying beside it, though tossed hither and thither by water and wind, yet retains its shape and grows, because its particles are bound by an internal and organic force.

Our woman's movement resembles strongly, in this matter, the gigantic religious and intellectual movement which for centuries convulsed the life of Europe; and had, as its ultimate outcome, the final emancipation of the human intellect and the freedom of the human spirit. Looked back upon from the vantage-point of the present, it presents the appearance of one vast, steady, persistent movement, proceeding always in one ultimate direction, as though guided by some controlling human intellect. But, to the mass of human individuals taking part in it, it presented an appearance far otherwise. It was fought out, now here, now there, by isolated individuals and small groups, and often for what appeared small and almost personal ends, having sometimes, superficially, little in common. Now it was a Giordano Bruno, burnt in Rome in defense of abstract theory with regard to the nature of the First Cause; then an Albigense hurled from his rocks because he refused to part with the leaves of his old Bible; now a Dutch peasant woman, walking serenely to the stake because she refused to bow her head before two crossed rods; then a Servetus burnt by Protestant Calvin at Geneva; or a Spinoza cut off from his tribe and people because he could see nothing but God anywhere; and then it was an exiled Rousseau or Voltaire, or a persecuted Brad-laugh; till, in our own day, the last sounds of the long fight are dying about us, as fading echoes, in the guise of a few puerile attempts to enforce trivial disabilities on the ground of abstract convictions. The vanguard of humanity has won its battle for freedom of thought.

But to the men and women taking part in that mighty movement during the long centuries of the past, probably nothing was quite clear, in the majority of cases, but their own immediate move. Not the leaders—most certainly not good old Martin Luther, even when he gave utterance to his immortal "I can no otherwise" (the eternal justification of all reformers and social innovators!), understood the whole breadth of the battlefield on which they were engaged, or grasped with precision the issues which were involved. The valiant Englishman, who, as the flames shot up about him, cried to his companion in death, "Play the man, Master Ridley; we shall by God's grace this day light such a candle in England, as shall never be put out!" undoubtedly believed that the candle lighted was the mere tallow rushlight of a small sectarian freedom for England alone; nor perceived that what he lighted was but one ray of the vast, universal aurora of intellectual and spiritual liberty, whose light was ultimately to stream, not only across England, but across the earth. Nevertheless, undoubtedly, behind all these limited efforts, for what appeared, superficially, limited causes, lay, in the hearts of the men and women concerned, through the ages, a profound if *vague* consciousness of ends larger than they clearly knew, to be subserved by their action; of a universal social duty and a great necessity.

That the woman's movement of our day has not taken its origin from any mere process of theoretic argument; that it breaks out, now here and now there, in forms divergent and at times superficially almost irreconcilable; that the majority of those taking part in it are driven into action as the result of the immediate pressure of the conditions of life, and are not always able logically to state the nature of all causes which propel them, or to paint clearly all results of their action; so far from removing it from the category of the vast reorganizing movements of humanity, places it in a line with them, showing how vital, spontaneous, and wholly organic and unartificial is its nature.

The fact that, at one point, it manifests itself in a passionate, and at times almost incoherent, cry for an accredited share in public and social duties, while at another it makes itself felt as a determined endeavor after self-culture; that in one land it embodies itself mainly in a resolute endeavor to enlarge the sphere of remunerative Labour for women, while in another it manifests itself chiefly as an effort to recoordinate the personal relation of the sexes; that in one individual it manifests itself as a passionate and sometimes noisy struggle for liberty of personal action, while in another it is being fought out silently in the depths of the individual consciousness—that primal battleground, in which all questions of reform and human advance must ultimately be fought and decided; all this diversity, and the fact that the average woman is entirely concerned in Labour in her own little field, shows, not the weakness, but the strength of the movement, which, taken as a whole, is a movement steady and persistent in one direction, the direction of increased activity and culture, and towards the negation of all possibility of parasitism in the human female. Slowly, and unconsciously, as the child is shaped in the womb, this movement shapes itself in the bosom of our time, taking its place beside those vast human developments, of which men, noticing their spontaneity and the co-ordination of their parts, have said, in the phraseology of old days, "This thing is not of man, but of God."

He who to-day looks at some great Gothic cathedral in its final form, seems to be looking at that which might have been the incarnation of the dream of some single soul of genius. But in truth, its origin was far otherwise. Ages elapsed from the time the first rough stone was laid as a foundation till the last spire and pinnacle were shaped, and the hand which laid the foundation-stone was never the same as that which set the last stone upon the coping. Generations often succeeded one another, Labouring at gargoyle, rose-window, and shaft, and died, leaving the work to others; the master-builder who drew up the first rough outline passed away, and was succeeded by others, and the details of the work as completed bore sometimes but faint resemblance to the work as he devised it; no man fully understood all that others had done or were doing, but each Laboured in his place; and the work as completed had unity; it expressed not the desire and necessity of one mind, but of the human spirit of that age; and not less essential to the existence of the building was the Labour of the workman who passed a life of devotion in carving gargoyles or shaping rose-windows, than that of the greatest master who drew general outlines: perhaps it was yet more heroic; because, for the master-builder, who, even if but vaguely, has an image of what the work would be when the last stone was laid and the last spire raised, it was easy to Labour with devotion and zeal, though well he might know that the placing of that last stone and the raising of that last spire would not be his, and that the building in its full beauty and strength he should never see; but for the journeyman Labourer who carried on his duties and month by month toiled at carving his own little gargoyle or shaping the traceries in his own little oriel window, without any complete vision, it was not so easy; nevertheless, it was through the conscientious Labours of such alone, through their heaps of chipped and spoiled stones, which may have lain thick about them, that at the last the pile was reared in its strength and beauty.

For a Moses who could climb Pisgah, and, though it were through a mist of bitter tears, could see stretching before him the land of the inheritance, a land which his feet should never tread and whose fruit his hand should never touch, it was yet, perhaps, not so hard to turn round and die; for, as in a dream, he had seen the land; but for the thousands who could climb no Pisgah, who were to leave their bones whitening in the desert, having even from afar never seen the true outline of the land; those who, on that long march, had not even borne the Ark nor struck the timbrel, but carried only their small household vessels and possessions, for these it was perhaps not so easy to lie down and perish in the desert, knowing only that far ahead somewhere, lay a Land of Promise. Nevertheless, it was by the slow and sometimes wavering march of such as these, that the land was reached by the people at last.

For her whose insight enables her to see, however vaguely, through the distance, those large beatitudes towards which the struggles and suffering of the women of to-day may tend; who sees beyond the present, though in a future she knows she herself will never enter, an enlarged and strengthened womanhood bearing forward with it a strengthened and expanded race, it is not too hard to renounce and Labour with unshaken purpose; but for those who have not that view, and struggle on, animated at most by a vague consciousness that somewhere ahead lies a large end, towards which their efforts tend; who Labour on patiently year after year at sc ne poor little gargoyle of a Franchise Bill, or the shaping of some rough little foundation-stone of reform in education, or dress a stone (which perhaps never quite fits the spot it was intended for, and has to be thrown aside !); or who carve away all their lives to produce a corbel of some new and beautiful condition in sexual relations, in the end to find it break under the chisel; who, out of many failures attain, perhaps, to no success, or but to one, and that so small and set so much in the shade that no eye will ever see it; for such as these, it is perhaps not so easy to Labour without growing weary.

Nevertheless, it is through the Labours of these myriad toilers, each working in her own minute sphere, with her own small outlook, and out of endless failures and miscarriages, that at last the enlivened and beautified relations of woman to life must rise, if they are ever to come.

When a star-fish lies on the ground at the bottom of a sloping rock it has to climb, it seems to the onlooker as though there were nothing which could stir the inert mass, and no means for taking it to the top. Yet watch it. Beneath its lower side, hidden from sight, are a million fine tentacles; impulses of will from the center radiate throughout the whole body, and each tiny fiber, fine as a hair, slowly extends itself, and seizes on the minute particle of rough rock nearest to it; now a small tentacle slips its hold, and then it holds firmly, and then slowly the whole inert mass rises to the top.

It is often said of those who lead in this attempt at the readaption of woman's relation to life, that they are "New Women"; and they are at times spoken of as though they were a something portentous and unheard of in the order of human life.

But, the truth is, we are not new. We who lead in this movement to-day are of that old, old Teutonic womanhood, which twenty centuries ago plowed its march through European forests and morasses beside its male companion; which marched with the Cimbri to Italy, and with the Franks across the Rhine, with the Varagians into Russia, and the

Alamani into Switzerland; which peopled Scandinavia, and penetrated to Britain; whose priestesses had their shrines in German forests, and gave out the oracle for peace or war. We have in us the blood of a womanhood that was never bought and never sold; that wore no veil, and had no foot Bound; whose realized ideal of marriage was sexual companionship and an equality in duty and Labour; who stood side by side with the males they loved in peace or war, and whose children, when they had borne them, sucked manhood from their breasts, and even through their fetal existence heard a brave heart beat above them. We are women of a breed whose racial ideal was no Helen of Troy passed passively from male hand to male hand, as men pass gold or lead; but that Brynhild whom Segurd found, clad in helm and byrnie, the warrior maid, who gave him counsel, "the deepest that ever yet was given to living man," and "wrought on him to the performing of great deeds"; who, when he died, raised high the funeral pyre and lay down on it beside him, crying, "Nor shall the door swing to at the heel of him as I go in beside him!" We are of a race of women that of old knew no fear, and feared no death; and if to-day some of us have fallen on evil and degenerate times, there moves in us yet the throb of the old blood. If it be to-day on no physical battlefield that we stand beside our men, and on no march through an external forest or morass that we have to lead; it is yet the old spirit which, undimmed by two thousand years, stirs within us in deeper and subtler ways; it is yet the cry of the old, free Northern woman which makes the world to-day. Though the battle be now for us all, in the Labouratory or the workshop, in the forum or the study, in the assembly and in the mart, with the pen and not the sword, of the head and not the arm; we still stand side by side with the men we love, "to dare with them in war and to suffer with them in peace," as the Roman wrote of our old Northern womanhood.

Those women of whom the old writers tell us, who, barefooted and white robed, led their northern hosts on that long march to Italy, were animated by the thought that they led their people to a land of warmer sunshine and richer fruitage; we, to-day, believe we have caught sight of a land bathed in a nobler than any material sunlight, with a fruitage richer than any which the senses only can grasp. And behind us, we believe, there follows a longer train than any composed of our own race and people; the sound of the tread we hear behind us is that of all earth's women, bearing within them the entire race. The footpath, yet hardly perceptible, which we tread down to-day, will, we believe, be life's broadest and straightest road, along which the children of men will pass to a higher coordination and harmony. The banner which we unfurl to-day is not new: it is the stand-ard of the old, free, monogamous, Labouring woman, which, twenty hundred years ago, floated over the forests of Europe. We shall bear it on, each generation as it falls passing it into the hand of that which follows, till we plant it so high that all nations of the world shall see it; till the women of the humblest human races shall be gathered beneath its folds, and no child enter life that was not born within its shade.

We are not new! If you would understand us, go back two thousand years, and study our descent; our breed is our explanation. We are the daughters of our fathers as well as of our mothers. In our dreams we still hear the clash of the shields of our forebears as they struck them together before battle and raised the shout of "Freedom !" In our dreams it is with us still, and when we wake it breaks from our own lips! We are the daughters of those men.

But, it may be said, "Are there not women among you who would use the shibboleth of freedom and Labour merely as a means for opening a door to a greater and more highly flavored self-indulgence, to a more lucrative and enjoyable parasitism? Are there not women who, under the guise of 'work,' are seeking only increased means of pleasure and self-indulgence; to whom intellectual training and the opening to new fields of Labour side by side with man, mean merely new means of self-advertisement and parasitic success?"

We answer: There may be such truly; among us—but not of us! This at least is true, that we, ourselves, are seldom deceived by them; the sheep generally recognize the wolf however carefully fitted the sheepskin under which he hides, though the onlookers may not; and though the sheep may not always be able to drive him from the flock I The outer world may be misled; we, who stand shoulder to shoulder with them, know them; they are not many; neither are they new. They are one of the oldest survivals, and among the most primitive relics in the race. They are as old as Loki among the gods, as Lucifer among the Sons of the Morning, as the serpent in the Garden of Eden, as pain and dislocation in web of human life.

Such women are as old as that first primitive woman who, when she went with her fellows to gather wood for the common household, put grass in the center of the bundle that she might appear to carry as much as they, yet carry nothing; she is as old as the first man who threw away his shield in battle, and yet, when it was over, gathered with the victors to share the spoils; as old as cowardice and lust in the human and animal world; only to cease from being when, perhaps, an enlarged and expanded humanity shall have cast the last slough of its primitive skin.

Every army has its camp-followers, not among its accredited soldiers, but who follow in its train, ready to attack and rifle the fallen on either side. To lookers-on, they may appear soldiers; but the soldier knows who they are. At the Judean supper there was one Master, and to the onlooker there may have seemed twelve apostles; in truth only twelve were of the company, and one was not of it. There has always been this thirteenth figure at every sacramental gathering, since the world began, wherever the upholders of a great cause have broken spiritual bread; but it may be questioned whether in any instance this thirteenth figure has been able to destroy, or even vitally to retard, any great human movement. Judas could betray his Master by a kiss; but he could not silence the voice which for a thousand years rang out of that Judean grave. Again and again, in social, political, and intellectual movements, the betrayer betrays; and the cause marches on over the body of the man.

There are women, as there are men, whose political, social, intellectual, or philanthropic Labours are put on, as the harlot puts on paint, and for the same purpose, but they can no more retard the progress of the great bulk of vital and sincere womanhood, than the driftwood on the surface of a mighty river can ultimately prevent its waters from reaching the sea.

●●

11
Woman and War

It may also be said, "Granting fully that you are right, that, as woman's old fields of Labour slip from her, she must grasp new, or must become wholly dependent on her sexual function alone, all the other elements of human nature in her becoming atrophied and arrested through lack of exercise, and granting that her evolution being arrested, the evolution of the whole race will be also arrested in her person; granting all this to the full, and allowing that the bulk of human Labour tends to become more and more intellectual and less and less purely mechanical as perfected machinery takes the place of crude human exertion; and that therefore if woman is to be saved from degeneration and parasitism, and the body of humanity from arrest, she must receive a training which will cultivate all the intellectual and all the physical faculties and be allowed freely to employ them; nevertheless, would it not be possible, and be well, that a dividing line of some kind should be drawn between the occupations of men and of women? Would it not be possible that woman should retain agriculture, textile manufactory, trade, domestic management, the education of youth, and medicine, in addition to child-bearing, as her exclusive fields of toil; while to the male should be left the study of abstract science, law and war, and statecraft; as of old, man took war and the chase, and woman absorbed the further Labours of life? Why should there not be again a fair and even division in the field of social Labour?"

Superficially, this suggestion appears rational, having at least this to recommend it, that it appears to harmonize with the course of human evolution in the past; but closely examined, it will, we think, be found to have no practical or scientific basis, and to be out of harmony with the conditions of modern life. In ancient and primitive societies, the mere larger size and muscular strength of man in certain mechanical directions, and woman's incessant physical activity in child-bearing and suckling, made almost inevitable such a sexual division of Labour in almost all countries, save perhaps in ancient Egypt. Woman naturally took the heavy agricultural and domestic Labours, which were yet more consistent with the continual dependence of infant life on her own, than those of man in war and the chase. There was nothing artificial in such a division; it threw the heaviest burden of the most wearying and unexciting forms of social Labour on woman, but under it both sexes Laboured, and each transmitted to the other, through inheritance, the fruit of its slowly expanding and always exerted powers; and the race progressed.

Individual women might sometimes, and even often, become the warriors or chiefs of tribes; the King of Ashantee might train his terrible regiment of females; and men might now and again plant and weave for their children: but in the main, and in most societies, the division of Labour was just, natural, beneficial, and it was inevitable that such a division should take place. Were to-day a band of civilized, men, women, and infants thrown down absolutely naked and defenseless in some desert, and cut off hopelessly from all external civilized life, undoubtedly very much the old division of Labour would, at least for a time, reassert itself. Men would look about for stones and sticks with which to make weapons, with which to repel wild beasts and enemies, and would go a-hunting meat and tend the beasts when tamed; women would suckle their children, cook the meat men brought, build shelters, look for roots and if possible cultivate them. There certainly would be no parasite in the society. The woman who refused to Labour for her offspring, and the man who refused to hunt or defend society would not be supported by their fellows, would soon be extinguished by want. As wild beasts were extinguished and others tamed and the materials for war improved, fewer men would be needed for hunting and war; then they would remain at home and aid in building and planting; many women would retire into the house to perfect domestic toil and handicrafts, and on a small scale the common ancient evolution of society would practically repeat itself. But for the present we see no such natural and spontaneous division of Labour based on natural sexual distinctions in the new fields of intellectual or delicately skilled manual Labour, which are taking the place of the old.

It is possible, though at present there is nothing to give indication of such a fact, and it seems highly improbable, that, in some subtle manner now incomprehensible, there might tend to be a subtle correlation between that condition of the brain and nervous system which accompanies ability in the direction of certain forms of mental, social Labour and the particular form of reproductive function possessed by an individual. It may be that, inexplicable as it seems, there may ultimately be found to be some connection between that condition of the brain and nervous system which fits the individual for the study of the higher mathematics, let us say, and the nature of their sex attributes. The mere fact that, of the handful of women who, up to the present, have received training and been allowed to devote themselves to abstract study, several have excelled in the higher mathematics, proves of necessity no pre-eminent tendency on the part of the female sex in the direction of mathematics, as compared to Labour in the fields of statesmanship, administration, or law, as into these fields, there has been practically no admittance for women. It is sometimes stated, that as several women of genius in modern times have sought to find expression for their creative powers in the art of fiction, there must be some inherent connection in the human brain between the ovarian sex function and the art of fiction. The fact is that modern fiction, being merely a description of human life in any of its phases, and being the only art that can be exercised without special training or special appliances, and produced in the moments stolen from the multifarious, brain-destroying occupations which fill the average woman's life, they have been driven to find this outlet for their powers as the only one presenting itself. How far otherwise might have been the directions in which their genius would naturally have expressed itself can be known only to the women themselves; what the world has lost by that compulsory expression of genius, in a form which may not have been its most natural form of expression, or only one of its forms, no one can ever know. Even in the little third-rate novelist whose works cumber the ground, we see often a pathetic figure when we recognize that beneath that failure in a complex and difficult art, may lie buried a sound legislator, an able architect, an original scientific investigator, or a good judge. Scientifically speaking, it is as unproven that there is any organic relation between the brain of the female and the production of art in the form of fiction, as that there is an organic relation between the hand of woman and the typewriter. Both the creative writer and the typist, in their respective spheres, are merely finding outlets for their powers in the direction of least mental resistance. The tendency of women at the present day to undertake certain forms of Labour proves only that in the crabbed, walled-in, and bound conditions surrounding woman at the present day, these are the lines along which action is most possible to her.

It may possibly be that, in future ages, when the male and female forms have been placed in like intellectual conditions, with like stimuli, like trainings and like rewards, some aptitudes may be found running parallel with the line of sex function when humanity is viewed as a whole. It may possibly be that, when the historian of the future looks back over the history of the intellectually freed and active sexes for many generations, a decided preference of the female intellect for mathematics, engineering, or statecraft may be made clear; and that a like marked inclination in the male to excel in acting, music, or astronomy may by careful and large comparison be shown. But, for the present, we have no adequate scientific data from which to draw any conclusion, and any attempt to divide the occupations in which male and female intellects and wills should be employed, must be to attempt a purely artificial and arbitrary division: a division not more rational and scientific than an attempt to determine by the color of his eyes and the shape and strength of his legs, whether a lad should be an astronomer or an engraver.

Those physical differences among mankind which divide races and nations—not merely those differences, enormously greater as they are generally, than any physical differences between male and female of the same race which divide the Jew and the Swede, the Japanese and the Englishman, but even those subtle physical differences which divide closely allied races such as the English and German—often appear to be allied with subtle differences in intellectual aptitudes. Yet even with regard to these differences, it is almost impossible to determine scientifically in how far they are the result of national traditions, environment, and education, and in how far they run parallel with the differences in physical conformation.

No study of the mere physical differences between individuals of different races would have enabled us to arrive at any knowledge of their mental aptitude; nor does the fact that certain individuals of a given human variety have certain aptitudes form a rational ground for compelling all individuals of that variety to undertake a certain form of Labour.

No analysis, however subtle, of the physical conformation of the Jew could have suggested *a priori,* and still less could have proved, apart from ages of practical experience, that, running parallel with any physical characteristics which may distinguish him from his fellows, was an innate and unique intellectual gift in the direction of religion. The fact that, during three thousand years, from Moses to Isaiah, through Jesus and Paul, on to Spinoza, the Jewish race has produced men who have given half the world its religious faith and impetus, proves that, somewhere and somehow, whether connected organically with that physical organization that marks the Jew, or as the result of his traditions and training, there does go this gift in the matter of religion. . But, on the other hand, we find millions of Jews who are totally and markedly deficient in it, and to base any practical legislation for the individual even on this proven intellectual aptitude of the race as a whole would be manifestly as ridiculous as abortive.

Yet more markedly, with the German— no consideration of his physical peculiarities, though it proceeded to the subtlest analysis of nerve, bone, and muscle, could in the present stage of our knowledge have proved to us what generations of experience appear to have proved, that, with that organization which constitutes the German, goes a unique aptitude for music. There is always the possibility of mistaking the result of training and external circumstance for inherent tendency, but when we consider the passion for music which the Grerman has shown, and when we consider that the greatest musicians the world has seen, from Bach, Beethoven, and Mozart to Wagner, have been of that race, it appears highly probable that such a correlation between the Grerman organization and the intellectual gift of music does exist. Similar intellectual peculiarities seem to be connoted by the external differences which mark off oilier races from each other. Nevertheless, if persons of all of these nationalities gathered in one colony, any attempt to legislate for their restriction to certain forms of intellectual Labour on the ground of their apparently proved national aptitudes or disabilities, would be regarded as insane. To insist that all Jews, and none but Jews, should lead and instruct in religious matters; that all Englishmen, and none but Englishmen, should engage in trade; that each Grerman should make his living by music, and none but a Grerman allowed to practise it, would drive to despair the unfortunate individual Englishman, whose most marked deficiency might be in the direction of finance and bartering trade power; the Jew, whose religious instincts might be entirely rudimentary; or the German, who could not distinguish one note from another; and the society as a whole would be an irremediable loser, in one of the heaviest of all forms of social loss—the loss of the full use of the highest capacities of all its members.

It may be that with sexes as with races, the subtlest physical differences between them may have their mental correlatives; but no abstract consideration of the human body in relation to its functions of sex can, in the present state of our knowledge, show us what intellectual capacities tend to vary with sexual structure, and nothing in the present or past condition of male or female gives us more than the very faintest possible indication of the relation of their intellectual aptitudes and their sexual functions. And even if it were proved by centuries of experiment that with the possession of the uterine function of sex tends to go exceptional intellectual capacity in the direction of mathematics rather than natural history, or an inclination for statecraft rather than for mechanical invention; were it proved that, generally speaking and as a whole, out of twenty thousand women devoting themselves to law and twenty thousand to medicine, they tended to achieve relatively more in the field of law than of medicine, there would yet be no possible healthy or rational ground for restricting the activities of the individual female to that line in which the average female appeared rather more frequently to excel.

That even one individual in a society should be debarred from undertaking that form of social toil for which it is most fitted, makes an unnecessary deficit in the general social assets. That one male Froebel should be prohibited or hampered in his Labour as an educator of infancy, on the ground that infantile instruction was the field of the female; that one female with gifts in the direction of state administration, should be compelled to instruct an infants' school, perhaps without any gift for so doing, is a running to waste of social lifeblood.

Free trade in Labour and equality of training, intellectual or physical, is essential if the organic aptitudes of a sex or class are to be determined. And our demand to-day is that natural conditions, inexorably, but beneficently, may determine the Labours of each individual, and not artificial restrictions.

As there is no need to legislate that Hindus, being generally supposed to have a natural incapacity for field sports, shall not betake themselves to them—for, if they have no capacity, they will fail; and, as in spite of the Hindus' supposed general incapacity for sport, it is possible for an individual Hindu to become the noted batsman of his age; so, there is no need to legislate that women should be restricted in her choice of fields of Labour; for the organic incapacity of the individual, if it exist, will legislate far more strongly than any artificial, legal, or social obstruction can do; and it may be that the one individual in ten thousand who selects a field not generally sought by their fellows will enrich humanity by the result of an especial genius. Allowing all to start from the one point in the world of intellectual culture and Labour, with our ancient Mother Nature sitting as umpire, distributing the prizes and scratching from the lists the incompetent, is all we demand, but we demand it determinedly. Throw the puppy into the water: if it swims, well; if it sinks, well; but do not tie a rope round its throat and weight it with a brick, and then assert its incapacity to keep afloat.

For the present, *we take all Labour for our province!*

From the judge's seat to the legislator's chair; from the statesman's closet to the merchant's office; from the chemist's Labouratory to the astronomer's tower, there is no post or form of toil for which it is not our intention to attempt to fit ourselves; and there is no closed door we do not intend to force open; and there is no fruit in the garden of knowledge it is not our determination to eat. Acting in us, and through us, nature will mercilessly expose to us our deficiencies in the field of human toil and reveal to us our powers. *And, for to-day, we take all Labour for our province!*

But, it may be said: "What then of war, that struggle of the human creature to attain its ends by physical force and at the price of the life of others: will you take part in that also?" We reply: Yes; more particularly in that field we intend to play our part. We have always borne part of the weight of war, and the major part. It is not that in primitive times we suffered from the destruction of the fields we tilled and the houses we built; it is not that later as domestic Labourers and producers, though unwaged, we, in taxes and material loss and additional Labour, paid as much as our male towards the cost of war; it is not that in a comparatively insignificant manner, as nurses of the wounded in modern times, or now and again as warrior chieftainesses and leaders in primitive and other societies, we have borne our part; nor is it even because the spirit of resolution in its women, and their willingness to endure, has in all ages, again and again largely determined the fate of a race that goes to war, that we demand our controlling right where war is concerned. Our relation to war is far more intimate, personal, and indissoluble than this. Men have made boomerangs, bows, swords, or guns with which to destroy one another; we have made the men who destroyed and were destroyed ! We have in all ages produced, at an enormous cost, the primal munitions of war, without which no other would exist. There is no battlefield on earth, nor ever has been, howsoever covered with slain, which it has not cost the women of the race more in actual bloodshed and anguish to supply, than it has cost the men who lie there. *We pay the first cost on all human life.*

In supplying the men for the carnage of a battlefield, women have not merely lost actually more blood, and gone through a more acute anguish and weariness, in the long months of bearing and in the final agony of child-birth, than has been experienced by the men who cover it; but, in the long months of rearing that follow, the women of the race go through a long, patiently endured strain which no knap sacked soldier on his longest march has ever more than equalled; while, even in the matter of death, in all civilized societies, the probability that the average woman will die in child-birth is immeasurably greater than the probability that the average male will die in battle.

There is, perhaps, no woman, whether she have borne children, or be merely potentially a child-bearer, who could look down upon a battlefield covered with slain, but the thought would rise in her, "So many mothers' sons ! So many young bodies brought into the world to lie there ! So many months of weariness and pain while bones and muscles were shaped within! So many hours of anguish and struggle that breath might be! So many baby mouths drawing life at women's breasts;—all this, that men might lie with glazed eyeballs, and swollen faces, and fixed, blue, unclosed mouths, and great limbs tossed—this, that an acre of ground might be manured with human flesh, that next year's grass or poppies or karoo bushes may spring up greener and redder, where they have lain, or that the sand of a plain may have a glint of white bones!" And we cry, "Without an inexorable cause, this must not be!" No woman who is a woman says of a human body, "It is nothing!"

On that day when the woman takes her place beside the man in the governance and arrangement of external affairs of her race will also be that day that heralds the death of war as a means of arranging human differences. No tinsel of trumpets and flags will ultimately seduce women into the insanity of recklessly destroying life, or gild the willful taking of life with any other name than that of murder, whether it be the slaughter of the million or of one by one. And this will be, not because with the sexual function of maternity necessarily goes in the human creature a deeper moral insight, or a loftier type of social instinct than that which accompanies the paternal. Men have in all ages led as nobly as women in many paths of heroic virtue, and toward the higher social sympathies; in certain ages, being freer and more widely cultured, they have led further and better. The fact that woman has no inherent all-round moral superiority over her male companion, or naturally on all points any higher social instinct, is perhaps most clearly exemplified by one curious very small fact: the two terms signifying intimate human relationships which in almost all human languages bear the most sinister and antisocial significance are both terms which have as their root the term "mother," and denote feminine relationships—the words "mother-in-law" and "step-mother."

In general humanity, in the sense of social solidarity, and in magnanimity, the male has continually proved himself at least the equal of the female.

Nor will women shrink from war because they lack courage. Earth's women of every generation have faced suffering and death with an equanimity that no soldier on a battlefield has ever surpassed and few have equalled; and where war has been to preserve life, or land, or freedom, rather than for aggrandisement and power, unparasitised and Labouring women have in all ages known how to bear an active part, and die.

Nor will woman's influence militate against war because in the future woman will not be able physically to bear her part in it. The smaller size of her muscle, which might severely have disadvantaged her when war was conducted with a battle-axe or sword and hand to hand, would now little or not at all affect her. I If intent on training for war, she might acquire the skill for guiding a Maxim or shoot-Zing down a foe with a Lee-Metford at four thousand yards as ably as any male; and undoubtedly, it has not been only the peasant girl of France, who has carried latent and hid in her person the gifts that would make the great general. If our European nations should continue in their present semi-civilized condition a few generations longer, it is highly probable that as financiers, as managers of the commissariat department, as inspectors of provisions and clothing for the army, women may probably play a very leading part; and that the nation which is the first to employ women may be placed at a vast advantage over its fellows in time of war. It is not because of woman's cowardice, incapacity, nor, above all, because of her general superior virtue, that she will end war when her voice is fully and clearly heard in the governance of states—it is because, on this one point, and on this point almost alone. the knowledge woman simply as woman, is superior to that of man: she knows the history of human flesh; she knows its cost; he does not.

In a besieged city, it might well happen that men in the streets might seize upon statues and marble carvings from public buildings and galleries and hurl them in to stop the breaches made in their ramparts by the enemy, unconsideringly and merely because they came first to hand, not valuing them more than had they been paving-stones. One man, however, could not do this—the sculptor. He, who, though there might be no work of his own chisel among them, yet knew what each of these works of art had cost, knew by experience the long years of struggle and study and the infinitude of toil which had gone to the shaping of even one limb, to the carving of even one perfected outline, he could never so use them without thought or care. Instinctively he would seek to throw in household goods, even gold and silver, all the city held, before he sacrificed its works of art!

Men's bodies are our woman's works of art, Given to us power to control, we will never" carelessly throw them in to fill up the gaps in human relationships made by international ambitions and greeds. The thought would never come to us as women, "Cast in men's bodies; settle the thing so!" Arbitration and compensation would as naturally occur to her as cheaper and simpler methods of bridging the gaps in national relationships, as to the sculptor it would occur to throw in anything rather than statuary, though he might be driven to that at last!

This is one of those phases of human life, not very numerous, but very important, towards which the man as man, and the woman as woman, on the mere ground of their different sexual function with regard to reproduction, stand, and must stand, at a somewhat differing angle. The physical creation of human life, which, in as far as the male is concerned, consists in a few moments of physical pleasure, to the female must always signify months of pressure and physical endurance, crowned with danger to life. To the male, the giving of life is a laugh; to the female, blood, anguish, and sometimes death. Here we touch one of the few yet important differences between man and woman as such.

The twenty thousand men prematurely slain on a field of battle, mean, to the women of their race, twenty thousand human creatures to be borne within them for months, given birth to in anguish, fed from their breasts and reared with toil, if the numbers of the tribe and the strength of the nation are to be maintained. In nations continually at war, incessant and unbroken child-bearing is by war imposed on all women if the state is to survive; and whenever war occurs, if numbers are to be maintained, there must be an increased child-bearing and rearing. This throws upon woman as woman a war tax, compared with which all that the male expends in military preparations is comparatively light.

The relations of the female towards the production of human life influence undoubtedly even her relation towards animal and all life, "It is a fine day, let us go out and kill something!" cries the typical male of certain races, instinctively; "There is a living thing, it will,, die if it is not cared for," says the average woman, almost equally instinctively. It is true that the woman will sacrifice as mercilessly, as cruelly, the life of a hated rival or an enemy, as any male; *but she always knows what she is doing, and the value of the life she takes!* There is no light-hearted, careless enjoyment in the sacrifice of life to the normal woman; her instinct, instructed by experience, steps in to prevent it. She always knows what life costs; and that it is more easy to destroy than create it.

It is also true, that, from the loftiest standpoint, the condemnation of war which has arisen in the human spirit, is in no sense related to any particular form of sex function. The man and the woman alike, who with Isaiah on the hills of Palestine, or the Indian Buddha under his botree, have seen the essential unity of all sentient life; and who therefore see in war but a symptom of that crude disco-ordination of life on earth, not yet at one with itself, which affects humanity in these early stages of its growth; and who are compelled to regard as the ultimate goal of the race, though yet perhaps far distant across the ridges of innumerable coming ages, that harmony between all forms of conscious life, metaphorically prefigured by the ancient Hebrew, when he cried, "The wolf shall dwell with the lamb; and the leopard shall lie down with the kid; and the calf and the young lion and the fatling together, and a little child shall lead them!" — to the individual, whether man or woman, who has reached this standpoint, there is no need for enlightenment from the instincts of the child-bearers of society as such; their condemnation of war, rising not so much from the fact that it is a wasteful destruction of human flesh, as that it is an indication of the non-existence of that co-ordination, the harmony which is summed up in the cry, "My little children, love one another."

But for the vast bulk of humanity, probably for generations to come, the instinctive antagonism of the human child-bearer to reckless destruction of that which she has at so much cost produced will probably be necessary to educate the race to any clear conception of the bestiality and insanity of war.

War will pass when intellectual culture and activity have made possible to the female an equal share in the control and governance of modern national life; it will probably not pass away much sooner; its extinction will not be delayed much longer.

It is especially in the domain of war that we, the bearers of men's bodies, who supply its most valuable munition, who, not amid the clamor and ardor of battle, but singly, and alone, with a three-in-the-morning courage, shed our blood and face death that the battlefield might have its food, a food more precious to us than our heart's blood; it is we especially who, in the domain of war, have our word to say, a word no man can say for us. It is our intention to enter into the domain of war and to Labour there till in the course of generations we have extinguished it.

If to-day we claim all Labour for our province, yet more especially do we claim those fields in which the difference in the reproductive function between man and woman may place male and female at a slightly different angle with regard to certain facts of human life.

●●

12
Sex Differences

If we examine the physical phenomenon of sex as it manifests itself in the human creature, we find, in the first stages of the individual's existence, no difference discernible, by any means we have at present at our command, between those germs which are ultimately to become male or female. Later, in the fetal life, at birth, and through infancy, though the organs of sex serve to distinguish the male from the female, there is in the general structure and working of the organism little or nothing to divide the sexes.

Even when puberty is reached, with its enormous development of sexual and reproductive activity modifying those parts of the organism with which it is concerned, and producing certain secondary sexual characteristics, there yet remains a major extent of the human body and of physical function little, or not at all, affected by sex modification. The eye, the ear, the sense of touch, the general organs of nutrition and respiration and volition are in the main identical, and often differ far more in persons of the same sex than in those of opposite sexes; even on the dissecting-table the tissues of the male and female are often wholly indistinguishable.

It is when we consider the reproductive organs themselves and their forms of activity, and such parts of the organism modified directly in relation to them, that a real and important difference is found to exist, radical though absolutely complementally. It is exactly as we approach the reproductive functions that the male and female bodies differ; exactly as We recede from them that they become more and more similar, and even absolutely identical. Taking the eye, perhaps the most highly developed, complex organ in the body, and, if an organ may be allowed the term, the most intellectual organ of sense, we find it remains the same in male and female in structure, in appearance, and in function throughout life; while the breast, closely connected with reproduction, though absolutely identical in both forms in infancy, assumes a widely different organization when reproductive activity is actually concerned.

When we turn to the psychic phase of human life, an exactly analogous phenomenon presents itself. The intelligence, emotions, and desires of the human infant at birth differ not at all perceptibly, as its sex may be male or female; and such psychic differences as appear to exist in later childhood are undoubtedly very largely the result of artificial training, forcing on the appearance of psychic sexual divergencies long before they would tend spontaneously to appear; as where sports and occupations are interdicted to young children on the ground of their supposed sexual unfitness; as when an infant female is forcibly prevented from climbing or shouting, and the infant male from amusing himself with needle and thread or dolls. Even in the fully adult human, and in spite of difference of training, the psychic activities over a large extent of life appear to be absolutely identical. The male and female brains acquire languages, solve mathematical problems, and master scientific detail in a manner wholly indistinguishable; as illustrated by the fact that in modern universities the papers sent in by male and female candidates are as a rule identical in type.

Placed in like external conditions, their tastes and emotions, over a vast part of the surface of life, are identical; and, in an immense number of those cases where psychic sex differences appear to exist, subject to rigid analysis they are found to be artificial creations, for, when other races or classes are studied, they are found non-existent as sexual characteristics. The female is supposed by ignorant persons in modern European societies to have an inherent love for bright colors and ornaments, not shared by the male; while experience of other societies and past social conditions proves that it is as often the male who has been even more desirous of attiring himself in bright raiment and adorning himself with brilliant jewels; or as when, among certain tribes of savages, the use of tobacco is supposed to be a peculiarly female prerogative, while, in some modern societies, it is supposed to have some relation to masculinity.

But there remain certain psychic differences in attitude, on the part of male and female as such, which are, inherent and not artificial: and, in the psychic human world, it is exactly as we approach the sphere of sexual and reproductive activity. with those emotions and instincts connected with sex and the reproduction of the race, that a difference does appear.

In the animal world all forms of psychic variations are found allying themselves now with the male sex form, and then with the female. In the insect and fish worlds, where the female forms are generally larger and stronger than the male, the female is generally more pugnacious and predatory than the male. Among birds-of-prey, where the female form is larger and stronger than the male, the psychic differences seem very small. Among eagles and other allied forms, which are strictly monogamous, the affection of the female for the male is so great that she is said never to mate again if the male dies, and both watch over and care for the young with extreme solicitude. The ostrich male form, though perhaps larger than the female, shares with her the Labour of hatching the eggs, relieving the hen at a fixed hour daily: and his care for the young when hatched is as tender as hers. Among song-birds, in which the male and female forms are so alike as sometimes to be indistinguishable, and which are also monogamous, the male and female forms not only exhibit the same passionate affection for each other (in the case of the South African cock-o-veet, they have one answering love-song between them; the male sounding two or three notes and the female completing it with two or three more), but they build the nest together and rear the young with an equal care. In the case of the little kapok bird of the Cape, a beautiful white fluffy nest is made by both of the white down of a certain plant, and immediately below the entrance to the cavity in which the little female sits on the eggs is a small shelf or basket, in which the tiny male sits to watch over and guard them. It is among certain orders of birds that sex manifestations appear to assume their most harmonious and poetical forms on earth. Among gallinaceous birds, on the other hand, where the cock is much larger and more pugnacious than the female, and which are polygamous, the cock does not court the female by song, but seizes her by force, and shows little or no interest in his offspring, neither sharing in the brooding nor feeding of the young; and even at times seizing any tempting morsel which the young or the hen may have discovered.

Among mammals, the male form tends to be slightly larger than the female, though not always (the female whale, for instance, being larger than the male); the male also tends to be more pugnacious and less careful of the young; though to this rule also there are exceptions. In the case of the South African mierkat, for instance, the female is generally more combative and more difficult to tame than the male; and it is the males who from the moment of birth watch over the young with the most passionate and tender solicitude, keeping them warm under their persons, carrying them to places of safety in their mouths, and feeding them till full grown; and this they do not only to their own young, but to any young who may be brought in contact with them. We have known a male mierkat so assiduous in feeding young that were quite unrelated to himself, taking to them every morsel of food given him, that we have been compelled to shut him up in a room alone when feeding him, to prevent his starving himself to death: the male mierkat thus exhibiting exactly those psychic qualities which are generally regarded as peculiarly feminine; the females, on the other hand, being far more pugnacious towards each other than are the males.

Among mammals generally, except the tendency to greater pugnacity shown by the male towards other males, and the greater solicitude for the young shown generally by the female form, but not always, the psychic differences between the two sex forms are not great. Between the male and female pointer as puppies, there is as little difference in mental activity *as* in physical; and even when adult, on the hunting-ground, that great non-sexual field in which their highest mental and physical activities are displayed, there is little or nothing which distinguishes materially between the male and female; in method, manner, and quickness they are alike; in devotion to man, they are psychically identical. It is at the moment when the reproductive element comes fully into play that similarity and identity cease. In the intensity of initial sex instinct they are alike; the female will leap from windows, climb walls, and almost endanger her life to reach the male who waits for her, as readily as he will to gain her. It is when the bitch lies with her six young drawing life from her breast, and gazing with wistful and anguished solicitude at every hand stretched out to touch them, a world of emotion concentrated on the sightless creatures, and a whole body of new mental aptitudes brought into play in caring for them, it is then that between her and the male who begot them, but cares nothing for them, there does rise a psychic difference that is real and wide. Alike in the sports of puppydom and the non-sexual activities of adult age; alike in the possession of the initial instinct which draws the sex to the sex, the moment active sexual reproduction is concerned, there *is* opened to the female a world of sensations and experiences, from which her male companion is forever excluded.

So also is our human world: alike in the sports, and joys, and sorrows of infancy; alike in the non-sexual Labours of life; alike even in the possession of that initial instinct which draws sex to sex, and which, differing slightly in its forms of manifestation, is of equal intensity in both; the moment actual reproduction begins to take place, the man and the woman enter spheres of sensation,, perception, emotion, desire, and knowledge which are not, and cannot be, absolutely identical. Between the man who, in an instant of light-hearted enjoyment, begets the infant (who may even beget it in a state of half-drunken unconsciousness, and may easily know nothing of its existence for months or years after it is bony or even never at all; and who under no circumstances can have any direct sensational knowledge of its relation to himself) and the woman who bears it continuously for months within her body, and who gives birth to it in pain, and who, if it is to live, is compelled, or was in primitive times, to nourish it for months from the blood of her own being—between these, there exists of necessity, towards a limited but all-important body of human interests and phenomena, a distinct psychic attitude. At this one point, the two great halves of humanity stand confronting certain great elements in human existence, from angles that are not identical—From the moment the universal initial attraction of sex to sex becomes incarnate in the first concrete sexual act till the developed offspring attains maturity, no step in the reproductive journey, or in their relation to their offspring, has been quite identical for the man and the woman. And this divergence of experiences in human relations must react on their attitude towards that particular body of human concerns which directly is connected with the sexual reproduction of the race, and it is exactly in these fields of human activity, where sex as sex is concerned, that woman as woman has a part to play which she cannot resign into the hands of others.

It may be truly said that in the Labouratory, the designing-room, the factory, the mart, the mathematician's study, and in all fields of purely abstract and impersonal Labour, while the entrance of woman would add to the net result of human Labour in those fields, and though a grave injustice is done to the individual woman excluded from perhaps the only field she is fitted to excel in, yet woman as woman has probably little or nothing to contribute in those fields that is radically distinct from that which man might supply; there would be a difference in quality but probably none in kind, in the work done For the race.

But in those spheres of social activity dealing especially with certain relations between human creatures because of their diverse if complementary relation to the production. of human life, the sexes as sexes have of ten each a part to play which the other cannot play for them, have each a knowledge gained from phases of human experience which the other cannot "supply; here woman as woman has something radically distinct to contribute to the sum-total of human knowledge, and her activity is of importance, not merely individually, but collectively, and as a class.

That demand, which to-day in all democratic self-governing countries is being made by women, to be accorded their share in the electoral and ultimately in the legislative and executive duties of government, is based on two grounds: the wider, that they find nothing in the nature of their sex-function which exonerates them, as human beings, from their obligation to take part in the Labours of guidance and government in their state; the narrower, but yet important ground, that, in as far as in one direction, *i. e.,* in the special form of their sex function, they do differ from the male, they, in so far, form a class and are bound to represent the interests of, and to give the state the benefit of, the insight of their class, in certain directions. Those persons who imagine that the balance of great political parties in almost any society would be seriously changed by the admission of its women in public functions are undoubtedly wholly wrong.

The fundamental division of humans into those inclined to hold by the past and defend whatever is, and those hopeful of the future and inclined to introduce change, would probably be found to exist in much the same proportion were the males or the females of any given society compared: and females of each class will in the main share the faults, the virtues, and the prejudices of their class. The individual may lose by being excluded on the ground of sex from a share of public Labour, and by being robbed of a portion of their lawful individual weight in their own society; and the society as a whole may lose by having a smaller number to select her chosen Labourers from; yet, undoubtedly, on the mass of social, political, and international questions, the conclusions arrived at by one sex would be exactly those arrived at by the other.

Were a body elected to adjudicate upon Greek accents, or to pass a decision on the relative fineness of woolens and linens, the form of sex of the persons composing it would probably have no bearing on the result; there is no rational ground for supposing that, on a question of Greek accents or the thickness of cloths, equally instructed males and females would differ. Here sex plays no party. The experience and instructedness of the individuals would tell: their sexual attributes would be indifferent.

But there are points, comparatively small, even very small, in number, yet of vital importance to human life, in which sex does play a part.

It is not a matter of indifference whether the body called to adjudicate upon the question:— whether the temporary sale of the female body for sexual purposes shall or shall not be a form of traffic encouraged and recognized by the state; or whether one law shall exist for the licentious human female and another for the 'licentious human male; whether the claim of the female to the offspring she bears shall or shall not equal that of the male who begets it; whether an act of infidelity on the part of the male shall or shall not terminate the contract which binds his female companion to him as completely as an act of infidelity on her part would terminate her claim on him; it is not a matter of indifference whether a body elected to adjudicate on such points as these consists of males solely, or females solely, or of both com-bined. As it consists of one, or the other, or of both, so not only will the answers vary, but in some cases, will they he completely diverse. Here we come into the narrow, but important, region where sex as sex manifestly plays its part; where the male as male and the female as female have each their body of perceptions and experiences, which they do not hold in common; here one sex cannot adequately represent the other. It is here that each sexual part of the race has something radically distinct to contribute to the wisdom of the race. We, to-day, take all Labour for our province! We seek to enter the non-sexual fields of intellectual or physical toil, because we are unable to see to-day, with regard to them, any dividing wall raised by sex which excludes us from them. We are yet equally determined to enter those in which sex does play its part, because it is here that woman, the bearer of the race, must. stand side by side with man, the begetter; if a completed human wisdom, an insight that misses no aspect of human life, and an activity that is in harmony with the entire knowledge and the entire instinct of the human race, is to *exist.* It is here that the man cannot act for the woman nor the woman for the man; but both must, interact, It is here that each sexual half of the race, so closely and indistinguishably blended elsewhere, has its own distinct contribution to make to the sum total of human knowledge and human wisdom. Neither is the woman without the man, nor the man without the woman, the completed human intelligence.

●●

13

Certain Objections

It has been stated sometimes, though more often implicitly than in any direct or logical form. (this statement being one it is not easy to make definitely without its reducing itself to nullity !) that woman should seek no fields of Labour in the new world of social conditions that is arising about us, as she has her function as child-bearer: a Labour which, by her own! showing, is arduous and dangerous, though she may love it as a soldier loves his battle field; that woman, should perform her sex functions only, allowing man or the state to support her, even when she is only potentially a child-bearer and bears no children.

There is some difficulty in replying to a theorist so wholly delusive. Not only is he to be met by all the arguments against parasitism of class or race; but, at the present day, when probably much more than half the world's most Labourious and ill-paid Labour is still performed by women, from tea pickers and cocoa tenders in India and the islands, to the washerwomen, cooks, and drudging Labouring men's wives, who, in addition to the sternest and most unending toil, throw in their child-bearing as a little addition: and when in some civilized countries women exceed the males in numbers by one million, so that there would still be one million females for whom there was no legitimate sexual outlet, though each male in the nation supported a female, it is somewhat difficult to reply with gravity to the assertion, "Let Woman be contest to be the 'Divine Child-bearer,' and ask no more."

Were it worth replying gravely to so idle a theorist, we might answer:—Through all the ages of the past, when, with heavy womb and hard Labour-worn hands, we physically toiled beside man, bearing up by the Labour of our bodies the world about us, it was never suggested to us, "You, the child-bearers of the race, have in that one function a Labour that equals all others combined; therefore, toil no more in other directions, we pray of you. Neither plant, nor build, nor bend over the grindstone, nor far into the night, while we sleep, sit weaving the clothing we and our children are to wear! Leave it to us, to plant, to reap, to weave, to work, to toil for you, O sacred child-bearer! Work no more; every man of the race will work for you!" This cry in all the grim ages of our past toil we never heard.

And to-day the lofty theorist, who to-night stands before the drawing-room fire in spotless shirt-front and perfectly fitting clothes, and declaims upon the amplitude of woman's work in life as child-bearer, and the mighty value of that Labour which exceeds all other, making it unnecessary for her to share man's grosser and lower toils: does he always remember his theory? When waking to-morrow morning, he finds that the elderly house drudge, who rises at dawn while he yet sleeps, to make his tea and clean his boots, has brought his tea late, and polished his boots ill; may he not even sharply condemn her, and assure her she will have to leave unless she works harder and rises earlier? He does not exclaim to her, "Divine child-bearer! Potential mother of the race! Why should you clean my boots or bring up my tea, while I lie warm in bed? Is it not enough you should have the holy and mysterious power of bringing the race to life? Let that content you. Henceforth I shall get up at dawn and make my own tea and clean my own boots, and pay you just the same!" Nor, should his landlady, now about to give birth to her ninth child, send him up a poorly-cooked dinner or forget to bring up his scuttle of coal, does he send for her and thus apostrophize the astonished matron: "Child-bearer of the race! Producer of men! Cannot you be contented with so noble and lofty a function in life without toiling and moiling? Why carry up heavy coal-scuttles from the cellar and bend over hot fires, wearing out nerve and muscle that should be reserved for higher duties? We, we men of the race, will perform its mean, its sordid, its grinding toil! For woman is beauty, peace, repose! Your function is to give life, not to support it by Labour. The Mother, the Mother! How wonderful it sounds! Toil no more! Rest is for you; Labour and drudgery for us!" Would he not rather assure her that, unless she Laboured more assiduously and sternly, she would lose his custom and so be unable to pay her month's rent, and perhaps so, with children and an invalid or drunken husband whom she supports, be turned out into the streets? For it is remarkable, that, with theorists of this class, it is not toil, or the amount of toil, crushing alike to brain and body, which the female undertakes that he objects to; it is the form and the amount of the reward. It is not the hand-Labouring woman, even in his own society, worn out and prematurely aged at forty with grinding domestic toil that has no beginning and knows no end— "Man's work is from sun to sun, But woman's work is never done"— it is not the haggard, work-worn woman and mother who irons his shirts, or the potential mother who destroys health and youth in the sweater's den where she sews the garments in which he appears so radiantly in the drawing-room who disturbs him. It is the thought of the woman-doctor with an income of some hundreds a year, who drives round in her carriage to see her patients, or receives them in her consulting-rooms, and who spends the evening smoking and reading before her study fire or receiving her guests; it is the thought of the woman who, as legislator, may loll for perhaps six hours on the padded seat of legislative bench, relieving the tedium now and then by a turn in the billiard-or refreshment-room, when she is not needed to vote or speak; it is the woman as Greek professor, with three or four hundred a year, who gives half a dozen lectures a week, and has leisure to enjoy the society of her husband and children, and to devote to her own study and life of thought; it is she who wrings his heart. It is not the woman, who, on hands and knees, at tenpence a day, scrubs the floors of the public buildings, or private dwellings, that fills him with anguish for womanhood: that somewhat quadrupedal posture is for him truly feminine, and does not interfere with the ideal of the mother and child-bearer. That, in some other man's house, or perhaps his own, while he and the wife he keeps for his pleasure are visiting concert or entertainment, some weary woman paces till far into the night bearing with aching back and tired head the fretful teething child he brought into the world, for a pittance of twenty or thirty pound? a year, does not distress him. But that the same woman by work in an office should earn one hundred and fifty pounds, be able to have a comfortable home of her own and her evening free for study or pleasure, distresses him deeply. It is not the Labour, or the amount of Labour, so much as the amount of reward that interferes with his ideal of the eternal womanly; he is as a rule contented that the women of the race should Labour for him whether as tea-pickers or washerwoman, or toilers for the children he brings into the world, provided the reward they receive is not large, nor in such fields as he might himself desire to enter.

When master and ass, drawing a heavy burden between them, should have climbed a steep mountain range together; clambering over sharp rocks and across sliding gravel where no water is, and herbage is scant; if, when they were come out on the top of the mountain and before them stretch broad, green lands, and through wide half-open gates they caught the glimpse of trees waving, and there came the sound of running waters, if then the master should say to his ass, "Good beast of mine, lie down! I can push the whole burden myself now: lie down here; lie down my creature; you have toiled enough; I will go on alone!" then it might be even the beast would whisper (with that glimpse through the swinging gates of the green fields beyond)— "Good master, we two have climbed this mighty mountain together, and the stones have cut my hoofs as they cut your feet. Perhaps, if when we were at the foot you had found out that the burden was too heavy for me, and had then said to me, 'Lie down, my beastie; I will carry on the burden alone; lie down and rest!' I might then have listened. But now, just here, where I see the gates swinging open, a smooth road, and green fields before us, I think I shall go on a little farther. We two have climbed together; maybe we shall go on yet, side by side."

For the heart of Labouring womanhood cries out to-day to the man who would suggest she need not seek new fields of Labour, that child-bearing is enough for her share in life's Labour, "Do you dare say to us now, that we are fit to do nothing but child-bear, that when that is performed our powers are exhausted? To us, who yet through all the ages of the past, when child-bearing was persistent and incessant, regarded it hardly as a toil, but rather as the reward of Labour; has our right hand lost its cunning and our heart its strength, that to-day, when human Labour is easier and humanity's work grows fairer, you say to us, 'You can do nothing now but child-bear/ Do you dare to say this, to us, when the upward path of the race has been watered by the sweat of our brow, and the sides of the road by which humanity has climbed are whitened on either hand by the bones of the womanhood that has fallen there, toiling beside man? Do you dare say this, to us, when even to-day the food you eat, the clothes you wear, the comfort you enjoy, is largely given you by the unending muscular toil of woman?"

As the women of old planted and reaped and ground the grain that the children they bore might eat, as the maidens of old spun that they might make linen for their households and obtain the right to bear men; so, though we bend no more over grindstones, or Labour in the fields, or weave by hand, it is our intention to enter all the new fields of Labour, that we also may have the power and right to bring men into the world. It is our faith that the day comes in which not only shall no man dare to say, "It is enough portion for a woman in life that she bear a child," but when it will rather be said, "What noble Labour has that woman performed, that she should have the privilege of bringing a man or woman child into the world?" But, it may be objected, "What if the female half of humanity, though able, in addition to the exercise of its reproductive functions, to bear its share in the new fields of social Labour as it did in the old, be yet in certain directions a less productive Labourer than the male? What if, in the main, the result of the Labour of the two halves should not be found to be exactly equal?"

To this it may be answered that it is within the range of possibility that, mysteriously coordinated with the male reproductive function in the human, there may also be in many directions a tendency to possess gifts useful and beneficial to the race, in the stage of growth it has now reached, in excess of those possessed by the female. We see no reason why this should be so, and, in the present state of our knowledge, this is a point on which no sane person would dogmatize; but it is possible! It may, on the other hand, be that, taken in the bulk, when all the branches of productive Labour be considered, the value of the Labour of the two halves of humanity will be found so identical and so closely to balance that no superiority can possibly be asserted of either, as the result of the closest analysis. This also is possible.

But, it may also be that, when the bulk and sum-total of human activities is surveyed in future ages, it will be found that the value of the Labour of the female in the world that is rising about us has exceeded in quality or in quantity that of the male. We see no reason either why this should be; there is nothing in the nature of the reproductive function in the female human which of necessity implies such superiority.

Yet it may be that, with the smaller general bulk and the muscular fineness and the preponderance of brain and nervous system in net bulk over the fleshy and osseous parts of the organism, which generally, though by no means always, characterizes the female as distinguished from the male of the human species, go mental qualities which will peculiarly fit her for the Labour of the future. It may be that her lesser possession of the muscular and osseous strength, which were the elements of primary importance to humanity and which gave dominance in one stage of human growth, and which placed woman at a social disadvantage as compared with her companion, will, under new conditions of life, in which the value of crude mechanical strength as distinguished from high vitality and strong nervous activity is passing away, prove as largely to her advantage, as his muscular bulk and strength in the past proved to the male. It is quite possible, in the new world which is arising about us, that the type of human most useful to society and best fitted for its future conditions, and who will excel in the most numerous forms of activity, will be, not the muscularly powerful and bulky, but the highly versatile, active, vital, adaptive, sensitive, physically fine-drawn type: and, as that type, though, like the muscularly heavy and powerful, by no means peculiar to and confined to one sex, is yet rather more commonly found in conjunction with a female organism, it is quite possible that, taken in the bulk and on the whole, the female half of humanity may, by virtue of its structural adoptions, be found most fitted for the bulk of human Labours in the future!

As with individuals and races, so also with sexes, changed social conditions may render exactly those subtle qualities, which in one social state were a disadvantage, of the highest social advantage in another.

The skilled diplomatist or politician, so powerful in his own element, on board ship during a storm becomes at once of less social value or consideration than the meanest sailor who can reef a sail or guide a wheel; and, if we were to be reduced again suddenly to a state of nature, a company of highly civilized men and women would at once, as we have before remarked, find their social value completely inverted. Landed on a desert shore, unarmed and naked, to encounter wild beasts and savages, and to combat nature for food, the primitive scale of human values would at once reassert itself. It would not then be the mighty financier, the learned judge, or great poet and scholar who would be sought after, but the thickest-headed heavy who could throw a stone so exactly that he brought down a bird, and who could in a day raise a wall which would shelter the group, and the man so powerful that he could surely strike an enemy or wild beast dead with his club, would at once be objects of social regard and attain individual eminence, and perhaps dominance. It would not be the skilled dancer, who in one night in a civilized state earns her hundreds, nor the fragile, clinging beauty, but the girl of the broad back and the strong limb, who could collect wood and carry water, who would be the much considered and much sought after female in such a community.

Even in the animal world, there is the same inversion in values, according as the external conditions vary. The lion, while ruling over every other creature in his primitive wilds, by right of his untamable ferocity, size, and rapacity, is yet bound to become a prey to destruction and extermination when he comes into contact with the new condition brought by man; while the wild dog, so immeasurably his inferior in size, and ferocity, is tamed, survives and multiplies, exactly because he has been driven by his smaller structure and lesser physical force to develop those social instincts and those forms of intelligence which make him amenable to the new condition of life and valuable in them.

The same inversion in the value of qualities may be traced in the history of human species. The Jews, whose history has been one long story of oppression at the hands of more muscular, physically powerful, and pugilistic peoples; whom we find first making bricks under the lash of the Egyptian, and later hanging his harp as an exile among the willow-trees of Babylon; who, for eighteen hundred years, has been trampled, tortured, and despised beneath the feet of the more physically powerful and pugilistic, but not more vital, keen, intelligent, or persistent races of Europe; has, to-day, by the slow turning of the wheel of life, come uppermost. The Egyptian taskmaster and warrior have passed; what the Babylonian was we know no more, save for a few mud tablets and rock inscriptions recording the martial victories; but the once captive Jew we see to-day in every city and every street; until, at last, the descendants of those men who spat when they spoke his name, and forcibly drew his teeth to extract his money from him, wait patiently behind each other for admission to his offices and palaces; while nobles solicit his daughters in marriage and kings are proud to be summoned to his table in hope of golden crumbs, and great questions of peace and war are often held balanced in the hand of one little asthmatic Jew. After long ages of disgrace and pariahism, the time has come, whether for good or for evil, when just those qualities which the Jew possesses and which subtlety distinguish him from others, are in demand; while those he has not are sinking into disuse. Exactly that domination of the reflective faculties over the combative, which once made him slave, also saved him from becoming extinct in wars; and the intellectual quickness, the far-sighted keenness, the persistent mental activity and self-control, which could not in those ages save him from degradation or compensate for his lack of bone and muscle and combative instinct, are the very qualities the modern world demands and crowns. The day of Goliath with his club and his oaths is fast passing, and the day of David with his harp and skillfully constructed sling is coming near and yet nearer.

The qualities which give an animal, a race, an individual, a higher utility or social dominance must always be influenced by any change in the environment. As the wheel of life slowly revolves, that which was lowest comes continually uppermost, and that which was dominant becomes subservient.

It is possible that women, after countless ages, during which that smaller relative development in weight and muscularity which is incident to almost all females which suckle their young, and that lesser desire for pugilism inherent in almost all females who bear their young alive, rendered her lacking in the two qualities which made for individual dominance in her societies, may yet, in the future, discover that those changes in human conditions, which have done away with the primary necessity for muscular force and pugilistic arts, have also inverted her place in the scale of social values. It is possible that the human female, like the Jew, the male of that type farthest removed from the dominant male type of the past, may find that, so far from those qualities which, in an earlier condition, lessened her social value and power of Labour, continuing to do so, they will increase it. That the delicacy of hand, lightness of structure, which were fatal when the dominant Labour of life was to hurl a battle-axe or move a weight, may be no restraint but even an assistance in the intellectual and more delicate mechanical fields of Labour, that the preponderance of nervous and cerebral over muscular material, and the tendency towards preservative and creative activity over pugilistic and destructive, so far from shutting her off from the most important fields of human toil, may increase her fitness for them I We have no certain proof that it is so at present; but, if woman's long years of servitude and physical subjection, and her experience as child-bearer and protector of infancy, should, in any way, be found in the future to have endowed her, as a kind of secondary sexual characteristic, with any additional strength of social instinct, with any exceptional width of human sympathy and any instinctive comprehension; then, it is not merely possible, but certain, that, in the ages that are coming, in which the Labour of the human race will be not mainly destructive but conservative, in which the building up and consolidating of humanity, and not continually the inter-destruction of part by part, will be the dominant activity of the race, that woman as woman, and by right of that wherein she differs from the male, will have an all-important part to play in the activity of the race.

The matter is one of curious and subtle interest, but what practically concerns the human race is, not which of the two sexual halves which must always co-exist is best fitted to excel in certain human Labours in this or that direction, nor even which has most to contribute to the sum-total of human activities; but it is this, that every individual unit humanity contains, irrespective of race, sex, or type, should find exactly that field of Labour which may most contribute to its development, happiness, and health, and in which its peculiar faculties and gifts shall be most effectively and beneficially exerted for its fellows. It matters nothing, and less than nothing, to us as women, whether, of those children we bring into the world, our sons should excel in virtue, intelligence, and activity, our daughters, or our daughters our sons; so that, in each child we bring to life, not one potentiality shall be lost, nor squandered on a lesser when it might have been expended on a higher and more beneficent task. So that not one desirable faculty of the marvelous creatures we bring into existence be left uncultivated, to us as women, it matters nothing and less than nothing, which sex type excels in action, in knowledge, or in virtue, so both attain their best. There is one thing only on earth as precious to woman as the daughter who springs from her body—it is the son. There is one thing only dearer to the woman than herself—it is the man. As no sane human concerns himself as to whether the right or left ventricle of his heart works most satisfactorily, or is most essential to his well-being, so both be perfect in health and activity; as no sane woman distresses herself lest her right breast should not excel the left in beauty and use; so no sane man or woman questions over the relative perfections of male and female. In love there is no first nor last. What we request of life is that the tools should be given to his hand or hers who can handle them; that the least efficient should not be forced into the place of the more efficient, and that an artificially drawn line should never repress the activities of the individual creature which we as women bring into the world.

But it may also be said to us, "What, and if all your dreams and hopes for woman and the future of the race be based on air? What if, desirable as it is that woman should not become practically dependent on her sexual function alone, and should play at least as great a part in the productive Labour of the race in the future as she played in that of the past —what if woman *cannot* take the same vast share in the complex and largely mental Labour fields of the future as in the largely physical fields of the past? What if, in spite of all her effort and sacrifice to attain this end, exactly now when the Labour of civilized societies becomes mental rather than mechanical, woman be found wanting ?"

In Swiss valleys to-day the traveller comes sometimes on the figure of a solitary woman climbing the mountain-side, on her broad shoulders a mighty burden of fodder or manure she is bearing up for the cattle, or to the patch of cultivated land. Steady, unshrinking eyes look out at you from beneath the deeply seamed forehead, and a strand of hair, perhaps almost as white as the mountain snows on the peaks above, escapes from under the edge of the binding handkerchief. The face is seamed and seared with the stern marks of toil and endurance, as the mountain-side is with marks of storm and avalanche. It is the face of one who has brought men into the world in Labour and sorrow, and toiled mightily to sustain them; and dead must be the mind to the phases of human existence, who does not see in that toil worn figure one of the mighty pillars which have in the long ages of the past sustained the life of humanity on earth and made possible its later developments; and much must the tinsel of life have dazzled him, who fails to mark it with reverence and, metaphorically, to bow his head before it—the type of the mighty Labouring woman who has built up life.

But, it may be said, what if, in the ages to come, it should never again be possible for any man to stand bowed with the same respect in the presence of any other of earth's mighty toilers, who shall also be mother and woman? What if she, who could combine motherhood with the most unending muscular toil, will fall flaccid and helpless where the Labour becomes mental? What if, struggle as she will, she can become nothing in the future but the pet pug-dog of the race, lying on its sofa, or the Italian greyhound, shivering in its silken coat? What if woman, in spite of her most earnest aspirations and determined struggles, be destined to failure in the new world that is rising because of inherent incapacity?

There are many replies which may be made to such a suggestion. It is often said with truth that the ordinary occupations of woman in the past and present, and in all classes of society in which she is not parasitic, do demand, and have always demanded a very high versatility and mental activity, as well as physical. The medieval baron's wife who guided her large household probably had to expend far more pure intellect in doing so than the baron in his hunting and fighting. The wife of the city accountant probably expends today more reason, imagination, forethought, and memory on the management of her small household, than he in his simpler, monotonous arithmetical toil. As there is no cause for supposing that the tailor or shoemaker needs less intellect in his calling than the soldier or prize-fighter, so there is nothing to suggest that, in the past, woman has not expended as much pure intellect in the mass of her callings as the man in his.

As for those highly specialized intellectual occupations, in which long and uninterrupted training tending to one point is necessary, such as the liberal professions and arts, although woman has practically been excluded from the requisite training, and the freedom to place herself in the positions in which they can be pursued, yet, by force of innate genius and gifts in such directions, she has continually broken through the seemingly insuperable obstacles, and again and again taken her place beside man in those fields of Labour; showing thereby not merely aptitude but passionate and determined inclination in those directions.

With equal truth, it is often remarked that, when as an independent hereditary sovereign, woman has been placed in the only position in which she has been able freely and fully to express her own individuality, and though selected at random by fate from the mass of women, by the accident of birth or marriage, she has shown in a large percentage of cases that the female has the power to command, organize, and succeed in one of the most exacting and complex of human employments, the government of nations. From the days of Amalasontha to Isabella of Spain, Elizabeth of England, and Catherine of Russia, women have not failed to grasp the large impersonal aspects of life, and successfully and powerfully to control them, when placed in a position in which it was demanded.

It may also be stated, and is sometimes, with so much iteration as to become almost wearisome, that women's adequacy in the modern fields of intellectual or skilled manual Labour is no more to-day an open matter for debate, than the number of modern women who, as senior wranglers, doctors, etc., have already successfully entered the new fields, and the high standard attained by women in all university examinations to which they are admitted, and their universal success in the administration of parochial matters, wherever they have been allowed to share it, proves their intellectual and moral fitness for the new forms of Labour.

All these statements are certainly interesting, and may be unanswerable. And yet—if the truth be told, it is not ultimately on these grounds that many of us base our hope and our certitude with regard to the future of woman. Our conviction as to the plenitude of her powers for the adequate performance of lofty Labours in these new fields springs not at all from a categorical enumeration of the attainments or performances of individual women or bodies of women in the past or present; it has another source.

There was a bird's *egg* once, picked up by chance upon the ground, and those who found it bore it home and placed it under a barndoor fowl. And in time the chick bred out, and those who had found it chained it by the leg to a log, lest it should stray and be lost. And by and by they gathered round it, and speculated as to what the bird might be. One said, "It is surely a waterfowl, a duck, or it may be a goose; if we took it to the water it would swim and gabble." But another said, "It has no webs to its feet; it is a barn-yard fowl; should you let it loose it will scratch and cackle with the others on the dung-heap." But a third speculated, "Look now at its curved beak; no doubt it is a parrot, and can crack nuts!" But a fourth said, "No, but look at its wings; perhaps it is a bird of great flight." But several cried, "Nonsense! No one has ever seen it fly! Why should it fly? Can you suppose that a thing can do a thing which no one has ever seen it do?" And the bird, with its leg chained close to the log, preened its wings. So they sat about it, speculating, and discussing it: and one said this, and another that. And all the while as they talked the bird sat motionless, with its gaze fixed on the clear, blue sky above it. And one said, "Suppose we let the creature loose to see what it will do?"—and the bird shivered. But the others cried, "It is too valuable; it might get lost If it were to try to fly it might fall down and break its neck." And the bird, with its foot chained to the log, sat looking upward into the clear sky; the sky, in which it had never been—for the bird—the *bird*, knew what it would do—because it was an eaglet !

There is one woman known to many of us, as each human creature knows but one on earth; and it is upon our knowledge of that woman that we base our certitude.

For those who do not know her, and have not this ground, it is probably profitable and necessary that they painfully collect isolated facts and then speculate upon them, and base whatever views they should form upon these collections. It might even be profitable that they should form no definite opinions at all but wait till the ages of practical experience have put doubt to rest. For those of us who have a ground of knowledge which we cannot transmit to outsiders, it is perhaps more profitable to act fearlessly than to argue.

Finally, it may be objected to the entrance of woman to the new fields of Labour, and in effect it is often said—"What if all you have sought be granted you—if it be fully agreed that woman's ancient fields of toil are slipping from her, and that, if she do not find new, she must fall into a state of sexual parasitism, dependent on her reproductive functions alone; and granted, that, doing this, she must degenerate, and that from her degeneration must arise the degeneration and arrest of development of the males as well as of the females of her race; and granting also, fully, that in the past woman has borne one full half, and often more than one half, of the weight of the productive Labours of her societies, in addition to child-bearing; and allowing more fully that she may be as well able to sustain her share in the intellectual Labours of the future as in the more mechanical Labours of the past; granting all this, may there not be one aspect of the question left out of consideration which may reverse all conclusions as to the desirability, and the human good to be attained by woman's enlarged freedom and her entering into the new fields of toil? What if the increased culture and mental activity of woman necessary for her entrance into the new fields, however desirable in other ways for herself and the race, should result in a diminution, or an absolute abolition of the sexual attraction and affection, which in all ages of the past has bound the two halves of humanity together? What if, though the stern and unlovely manual Labours of the past have never affected her attractiveness for the male of her own society, nor his for her, yet the performance by woman of intellectual Labours, or complex and interesting manual Labour, and her increased intelligence and width, should render the male objectionable to her, and the woman undesirable to the male; so that the very race itself might become extinct through the dearth of sexual affection? What if the woman ceases to value the son she bears, and to feel desire for and tenderness to the man who begets him; and the man to value and desire the woman and her offspring? Would not such a result exceed, or at least equal, in its evil to humanity, anything which could result from the degeneration and parasitism of woman? Would it not be well, if there exist any possibility of this danger, that woman, however conscious that she can perform social Labour as nobly and successfully under the new conditions of life as the old, should yet consciously, and deliberately, with her eyes open, sink into a state of pure intellectual parasitism, with all its attendant evils, rather than face the more irreparable loss which her development and the exercise of her powers might entail? Would it not be well she should deliberately determine, as the lesser of two evils, to dwarf herself and limit her activities and the expansion of her faculties, rather than that any risk should be run of the bond of desire and emotion between the two sexual halves of humanity being severed? If the race is to decay and become extinct on earth, might it not as well be through the parasitism and decay of woman, as through the decay of sex instinct?

It is not easy to reply with rationality or even gravity to a supposition which appears to be based on the conception that a sudden and entire inversion of the deepest of those elements on which human, and even animal, life on the globe is based, is possible from so inadequate a cause: and it might well be passed silently, were it not that, under some form or other, this argument frequently recurs, now in a more rational and then in a more irrational form; constituting sometimes an objection, in even moderately intelligent minds, to the entrance of woman into the new fields of Labour. It must be at once frankly admitted that, were there the smallest danger in this direction, the sooner woman laid aside all endeavor in the direction of increased knowledge and the attainment of new fields of activity, the better for herself and for the race.

When one considers the part which sexual attraction plays in the order of sentient life on the globe, from the almost unconscious attractions which draw ameboid globule to ameboid globule, on through the endless progressive forms of life; till in monogamous birds it expresses itself in song and complex courtship and the life-long conjugal affection of mates; and which, in the human race itself, passing through various forms, from the imperative but almost purely physical attraction of savage male and female for each other, till in the highly developed male and female it assumes it esthetic and intellectual hut not less imperative form couching itself in the songs of the poet and the deathless fidelity of fully developed man and woman to each other, we find it not only everywhere forming the groundwork on which in based sentient existence, never eradicable, though infinitely varied in its external forms of expression. When we consider that in the human world, from the battles and dances of savages to the intrigues and entertainments of modern courts and palaces, the attraction of man and woman for each other has played an unending part; and that the most fierce ascetic religious enthusiasm through the ages, the flagellations and starvations in endless nunneries and monasteries, have never been able to extirpate nor seriously to-weaken for a moment the master dominance of this emotion; that the lowest and most brutal ignorance, and the highest intellectual culture leave mankind, equally, though in different forms, amenable to its mastery; that, whether in the brutal guffaw of sex laughter which rings across the drinking bars of our modern cities, and rises from the comfortable armchairs in fashionable clubs; or in the poet's dreams, and the noblest conjugal affection of men and women linked together for life, it plays still to-day on earth the part it played when hoary monsters plowed through Silurian slime, and that still it forms as ever the warp on which in the loom of human life the web is woven, and runs as a thread never absent through every design and pattern which constitutes an individual existence on earth:— not only does sexual attraction appear ineradicable, but it is ridiculous to suppose that that attraction of sex towards sex, which, with hunger and thirst, lie, as the triune instincts, at the base of animal life, should ever be ex-terminable or in any way modifiable by the comparatively superficial changes resulting from the performance of this or that form of Labour, or the little more or less of knowledge in one direction or another. That the female who runs steam-driven looms, producing scores of yards of linen in a day, should therefore desire less the fellowship of her corresponding male than had she toiled at a spinning-wheel with hand and foot to produce one yard; that the male should desire less of the companionship of the woman who spends the morning in doctoring babies in her consulting-room, according to the formularies of the pharmacopoeia, than she who of old spent it on the hillside collecting simples for remedies; that the woman who paints a modern picture or designs a modern vase should be less lovable by man than her ancestor who shaped the first primitive pot and ornamented it with zigzag patterns was to the man of her day and age; that the woman who contributes to the support of her family by giving legal opinions will less desire motherhood and wifehood than she who in the past contributed to the support of her household by bending on hands and knees over her grindstone, or scrubbing floors, and that the former should be less valued by man than the latter—these are suppositions which it is difficult to regard as consonant with any knowledge of human nature and the laws by which it is dominated.

On the other hand, if it be supposed that the possession of wealth or the means of earning it makes the human female objectionable to the male, all history and all daily experience negate it. The eager hunt for heiresses, in all ages and social conditions, makes it obvious that the human male has a strong tendency to value the female who can contribute to the family expenditure; and the case is yet, we believe, unrecorded of a male who, attracted to a female, becomes averse to her on finding she has material good. The female doctor or lawyer earning a thousand a year will always, and to-day certainly does, find more suitors than had she remained a governess or cook, Labouring as hard, earning thirty pounds. While if the statement that the female entering on new fields of Labour will cease to be lovable to the male be based on the fact that she will then be free, all history and all human experience yet more negate its truth. The study of all races in all ages proves that the greater the freedom of woman, the higher the sexual value put upon her by the males of that society. The three squaws who walk behind the Indian, whom he has captured in battle or bought for a few axes or lengths of tobacco, and over whom he exercises the right of life and death, are probably all three of infinitesimal value in his eyes, compared with the value of his single, free wife to one of our ancient, monogamous German ancestors; while the hundred wives and concubines purchased by a Turkish pasha have probably not even an approximate value in his eyes, when compared with the value thousands of modern European males set upon the one comparatively free woman, whom they have won, often only after a long and tedious courtship.

So axiomatic is the statement that the value of the female to the male varies as her freedom, that, given an account of any human society in which the individual female is highly valued, it will be perfectly safe to infer the comparative social freedom of woman; and, given a statement as to the high degree of freedom of woman in any society, it will be safe to infer the great sexual value of the individual woman to man.

Finally, if the suggestion, that men and women will cease to be attractive to one another if women enter modern fields of Labour, be based on the fact that her doing so may increase her intelligence and enlarge her intellectual horizon, it must be replied that the whole trend of human history absolutely negates the supposition. There is no ground for the assumption that increased intelligence and intellectual power diminish sexual emotion in the human creature of either sex. The ignorant savage, whether in ancient or modern societies, who violates and then clubs a female into submission, may be dominated, and is, by sex emotions of a certain class; but not less dominated have been the most cultured and powerful and highly differentiated male intelligences that the race has produced. A Mill, a Shelley, a Goethe, a Schiller, a

Pericles, have not been more noted for vast intellectual powers, than for the depth and intensity of their sexual emotions. And, if possible, with the human female, the relation between intensity of sexual emotion and highly intellectual gifts has been yet closer. The life of a Sophia Kovalevsky, a George Eliot, an Elizabeth Browning has not been more marked by a rare development of the intellect than by deep passionate sexual emotions. Nor throughout the history of the race has high intelligence and intellectual power ever tended to make either male or female unattractive to those of the opposite sex.

The merely brilliantly attired and unintelligent woman probably never awakened the same intensity of profound sex emotion, even among the men of her own type, which followed a George Sand, who attracted to herself with deathless force some of the most noted men of her generation, even when, nearing middle age, stout, and attired in rusty and inartistic black, she was to be found rolling her cigarettes in a dingy office, scorning all the external adornments with which feebler females seek to supply a hidden deficiency. Probably no more hopeless mistake could be made by an ascetic seeking to extirpate sex emotion and the attraction of the sexes for one another, than were he to imagine that in increasing virility, intelligence, and knowledge this end could be attained. He might thereby differentiate and greatly concentrate the emotions, but they would be intensified; as a widely spread, shallow, sluggish stream would not be annihilated but increased in force and activity by being turned into a sharply defined, clear-cut course.

And if, further, we turn to those secondary manifestations of sexual emotion, which express themselves in the relations of human progenitors to their offspring, we shall find, if possible more markedly, that increase of intelligence and virility -does not diminish but increases the strength of the affections. As the primitive, ignorant male, often willingly selling his offspring or exposing his female infants to death, often develops, with increase of culture and intelligence, into the often extremely devoted and self-sacrificing male progenitor of civilized societies; so, yet even more markedly, does the female relation with her offspring become intensified and permanent, as culture and intelligence and virility increase.

The Bushwoman, like the lowest female barbarians in our own societies, will often readily dispose of her infant son for a bottle of spirits or a little coin; and even among somewhat more mentally developed females, strong as is the affection of the average female for her newborn offspring, the closeness of the relation between mother and child tends rapidly to shrink as time passes, so that by the time of adolescence the relation between mother and son becomes little more than a remembrance of a close inter-union which once existed. It is, perhaps, seldom, till the very highest point of intellectual culture and mental virility has been reached by the human female, that her relation with her male offspring becomes a permanent and active and dominant factor in the lives of both.

The concentrated and all-absorbing affection and fellowship which existed between the greatest female intellect France has produced and the son she bore, dominating both lives to the end, the fellowship of the English historian with his mother, who remained his chosen companion and the sharer of all his Labours through life, the relation of St. Augustine to his mother, and countless others, are relations almost inconceivable where the woman is not of commanding and active intelligence, and where the passion of mere physical instinct is not completed by the passion of the intellect and spirit.

There appears, then, from the study of human nature in the past, no ground for supposing that if, as a result of woman's adopting new forms of Labour, she should become more free, more wealthy, or more actively intelligent, that this could in any way diminish her need of the physical and mental comradeship of man, nor his need of her; nor that it would affect their secondary sexual relations as progenitors, save by deepening, concentrating, and extending throughout life the parental emotions. The conception that man's and woman's need of each other could be touched, or the emotions binding the sexes obliterated, by any mere change in the form of Labour performed by the woman of the race, is as grotesque in its impossibility as the suggestion that the replacing of a shell on the seashore this way or that might destroy the action of the earth's great tidal wave.

But, it may be objected, "If there be absolutely no ground for the formation of such an opinion, how comes it that, in one form or another, it is so often expressed by persons who object to the entrance of woman into new or intellectual fields of Labour? Where there is smoke there must also be fire." To which it may be replied, "Without fire, no smoke; but very often the appearance of smoke wnere neither smoke nor fire exist!"

The fact that a statement is frequently made or a view held forms no presumptive ground of its truth; hut it is undoubtedly a ground for supposing that there in an *appearance* or semblance which makes it appear truth, and which suggests it, The universally entertained conception that the nun moved round the world was not merely false, but the reverse of the truth; all that was required for its inception was a fallacious appearance suggesting it.

When we examine narrowly the statement, that the entrance of woman into the new fields of Labour, with its probably resulting greater freedom of action, economic independence and wider culture, may result in a severance between the sexes, it becomes clear what that fallacious appearance, in, which suggests thin.

The entrance of a woman into new fields of Labour, though bringing her increased freedom and economic independence, and necessitating increased mental training and wider knowledge, could not extinguish the primordial physical instinct which draws sex to sex throughout all the orders of sentient life's and still less could it annihilate that subtler mental need, which, as humanity develops, draws sex to sex for emotional fellowship and else intercourse; but, it might, and undoubtedly would, powers fully react; and readjust the relations of certain men with certain women!

While the attraction, physical and intellectual, which binds sex to sex would remain the same in volume and intensity, the forms in which it would express itself, and, above all, the relative power of individuals to command the gratification of their instincts and desires, would be fundamentally altered, and in many cases inverted.

In the barbarian state of societies, where physical force dominates, it is the most muscular and pugillstically and brutally and animally successful male who captures and possesses the largest number of females; and no doubt he would be justified in regarding any social change which gave to woman a larger freedom of choice, and which would so perhaps give to the less brutal but perhaps more intelligent male whom the woman might select, an equal opportunity for the gratification of his sexual wishes and for the producing of offspring, as a serious loss. And, from the purely personal standpoint, he would undoubtedly be right in dreading anything which tended to free woman. But he would manifestly not have been justified in asserting that woman's increased freedom of choice, or the fact that the other men would share his advantage in the matter of obtaining female companionship, would in any way lessen the amount of sexual emotion or the tenderness of relation between the two halves of humanity. He would not by brute force possess himself of so many females nor have so large a circle of choice, under the new conditions; but what he lost, others would gain; and the intensity of the sex emotions and the nearness and passion of the relation between the sexes be in no way touched.

In our civilized societies, as they exist today, woman possesses (more often perhaps in appearance than reality!) a somewhat greater freedom of sexual selection; in modern societies she is no longer captured by muscular force, but there are still conditions entirely unconnected with sex attractions and affections, which yet largely dominate the sex relations.

It is not the man of the strong arm, but the man of the long purse, who unduly and artificially dominates in the sexual world to-day. Practically, wherever in the modern world woman is wholly or partially dependent for her means of support on the existence of her sexual functions, she is dependent more or less on the male's power to support her in their exercise, and her freedom of choice is practically so far limited. Probably three-fourths of the sexual unions in our modern European societies, whether in the illegal or recognized legal forms, are dominated by or largely influenced by the sex purchasing power of the male. With regard to the large and savage institution of prostitution, which still lies as a cancer embedded in the heart of all our modern civilized societies, this is obviously and nakedly the case; the wealth of the male as compared to the female being, with hideous obtrusiveness, its foundation and source of life. But the purchasing power of the male as compared with the poverty of the female is not less painfully, if a little less obtrusively, displayed in those layers of society lying nearer the surface. From the fair, effete young girl of the wealthier classes in her city boudoir, who weeps copiously as she tells you she cannot marry the man she loves, because he has only two hundred a year and cannot afford to keep her, to the father who demands frankly of his daughter's suitor how much he can settle on her before consenting to his acceptance, the fact remains, that, under existing conditions, not the amount of sex affection and attraction, but the extraneous question of the material possessions of the male, determines to a large extent the relation of the sexes. The parasitic, helpless youth who has failed in his studies, who possesses neither virility, nor charm of person, nor strength of mind, but who possesses wealth, has a far greater chance of securing the life companionship of the fairest maid, than her brother's tutor, who may be possessed of every manly and physical grace and mental gift; and the ancient libertine, possessed of material good, has, especially among the so-called upper classes of our societies, a far greater chance of securing the sex companionship of any woman he desires as wife, mistress, or prostitute, than the most physically attractive and mentally developed male, who may have nothing to offer to the dependent female but affection and sexual companionship.

To the male, whenever and wherever he exists in our societies, who depends mainly for his power for procuring the sex relation he desires, not on his power of winning and retaining personal affection, but on the purchasing power of his possessions as compared to the poverty of the females of his society, the personal loss would be seriously and at once felt, of any social change which gave to the woman a larger economic independence and therefore greater freedom of sexual choice. It is *not* an imaginary danger which the young dude—of that type which sits in the front row of the stalls in a theater, with sloping forehead and feeble jaw, sucking at intervals the top of his gilt-headed cane, and watching the unhappy women who dance for gold—sees looming before him, as he lisps out his deep disapproval of increased knowledge and the freedom of obtaining the means of subsistence in intellectual fields by woman, and expresses his vast preference for the uncultured ballet-girl over all types of cultured and productive, Labouring womanhood in the universe, A subtle and profound instinct warns him, that, with the increased intelligence and economic freedom of woman, he, and such as he, might ultimately be left sexually companionless; the undesirable, the residuary, male old-maids of the human race.

On the other hand, there is undoubtedly a certain body of females who would lose, or imagine they would lose, heavily by the advance of woman as a whole to a condition of free Labour and economic independence. That female, willfully or organically belonging to the parasite class, having neither the vigor of intellect nor the vitality of body to undertake any form of productive Labour, and desiring to be dependent only upon the passive performance of sex function merely, would, whether as prostitute or wife, undoubtedly lose heavily by any social change which demanded of woman increased knowledge and activity.

It is exactly by these two classes of persons that the objection is raised that the entrance of woman into the new fields of Labour and her increased freedom and intelligence will dislocate the relations of the sexes; and while, from the purely personal standpoint, they are undoubtedly right, viewing human society as a whole they are fundamentally wrong. The loss of a small and unhealthy section will be the gain of human society as a whole.

In the male voluptuary of feeble intellect and unattractive individuality, who depends for the gratification of his sexual instincts, not on his power of winning and retaining the personal affection and admiration of woman, but on her purchasable condition, either in the blatantly barbarous field of sex traffic that lies beyond the pale of legal marriage, or the not less barbarous though more veiled traffic within that pale, the entrance of woman into the new fields of Labour, with an increased intellectual culture and economic freedom, means little less than social extinction. But, to those males who, even at the present day, constitute the majority in our societies, and who desire the affection and fellowship of woman rather than a mere material possession; for the male who has the attributes and gifts of mind or body, which, apart from any weight of material advantage, would fit him to hold the affection of woman, however great her freedom of choice, the gain will be correspondingly great. Given a society in which the majority of women should be so far self-supporting, that, having their free share open to them in the modern fields of Labour, and reaping the full economic rewards of their Labour, marriage or some form of sexual sale was no more a matter of necessity to them; so far from this condition causing a diminution in the number of permanent sex unions, one of the heaviest bars to them would be removed. It is universally allowed that one of the disease spots in our modern social condition is the increasing difficulty which bars conscientious men from entering on marriage and rearing families, if limited means would in the case of their death or disablement throw the woman and their common offspring comparatively helpless into the fierce stream of our modern economic life. If the woman could justifiably be looked to, in case of the man's disablement or death, to take his place as an earner, thousands of valuable marriages which cannot now be contracted could be entered on; and the serious social evil, which arises from the fact that while the self-indulgent and selfish freely marry and produce large families, the restrained and conscientious are often unable to do so, would be removed, For the first time in the history of the modern world, prostitution, using that term in its broadest sense to cover all sexual relationships based, not on the spontaneous affection of the woman for the man, but on the necessitous acceptance by woman of material good in exchange for the exercise of her sexual functions, would be extinct; and the relation between men and women become a co-partnership between freemen.

So far from the economic freedom and social independence of the woman exterminating sexual love between man and woman, it would for the first time fully enfranchise it. The element of physical force and capture which dominated the most primitive sex relations, the more degrading element of seduction and purchase by means of wealth or material good offered to woman in our modern societies, would then give place to the untrammeled action of attraction and affection alone between the sexes, and sexual love, after its long pilgrimage in the deserts, would be enabled to return at last, a king crowned.

But, apart from the two classes of persons whose objection to the entrance of woman to new fields of Labour is based more or less instinctively on the fear of personal loss, there is undoubtedly a small, very small, number of sincere persons whose fear as to severance between the sexes to result from woman's entrance into the new field, is based upon a more abstract and impersonal ground.

It is not easy to do full justice in an exact statement to views held generally rather nebulously and vaguely, but we believe we should not mistake this view, by saying that there is a certain class of perfectly sincere and even moderately intelligent folk who hold a view which, expressed exactly, would come to something like this—that the entrance of woman into new fields would necessitate so large a mental culture and such a development of activity, mental and physical, in the woman, that she might ultimately develop into a being so superior to the male or so widely different from the man, that the bond of sympathy between the sexes might ultimately be broken and the man cease to be an object of affection and attraction to the woman, and the woman to the man through mere dissimilarity. The future these persons seem to see, more or less vaguely, is of a social condition, in which, the males of the race remaining precisely as they are, the corresponding females shall have advanced to undreamed-of heights of culture and intelligence; a condition in which the hand-worker and the ordinary official and small farmer shall be confronted with the female astronomer or Greek professor of astonishing learning and gifts as his only possible complementary sex companion. The vision naturally awakens certain misgivings as to sympathy between and suitability for each other, of these two widely dissimilar parts of humanity.

It must of course at once be admitted that, were the two sexual halves of humanity distinct species, which, having once entered on a course of evolution and differentiation, might continue to develop along those distinct lines for countless ages or even for a number of generations, without reacting through inheritance on each other, the consequences of such development might ultimately almost completely sever them.

The development of distinct branches of humanity has already brought about such a severance between races and classes which are in totally distinct stages of evolution. So wide is the hiatus between them often, that the lowest form of sex attraction can hardly cross it; and the more highly developed mental and emotional sex passion cannot possibly bridge it. In the world of sex, kind seeks kind, and too wide a dissimilarity completely bars the existence of the highest forms of sex emotion, and often even the lower and more purely animal.

Were it possible to place a company of the most highly evolved human females—George Sands, Sophia Kovalevskys, or even the average cultured females of a highly evolved race —on an island where the only males were savages of the Fuegan type, who should meet them on the shores with matted hair and prognathous jaws, and with wild shouts, brandishing their implements of death, to greet and welcome them, it is an undoubted fact that, so great would be the horror felt by the females towards them, that not only would the race become extinct, but if it depended for its continuance on any approach to sex affection on the part of the women, death would certainly be accepted by all, as the lesser of two evils. Hardly less marked would be the sexual division if, in place of cultured and developed females, we imagine males of the same highly evolved class thrown into contact with the lowest form of primitive females. A Darwin, a Schiller, a Keats, though all men capable of the strongest sex emotion and of the most durable sex affections, would probably be untouched by any emotion but horror, cast into the company of a circle of Bushmen females with greased bodies and twinkling eyes, devouring the raw entrails of slaughtered beasts.

But leaving out even such extreme instances of diversity, the mere division in culture and mental habits, dividing individuals of the same race but of different classes, tends largely to exclude the possibility of at least the nobler and more enduring forms of sex emotion. The highly cultured denizen of a modern society, though he may enter into passing and temporary and animal relations with the uncultured peasant or woman of the street, seldom finds awakened within him in such cases the depth of emotion and sympathy which is necessary for the closer tie of conjugal life; and it may be doubted whether the highest, most permanent, and intimate forms of sexual affection ever exist except among humans very largely identical in tastes, habits of thought, and moral and physical education.

Were it possible that the entrance of woman into the new fields of Labour should produce any increased divergence between man and woman in ideals, culture, or tastes, there would undoubtedly be a dangerous responsibility incurred by any who fostered such a movement. But the most superficial study of human life and the relation of the sexes negates such a conception.

The two sexes are not distinct species but the two halves of one whole, always acting and interacting on each other and reproducing each other and blending with each other in each generation. The human female is bound organically in two ways to the males of her society: collaterally they are her companions and the co-progenitors with her of the race; but she is also the mother of the males of each succeeding generation, bearing, shaping, and impressing her personality upon them. The males and females of each human society resemble two oxen tethered to one yoke: for a moment one may move slightly forward and the other remain stationary; but they can never move farther from each other than the length of the yoke that binds them; and they must ultimately remain stationary or move forward together. That which the women of one generation are mentally or physically, that by inheritance and education the males of the next tend to be: there can be no movement or change in one sex which will not instantly have its coordinating effect upon the other; the males of to-morrow are being cast in the mold of the women of to-day. If new ideals, new moral conceptions, new methods of action are found permeating the minds of the women of one generation, they will reappear in the ideals, moral conceptions, methods of action of the men of thirty years hence; and the idea that the males of a society can ever become permanently farther removed from its females than the individual man is from the mother who bore and reared him, is at variance with every law of human inheritance.

If, further, we turn from an abstract consideration of this supposition, and examine practically in the modern world men and women as they exist to-day, the irrationality of the supposition is yet more evident.

Not merely is the woman's movement of our age not a sporadic and abnormal growth, like a cancer bearing no organic relation to the development of the rest of the social organism, but it is essentially but one important phase of a general modification which the whole of modern life is undergoing. Further, careful study of the movement will show that, not only is it not a movement on the part of woman leading to severance and separation between the woman and the man, *but that it is essentially a movement of the woman toward the man, of the sexes towards closer union.*

Much is said at the present day on the subject of the "New Woman" (who, as we have seen, is essentially but the old non-parasitic woman of the remote past, preparing to draw on her new twentieth-century garb): and it cannot truly be said that her attitude finds a lack of social attention, On every hand she is examined, praised, blamed, mistaken for her counterfeit, ridiculed or deified—but nowhere can it be said, that the phenomenon of her existence is overlooked.

But there exists at the present day another body of social phenomena, quite as important, as radical, and if possible more far-reaching in its effects on the present and future, which yet attracts little conscious attention or animadversion, though it makes itself everywhere felt; as the shade of a growing tree may be sat under year after year by persons who never remark its silent growth.

Side by side with the "New Woman," corresponding to her, as the two sides of a coin cast in one mold, though differing from each other in superficial detail, are yet of one metal, one size, and one value, old in the sense in which she is old, being merely the reincarnation under the pressure of new conditions of the ancient forms of his race; new in the sense in which she is new, in that he is an adaptation to material and social conditions which have no exact counterpart in the past; more diverse from his immediate progenitors than even the woman is from hers, side by side with her today in every society and in every class in which she is found, stands—*the New Man!*

If he be asked, How comes it to pass, if, under the pressure of social conditions, man shows an analogous change of attitude toward life, that the change in woman should attract universal attention, while the corresponding change in the man of her society passes almost unnoticed?—it would seem that the explanation lies in the fact that, owing to woman's less independence of action in the past, any attempt at change or readaptation on her part has had to overcome great resistance, and it is the noise and friction of resistance, more than the amount of actual change which has taken place, which attracts attention. So, when an Alpine stream, after a long winter frost, breaks the ice, and with a crash and roar sweeps away the obstructions which have gathered in its bed, all men's attention is attracted to it, though when later a much larger body of water forces its way down, no man observes it. (An interesting practical illustration of this fact is found in the vast attention and uproar created when the first three women in England, some twenty odd years ago, sought to enter the medical profession. At the present day scores of women prepare to enter it yearly without attracting any general attention; not that the change which is going on is not far more in volume and social importance, but that, having overcome the first obstruction, it is now noiseless.)

Between the Emilias and Sophy Westerns of a bygone generation and the most typical of modern women, there exists no greater gap (probably not so great a one) as that which exists between the Tom Joneses and Squire Westerns of that day and the most typical of entirely modern men.

The sexual and social ideals which dominated the fox-hunting, hard-drinking, high-playing, recklessly loose-living country squire, clergyman, lawyer, and politician who headed the social organism of the past, are at least as distinct from the ideals which dominate thousands of their male descendants holding corresponding positions in the societies of to-day, as are the ideals of her great-great-grandmother's remote from those dominating the most modern of New Women.

That which most forces itself upon us as the result of a close personal study of those sections of modern European societies in which change and adaptation to the new conditions of life are now most rapidly progressing, is, not merely that equally large bodies of men and women are being rapidly modified as to their sexual and social ideals and as to their mode of life, but that this change is strictly complementary.

If the ideal of the modern woman becomes increasingly one inconsistent with the passive existence of woman on the remuneration which her sexual attributes may win from man, and marriage becomes for her increasingly a fellowship of comrades, rather than the relationship of the owner and the bought, the keeper and the kept; the ideal of the typically modern man departs quite as strongly from that of his forefathers in the direction of finding in woman active companionship and co-operation rather than passive submission. If the New Woman's conception of parenthood differs from the old in the greater sense of the gravity and obligation resting on those who are responsible for the production of the individual life, making her attitude toward the production of her race widely unlike the reckless, unreasoning, maternal reproduction of the woman of the past, the most typical male tends to feel in at least the same degree the moral and social obligation entailed by awakening lifehood: if the ideal which the New Woman shapes for herself of a male companion excludes the hard-drinking, hard-swearing, licentious, even if materially wealthy gallant of the past, the most typically modern male's ideal for himself excludes at least equally this type.

The brothel, the race-course, the gamingtable, and habits of physical excess among men are still with us; but the most superficial study of our societies will show that these have fallen into a new place in the scale of social institutions and manners. The politician, the clergyman, or the lawyer does not improve his social or public standing by violent addictions in these directions; to drink his companions under the table, to be known to have the largest number of illicit sex relations, to be recognized as an habitual visitant of the gambling saloon, does not, even in the case of a crowned head, much enhance his reputation, and may ultimately prove a *bar* to all success.

If the New Woman's conception of love between the sexes is one more largely psychic and intellectual than crudely and purely physical, and wholly of an affection between equals; the new man's conception, as expressed in the most typical literature and art, produced by typically modern males, gives voice with a force no woman has surpassed to the same new ideal. If to the typical modern woman the lifelong companionship of a Tom Jones or Squire Western would be more intolerable than death or the most complete celibacy, not less would the most typical of modern men shrink from the prospect of a lifelong betterment to the companionship of an always fainting and weeping Emilia or a Sophia of a bygone epoch.

If anywhere on earth exists the perfect ideal of that which the modern woman desires to be—of a Labouring and virile womanhood, free strong, fearless and tender—it will probably be found imaged deeply in the heart of the New Man; engendered there by his own highest needs and aspirations; and nowhere would the most highly developed modern male find a clearer image of that which forms his ideal of the most fully developed manhood, than in the ideal of man which haunts the heart of the New Woman.

Those have strangely overlooked some of the most important phenomena of our modern world, who see in the woman's movement of our day a movement of the female against the male, of the woman away from the man.

We have called the woman's movement of our age an endeavor on the part of women among modem civilized races to find new fields of Labour as the old slip from them, as an attempt to escape from parasitism and an inactive dependence upon sex function alone; but, viewed from another side, the woman's movement might not less justly be called a part of a great movement of the sexes towards each other, a movement towards common occupations, common interests, common ideals, and an emotional tenderness and sympathy between the sexes more deeply founded and more indestructible than any the world has yet seen.

It may be suggested, and the perception of a certain profound truth underlies this suggestion: How is it, if there be this close reciprocity between the lines along which the advanced and typical modern males and females are developing, that there does exist in our modern societies, and often among the very classes forming our typically advanced sections, so much of pain, unrest, and sexual disco-ordination at the present day?

The reply to this pertinent suggestion is, that the disco-ordination, struggle, and consequent suffering which undoubtedly do exist when we regard the world of sexual relationships and ideals in our modern societies, do not arise in any way from a disco-ordination between the sexes as such, but from the conflict between old ideals and new; a struggle which is going on in every branch of human life in our modern societies, and in which the determining element is not sex, but the point of evolution which the individual has reached.

It cannot be too often repeated, even at the risk of the most wearisome reiteration, that our societies are societies in a state of rapid evolution and change. The continually changing material conditions of life, with their reaction on the intellectual, emotional, and moral aspect of human affairs, render our societies the most complex and probably the most mobile and unsettled which the world has ever seen. As the result of this rapidity of change and complexity, there must exist a large amount of disco-ordination, and, consequently, of suffering.

In a stationary society where generation has succeeded generation for hundreds, or it may be for thousands, of years, with little or no change in the material conditions of life, the desires, institutions, and moral principles of men, their religious, political, domestic, and sexual institutions, have gradually shaped themselves in accordance with these conditions; and a certain harmony, and homogeneity, and tranquillity, pervades the society.

In societies in the rapid state of change in which our modern societies find themselves, where not merely each decade, but each year, and almost day, brings new forces and conditions to bear on life, not only is the amount of suffering and social rupture, which all rapid, excessive, and sudden change entails on an organism, inevitable; but, the new conditions, acting at different angles of intensity on the different individuals composing the society, according to their positions and varying intelligence, and producing a society of such marvelous complexity and dissimilarity in the different parts, the intensest rupture and disco-ordination between individuals is inevitable; and sexual ideals and relationships must share in the universal condition.

In a primitive society (if a somewhat prolix illustration may be allowed) where for countless generations the conditions of life had remained absolutely unchanged; where for ages it had been necessary that all males should employ themselves in subduing wild beasts and meeting dangerous foes, polygamy might universally have been a necessity, if the race was to exist and its numbers be kept up, and, society recognizing this, polygamy would be an institution universally approved and submitted to, however much suffering it entailed. If food were scarce, the destruction of superfluous infants and of the aged might also always have been necessary for the good of the individuals themselves as well as of society, and the whole society would acquiesce in it without any moral (doubt. If an eclipse of the sun had once occurred in connection with the appearance of a certain insect, they might universally regard that insect as a god causing it; and ages might pass without anything arising to disprove their belief. There would be no social or religious problem; and the view of one man would be the view of all men; and all would be more or less in harmony with the established institution and customs.

But, supposing the sudden arrival of strangers armed with superior weapons and knowledge, who should exterminate all wild beasts and render war and the consequent loss of male life a thing of the past; not only would the male be driven to encroach on the female's domain of domestic agriculture and Labour generally, but the males, not being so largely destroyed, would soon equal and surpass in numbers the females; and not only would it then become a moot matter, "a problem," which Labours were or were not to be performed by man and which by woman, but very soon, not the woman alone nor the man alone, but both, would be driven to speculate as to the desirability or necessity of polygamy, which, were men as numerous as women, would leave many males without sex companions. The more intelligent and progressive individuals in the community would almost at once arrive at the conclusion that polygamy was objectionable; the most fearless would seek to carry their theory into action; the most ignorant and unprogressive would determinately stick to the old institutions as inherited from the past, without reason or question. Differences of ideal would cause conflict and dissension in all parts of the body social, and suffering would ensue, where all before was fixed and determinate. So also if the strangers introduced new and improved methods of agriculture, and food became abundant, it would then at once strike the most far-seeing and readily adaptable members of the community, both male and female, that there was no necessity for the destruction of their offspring. Old men and women would begin seriously to object to being hastened to death when they realized that starvation did not necessarily stare them in the face if they survived to an extreme old age. The most stupid and hide-bound members of the community would still continue to sacrifice parents and offspring long after the necessity had ceased, under the influence of traditional bias; many persons would be in a state of much moral doubt as to which course of action to pursue, the old or the new; and hitter conflict might rage in the community on all these points. Were the strangers to bring with them telescopes, looking through which it might at once clearly be seen that an eclipse of the sun was caused merely by the moon's passing over its face, the more intelligent members of the community would at once come to the conclusion that the insect was not the cause of eclipses, would cease to regard it as a god, and might even kill it. The more stupid and immobile section of the community might refuse to look through the telescope, or looking might refuse to see that it was the moon which caused the eclipse, and their deep-seated reverence for the insect, which was the growth of ages, would lead them to regard as impious those individuals who denied its godhead, and might even lead to the physical destruction of the first unbelievers. The society, once so homogeneous and coordinated in all its parts, would become at once a society rent by moral and social problems; and endless suffering must come to individuals in the attempt to co-ordinate the ideals, manners, and institutions of the society to the new conditions I There might be immense gain in many directions; lives otherwise sacrificed would be spared, a higher and more satisfactory stage of existence might be entered on; but the disco-ordination and struggle would be inevitable until the society had established an equilibrium between its knowledge, its material conditions, and its social, sexual, and religious ideals and institutions.

An analogous condition, but of a far more complex kind, exists at the present day in our own societies. Our material environment differs in every respect from that of our grandparents, and bears little or no resemblance to that of a few centuries ago. Here and there, even in our civilized societies in remote agricultural districts, the old social conditions may remain undisturbed; but throughout the bulk of our societies the substitution of mechanical for hand-Labour, the wide diffusion of knowledge through the always increasing cheap printing-press, the rapidly increasing gathering of human creatures into vast cities, where not merely thousands but millions of individuals are gathered together under physical and mental conditions of life which invert every social condition of the past; the increasingly rapid means of locomotion; the increasing intercourse between races and lands, brought about by rapid means of intercommunication, widening and changing in every direction the human horizon—all these produce a society, so complex and so rapidly altering that social co-ordination between all its parts is impossible; and social unrest, and the strife of ideals, of faiths, of institutions, and consequent human suffering, is inevitable.

If the ancient guns and agricultural implements which our fathers taught us to use are valueless in the hands of their descendants, if the samplers our mothers worked and the stockings they knitted are become superfluous through the action of the modern loom, yet more are their social institutions, faiths, and manners of life become daily and increasingly unfitted to our use; and friction and suffering inevitable, especially for the most advanced and modified individuals in our societies. This suffering, if we analyze it closely, rises from three causes:

Firstly, it is caused by the fact that mere excessive rapidity of change tends always easily to become painful, by rupturing violently already formed habits and modes of thought, as a very rapidly growing tree ruptures its bark and exudes its internal juices.

Secondly, it arises from the fact that individuals of the same human society, not adapting themselves at the same rate to the new conditions, or being exposed to them in different degrees, a wide and almost unparalleled dissimilarity has to-day arisen between the different individuals composing our societies. Side by side with men and women who have so rapidly adapted or are so successfully seeking to adapt themselves to the new conditions of knowledge and new conditions of life, that, were they to reappear in future ages in more coordinated societies, they might hardly appear wholly antiquated, are to be found men and women whose social, religious, and moral ideals would not constitute them out of harmony if they returned to the primitive camps of the remote forbears of the human race; while, between these extreme classes, lies that large mass of persons in an intermediate state of development. This diversity is bound to cause friction and suffering in the interactions of the members of our societies; more especially as the individuals composing each type are *not* sorted out into classes and families, but are found scattered through all classes and grades in our societies. Persons bound by the closest ties of blood or social contiguity and compelled to a continual intercourse are often those most widely dissevered in their amount of adaptation to the new conditions of life. The amount of social friction and consequent human suffering arising from this fact is so subtle and almost incalculable, that perhaps it is impossible adequately to portray it in dry didactic language-It is perhaps only describable in the medium of art, where actual concrete individuals are shown acting and reacting on each other—as in the novel or the drama. We are like a company of chess-men, not sorted out in kinds, pawns together, kings and queens together, and knights and rooks together, but simply thrown at haphazard into a box, and jumbled side by side. In the stationary societies, where all individuals were permeated by the same political, religious, moral, and social ideas; and where each class had its own hereditary and fixed traditions of action and manners, this cause of friction and suffering had of necessity no existence; individual differences and discord might be occasioned by personal greed's, ambitions, and selfishnesses, but not by conflicting conceptions of right and wrong, of the desirable and undesirable, in all branches of human life. Thirdly, the unrest and suffering peculiar to our age is caused by conflict going on within the individual himself. So intensely rapid is the change which is taking place in our environment and knowledge that in the course of a single life a man may pass through half a dozen phases of growth. Born and reared in possession of certain ideas and manners of action, he or she may, before middle life is reached, have had occasion repeatedly to modify, enlarge, and alter, or completely throw aside those traditions. Within the individuality itself of such persons goes on, in an intensified form, that very struggle, conflict, and disco-ordination which is going on in society at large between its different members and sections; and agonizing moments must arise, when the individual, seeing the necessity for adopting new courses of action, or for accepting new truths, or conforming to new conditions, will yet be tortured by the hold of traditional convictions; and the men or women who attempt to adapt their life to the new material conditions and to harmony with new knowledge are ulmost bound at some time to rupture the continuity of their own psychological existence.

It is these conditions which give rise to the fact so often noticed, that the art of our age tends persistently to deal with subtle psychological problems, religious, political, and sexual, to which the art of the past holds no parallel; and it is so inevitably, because the artist who would obey the artistic instinct to portray faithfully the world about him, must portray that which lies at the core of its life. The "problem" play, novel, and poem are as in- evitable in this age, as it was that the artist of the eleventh century should portray tournaments, physical battles, and chivalry, because they were the dominant element in the life about him.

It is also inevitable that this suffering and conflict must make itself felt in its acutest form in the person of the most advanced individual of our societies. It is the swimmer who first leaps into the frozen stream who is cut sharpest by the ice; those who follow him find it broken, and the last find it gone. It is the men or women who first tread down the path which the bulk of humanity will ultimately follow, who must find themselves at last in solitudes where the silence is deadly.

The fact that any course of human action leading to adjustment leads also to immediate suffering is no argument against it; that suffering is the crown of thorns which marks the kingship of earth's Messiahs: it is the mark of the leader.

Thus social disco-ordination, and subjective conflict and suffering, pervade the life of our age, making themselves felt in every division of human life, religious, political, and domestic.

If they are more noticeable, and make themselves more keenly felt in the region of sex than in any other, even the religious, it is because when we enter the region of sex we touch, as it were, the spinal cord of the human existence, its great nerve center, where sensation is most acute, and pain and pleasure most keenly felt. It is not sex disco-ordination that is at the root of our social unrest; it is the universal disco-ordination which affects even the world of sex phenomena.

Also it is necessary to note that the line which divides the progressive sections of our communities, seeking to co-ordinate themselves to the new conditions of life, from the retrogressive is not a line running coincidentally with that of sex. A George Sand and a Henrick Ibsen belong more essentially to the same class in the order of modern development, than either belongs to any class composed entirely of their own sex. If we divide humanity into classes according to type, in each division will be found the male with his complementary female. Side by side with the old harlot at the street corner anxious to sell herself, stands the old aboriginal male, whether covered or not with a veneer of civilization, eager and desiring to buy. Side by side with the parasitic woman, seeking only increased pleasure and luxury from her relations with man, stands the male seeking only pleasure and self-indulgence from his relations with her. Side by side with the New Woman, anxious for Labour and seeking from man only such love and fellowship as she gives, stands the New Man, anxious to possess her only on the terms she offers. If the social movement, through which the most advanced women of our day are attempting to bring themselves into coordination with the new conditions of life, removes them immeasurably from certain types of the primitive male; the same movement equally removes the new male from the old female. The sexual tragedy of modern life lies, not in the fact that woman as such is tending to differ fundamentally from man as such; but that, in the unassorted confusion of our modern life, it is continually the modified type of man or woman who is thrown into the closest personal relations with the antiquated type of the opposite sex; that between father and daughter, mother and son, brother and sister, husband and wife, may sometimes be found to intervene not merely years, but even centuries of social evolution.

It is not man as man who opposes the attempt of woman to readjust herself to the new conditions of life: that opposition arises, perhaps more often, from the retrogressive members of her own sex. And it is a fact which will surprise no one who has studied the conditions of modern life, that among the works of literature in all European languages which most powerfully advocate the entrance of woman into the new fields of Labour, which most uncompromisingly demand for her the widest training and freedom of action, and which most passionately seek for the breaking down of all artificial lines which sever the woman from the man, many of the ablest and most uncompromising are the works of men.

The New Man and Woman do not resemble two people, who, standing on a level plain, set out on two roads, which, diverging at different angles and continued in straight lines, must continue to take them farther and farther from each other the longer they proceed in them; rather, they resemble two persons who start to climb a spur of the same mountain from opposite sides; where, the higher they climb, the nearer they come to each other, being bound ultimately to meet at the top.

Even that opposition often made by males to the entrance of woman into the new fields of Labour, of which they at present hold the monopoly, is not fundamentally sexual in its nature. The male who opposes the entrance of woman into the trade or profession in which he holds more or less a monopoly, would oppose with equal, and perhaps even greater bitterness, the opening of its doors to numbers of his own sex who had before been excluded, and who would limit his gains and share his privileges. It is the primitive brute instinct to retain as much as possible for the ego, irrespective of justice or humanity, which dominates all the lower moral types of humanity, both male and female, which acts here. "The lawyer or physician who objects to the entrance of women to his highly fenced professional enclosure, would probably object yet more strenuously if it were proposed to throw down the barriers of restraint and monetary charges which would result in the flooding of his profession by other males: while the mechanic, who resists the entrance of woman into his especial field, is invariably found even more persistently to oppose any attempt at entrance on the part of other males, when he finds it possible to do so.

This opposition of the smaller type of male, to the entrance of woman into the callings hitherto apportioned to himself, is sometimes taken as implying the impossibility of fellowship and affection existing between the men and women employed in common Labour; it is said sometimes that the professional jealousy of the man must necessitate his feeling a hatred and antagonism towards the woman who shares his fields of Labour. But the most superficial study of human life negates such a supposition. Among men, in spite of the occasional existence of the petty professional jealousies and antagonism, we find, viewing society as a whole, that common interests, and above all common Labours, are the most potent means of bringing them into close and friendly relations, and, in fact, they seem generally essential for the formation of the closest and most permanent human friendships. In every walk of human life, whether trade or profession, we find men associating by choice mainly with, and entertaining often the profoundest and most permanent friendship for, men engaged in their own callings. The inner circle of a barrister's friendships almost always consists of his fellow-barristers; the broker, who is free to select his society where he will, will be oftenest found in company with his fellow-man-of-business; the medical man's closest friendship is, in a large number of cases, for some man who was once his fellow-student and has passed through the different stages of his professional life with him; the friends and chosen companions of the actor are commonly actors; of the savant, savants; of the farmer, farmers; of the sailor, sailors. So generally is this the case that it would almost attract attention and cause amusement were the boon companion of the sea captain a leading politician, and the intimate friend of the clergyman an actor, or the dearest friend of the farmer an astronomer. Kind seeks kind. The majority of men by choice frequent clubs where those of their own calling are found, and especially as life advances and men sink deeper into their professional grooves, they are found to seek fellowship mainly among their fellow-workers. That this should be so is inevitable; common amusements may create a certain bond between the young, but the performance of common Labours, necessitating identical knowledge, identical habits, and modes of thought, forms a far stronger bond, drawing men far more powerfully towards social intercourse and personal friendship, than the centrifugal force of professional jealousies can divide them.

That the same condition would prevail where women became fellow-workers with men might be inferred on abstract grounds: but practical experience confirms this. The actor oftenest marries the actress; the male musician the female; the reception-room of the literary woman or female painter is found continually frequented by men of her own calling; the woman-doctor associates continually with and often marries one of her own confreres; and as women in increasing numbers share the modern fields of Labour with men, which have hitherto been apportioned to them alone, the nature and strength of the sympathy arising from common Labours will be increasingly clear. The sharing by men and women of common Labours, necessitating a common culture and therefore common habits of thought and interests, would tend to fill that painful hiatus which arises so continually in modern conjugal life, dividing the man and woman as soon as the first sheen of physical sexual attraction which glints only over the unknown begins to fade, and from which springs so large a part of the tragedy of modern conjugal relations. The primitive male might discuss with her his success in hunting and her success in finding roots; as the primitive peasant may discuss to-day with his wife the crops and cows in which both are equally interested and which both understand; there is nothing in their order of life to produce always increasingly divergent habits of thought and interest-In modern civilized life, in many sections, the lack of any common Labour and interests and the wide dissimilarity of the life led by the man and the woman, tend continually to produce increasing divergence, so that, long before middle life is reached, they are left without any bond of cohesion but that of habit.

The comradeship and continual stimulation, rising from intercourse with those sharing our closest interests and regarding life from the same standpoint, the man tends to seek in his club and among his male companions, and the woman accepts solitude, or seeks dissipations which tend yet further to disrupt the common conjugal life. A certain mental camaraderie and community of impersonal interests is imperative in conjugal life in addition to a purely sexual relation, if the union is to remain a living and growing reality. It is more especially because the sharing by woman of the Labours of man will tend to promote camaraderie and the existence of common, impersonal interests and like habits of thought and life, that the entrance of women into the fields shared by men, and not into others peculiarly reserved for her, is so desirable.

It is a gracious fact, to which every woman who has achieved success or accomplished good work in any of the fields generally apportioned to men will bear witness, whether that work be in the field of literature, of science, or the organized professions, that the hands which have been most eagerly stretched out to welcome her have been those of men; that the voices which have most generously acclaimed her success have been those of male fellow-workers in the fields into which she has entered.

There is no door at which the hand of woman has knocked for admission into a new field of toil but there have been found on the other side the hands of strong and generous men eager to turn it for her almost before she knocks.

To those of us who, at the beginning of a new century, stand with shaded eyes, gazing into the future, striving to descry the outlines of the shadowy figures which loom before us in the distance, nothing seems of so gracious a promise as the outline we seem to discern of a condition of human life in which a closer union than the world has yet seen shall exist between the man and the woman: where the Walhalla of our old Northern ancestors shall find its realization in a concrete reality, and the Walkurie and her hero feast together at one board in a brave fellowship.

Always in our dreams we hear the turn of the key that shall close the door of the last brothel; the clink of the last coin that pays for the body and soul of a woman; the falling of the last wall that encloses artificially the activity of woman and divides her from man; always we picture the love of the sexes as once a dull, slow, creeping worm; then a torpid, earthy chrysalis; at last the full-winged insect, glorious in the sunshine of the future.

To-day, as we row hard against the stream of life, is it only a blindness in our eyes, which have been too long strained, which makes us see, far up the river where it fades into the distance, through all the mists that rise from the river-banks, a clear, a golden light? Is it only a delusion of the eyes which makes us grasp our oars more lightly and bend our backs lower; though we know well that, long before the boat reaches those stretches, other hands than ours will man the oars and guide its helm? Is it all a dream?

The ancient Chaldean seer had a vision of a Garden of Eden which lay in a remote past-It was dreamed that man and woman once lived in joy and fellowship, till woman ate of the tree of knowledge and gave to man to eat; and that both were driven forth to wander, to toil in bitterness; because they had eaten of the fruit.

We also have our dream of a Garden, but it lies in a distant future. We dream that woman shall eat of the tree of knowledge together with man, and that side by side and hand close to hand, through ages of much toil and Labour, they shall together raise about them an Eden nobler than any the Chaldean dreamed of; an Eden created by their own Labour and made beautiful by their own fellowship.

In his apocalypse there was one who saw a new heaven and a new earth; we see a new earth; but therein dwells love—the love of comrades and co-workers.

It is because so wide and gracious to us are the possibilities of the future; so impossible is a return to the past, so deadly is a passive acquiescence in the present, that to-day we are found everywhere raising our strange new cry —"Labour and the training that fits us for Labour!"

Index

A

Abigail Adams 74
Adolescent period 102
Alice Freeman Palmer 77
Andrew D. White 33
Anthony 77
Augustine 19
Augustus Caesar 166

B

Bushwoman 245

C

Carrie Chapman Catt 75
Catherine Beecher 30
Catherine of Russia 236
Catholic Church 109
Charlotte Perkins Gilman 77
Christianity 17
Cimbrian women 167
Civilized life 200
Civilized societies 208
Clara Barton 22
Clara L. Cambell 89
Classical times 27
Conditions in Colorado 92

D

Degradation and dependency 181
Developing civilization 3
Divine Child-bearer 223
Dorothea Dix 22
Dutch peasant woman 189

E

Eastern Kingdoms 15
Economic conditions 28
Economic independence 247, 249
Ellen Key 4, 111
Entrance of woman 246
Ernestine L. Rose 74
Exact material condition 170

F

Female parasitism 177
Fields of Labour 252
Frances Wright 22

G

Garden of Eden 274
George Sand 244
George Sands 253
Gnauck-Kuhne 101
Gothic cathedral 192
Grecian greatness 162
Grerman organization 204

H

Helen Sumner 86
Henry Ward Beecher 75
Human activities 228
Human creature 207
Human growth 12
Human species 231

I

Impersonal obligation 182
Industrial efficiencies 120
Industrial problem 99
Industrial reorganization 23
Instinctive comprehension 233
Institution of marriage 107
Institutional regulation 79

J

Jane Addams 69

L

Labour movement 181
Labour problem 157
Lee-Metford 210
Legal restrictions 49

M

Madame Curie 6
Mary A. Wright 89
Mary Lyon 30
Mary Sheldon Barnes 77
Matthew Vassar 31
Methodism to Christian Science 7
Modern democracies 62, 74
Modern men 10
Modern social conditions 152

N

Natural conditions 206
Nervous breakdown 144
New Woman's conception 259
Non-Labouring females 179

O

Olive Schreiner 113

P

Parasite woman 187
Parasitism 134
Patriarchal Deity 16
Physical conformation 203
Physical education 254
Physical force 247
Physical phenomenon 214
Physical sexual attraction 272
Physical sympathy 108
Political life 85
Primitive life 41
Primitive society 261
Primitive woman 197
Productive Labourer 151
Property rights 42
Protestant Revolution 110
Psychological existence 267
public consciousness 98, 99

Q

Queen Victoria 69

R

Religious enthusiasm 241
Richard Coeur de Lion 139
Roman Empire 174

S

Sacramental significances 110

Self-governing countries 220
Self-realization 2
Sex adjustments 132
Sex characteristics 9
Sex-parasitism 178
Sexual attraction 239
Sexual halves 253
Sioux Falls 116
Social conditions 229
Social duty 190
Social phenomena 256
Sophia Kovalevsky 244
Sophia Kovalevskys 253
Sophy Westerns 258
South African 217
St. Jerome 19
Stationary society 261
Susan B. Anthony 75

T

Theological changes 27
Thessaly to Sparta 163
Tradition of government 66

U

Unattractive individuality 250

W

William Kingdon Clifford 186
Woman's Labour Problem 144
Woman's Movement 153
Woman's movement 182
Woman's Rights Convention 75
Woman's work 225